INTERACTION
Interpersonal Relationships in Organizations

ROBERT C. SEDWICK
Professor of Business Administration
George Washington University

PRENTICE-HALL, INC., ENGLEWOOD CLIFFS, NEW JERSEY

Library of Congress Cataloging in Publication Data

SEDWICK, ROBERT C

Interaction: interpersonal relationships in organizations.

Bibliography: p.

1. Industrial relations. 2. Interpersonal relations. 3. Organization. I. Title.

HD6971.S37 158'.26 73-21916

ISBN 0-13-469163-6

ISBN 0-13-469155-5 (pbk.)

Printed in the United States of America

10 9 8 7 6 5 4 3 2 1

All names used in this book are fictitious. Any similarity to persons living or dead is purely coincidental.

Prentice-Hall International, Inc., *London*
Prentice-Hall of Australia, Pty. Ltd., *Sydney*
Prentice-Hall of Canada, Ltd., *Toronto*
Prentice-Hall of India Private Limited, *New Delhi*
Prentice-Hall of Japan, Inc., *Tokyo*

To Angie

Contents

Preface

Interaction—the life blood of the organization—the interpersonal relationships that develop between individuals, between individuals and groups, and between groups—the communication patterns that can spell success or failure—it must be successful or the organization is doomed.

In this day and age successful interaction is what it's all about. The older generation *must* develop it for survival; the younger generation *insists* on developing it for personal growth. Although both want it, their objectives are different. And this is exactly where successful interaction fails. We fail to realize that every individual has acquired a unique personal philosophy based upon his own value system and frame of reference and a unique managerial philosophy based upon training and experience. We often tend to assume that everyone believes, thinks, and acts or reacts as we do. We fail to see the other person's point of view or the fact that his objectives may be different from ours. We charge ahead thinking mostly about ourselves. The results—frustrating interaction—outward with our co-workers —upward with our boss—and inward within ourselves.

The purpose of this book, therefore, is to develop an understanding of interpersonal relationships in organizations so that successful interaction can be achieved. Unfortunately, an understanding of interpersonal relationships cannot be taught; however, it *can* be learned. It is hoped that this book will assist in the learning process.

Part I explores the uniqueness of individuals. First, the development of beliefs and attitudes is examined. We see that as the beliefs and attitudes acquired throughout the formative years are modified by a value system acquired from parents, peers, and the school system, a philosophy emerges. Each person's philosophy is further modified by a particular need at any specific time, by a frame of reference, by past experiences, by present situations, and by future expectations to give a characteristic behavior pattern. Furthermore, each individual's behavior pattern and philosophy are unique. No other person will act and react in exactly the same manner. Each of us, then, brings to every organization a unique philosophy and behavior pattern. Is it any wonder that successful interaction is hard to achieve?

Part II develops an understanding of groups. We find that groups—and all of us belong to one or more—have their own norms, values, and role situations, which may cause us to modify our own behavior in order to be accepted or may cause a change in certain characteristics of the group.

Part III presents the development of managerial philosophies in different frames of reference. By comparing the lectures given in the different time periods, Part III also traces the transition of man's thinking about man from the interchangeable part concept of the turn of the century to the self-actualizing behavioral science concept being taught today. Based on knowledge of frames of reference and the ages of peers and supervisors, we should be able to predict whether interaction will be positive and productive or whether conflicts will develop.

Finally, Part IV sets forth a modus operandi for successful interpersonal relationships in organizations based upon knowledge of individuals, groups, and managerial philosophies. The emphasis is on interaction from the bottom up—between co-workers and the boss—a down-under point of view. This point of view—interaction outward and upward (IOU)—has been taken as a new approach. Most behavioral science textbooks are written from the manager's point of view, which is a downward approach, yet most of the action occurs between peers, co-workers, and supervisors, which is an outward and upward point of view; thus, the emphasis in the book.

Three basic premises have been followed in preparing the manuscript:

1. all background information pertains to the United States;
2. the word "man" is used in most of the examples and discussions throughout the text as a biological term in place of the rather awkward "homo-sapiens"; it is meant to include woman, worker, person, or individual as the case may be;
3. the examples used in Chapter 12 involve *knowledge* workers, not *manual* workers.

In preparing this novel approach to the study of human relations in organizations—that is, from the point of view of the lower level employee rather than the manager—I am indebted to James Howerton who gave me advice and encouragement and Jo Anne Squires who bolstered up the entire effort and Chapter 2 in particular. In addition, I would like to express my appreciation to Professors Gary W. Falkenberg, Oakland (Michigan) Community College; Robert H. Kessner, University of Hawaii; William C. Miller, Burlington (New Jersey) County College; Albert A. Salerno, Clark (Ohio) Technical College; and R. E. C. Wegner, University of Saskatchewan for their help in reviewing the book. I would also like to thank Fred Easter for his faith; Julia Casamajor and Michele Bitters for their help in obtaining library reference material; Louie Andrews for supplying theological background; Joan Langlais for her expert typing; Virginia Manley, my secretary, for helping with compilation; and Annabelle Sedwick, my mother, for proofing the manuscript and researching the decades. My daughter Betsi drew all the chapter opening frontispieces and I would like to give her a special note of thanks.

Finally, and most important, I thank my wife Angie for editing the final manuscript and for being there when I needed her.

ROBERT C. SEDWICK

part I

UNDERSTANDING THE INDIVIDUAL

The individual is the building block of the organization—the smallest identifiable human element. Understanding of the individual (and one's self) is the first essential element in developing a plan for successful interpersonal relationships in organizations.

The objectives of Part I are to enable you to

1. *appreciate* the fact that each human being is unique;
2. *understand* how each individual acquires beliefs, attitudes, and values that combine to give a general philosophy;
3. *realize* how philosophy is modified by needs and affected by a frame of reference, past experience, the present situation, and future expectations to give a unique behavior;
4. *identify* your own behavior and philosophy and learn how it was acquired;
5. *explore* whether you are "your own man";
6. *develop* the first part of a plan of action for successful interaction.

THE OLD WAY
ROUTING
A
C
C
Y
D-3
BD-2
D-1

1

Setting the Stage

Jim Dee's thoughts of last night's date were interrupted by a familiar voice.

"Jim, old boy, I've finally made up my mind."

Jolted back to reality, Jim mumbled a weak, "What did you say, Al?"

"I said I've made up my mind—I'm going to do it."

"OK, Al, calm it down. What are you going to do?"

"Well, I've finally decided I'm going to approach the old man about rerouting our delivery trucks."

"You're going to do *What?"*

"I'm going to approach the old man about rerouting the delivery trucks. You know I've been talking to you about it for the last couple of weeks or so."

"Sure, I remember, but I thought you'd decided to give that up."

"I know—you almost had me convinced that I ought to, Jim; but I just can't. When I see a chance for the company to save some money just by changing a schedule, it seems to me that I just have to point it out to the old man. You know it's logical."

"All right, Al, I'll agree; you worked it out on paper like your book says. And I saw the example you showed me all worked out, but you know what I told you I thought your troubles might be."

"Yes, Jim, I remember. First you told me that the drivers have been doing it this way for a long time and that they might not like to change their schedules, and that the old man has the trucks paid for and wouldn't want to buy new ones, and that he doesn't appreciate new ideas or younger people trying to make suggestions. I know, I heard all that, but this is a problem right out of my textbook. I know I can convince him."

"All right, Al," replied Jim in measured tones, "but I told you you're going to have problems with your own group as well as with the old man. I've been here for five years and I know. The men in Shipping and Receiving have worked together too long and they're all rather set in their ways. They're not going to look kindly on your wanting to shake everything up after such a short time with the company."

"I know, Jim," Al shot back. "I've been here only a month, and I have to wait and I can't do things overnight, but this is so logical. It's right there in black and white; it's in the book if you use the example at the end of the chapter. I put in our statistics, and it comes out that we can save $120 a month. Now that seems worth it to me."

"OK, Al, go ahead, but don't say I didn't warn you."

After finishing their coffee, Jim went back to the accounting department and Al disappeared down the corridor toward the shipping and receiving office.

As soon as Al Allen got back to his desk, he picked up his phone and dialed the plant manager's office. After one buzz, a cheery voice answered, "Mr. Able's office."

"Sally, this is Al Allen down in Shipping and Receiving."

"Oh, hello, Mr. Allen. What can I do for you?"

"Well, I was wondering if you could check Mr. Able's calendar and see if I could see him sometime today."

"Just a minute." In about half a minute Sally's voice came back over the phone. "Yes, Mr. Allen, I can make an appointment for you at two o'clock this afternoon if that would be convenient for you."

"Sure, Sally—thanks. See you then."

"All right, see you at two o'clock."

At five minutes of two Al approached the plant manager's office with his textbook and a sheet of notes stuck under his arm. He grinned as he approached Sally's desk.

Before he could speak, Sally looked up and said, "He's expecting you; go right on in."

As Al walked through the door of the general manager's office, Mr. Able looked up from his desk, nodded, and greeted him with "Have a chair, Al," pointing to a chair across from his desk. "What can I do for you this afternoon?"

"Well, Mr. Able, I've been doing a little analysis work on our shipping operation, and I believe I have uncovered a method that might save us about $100 a month," Al began rather gingerly.

"Sounds interesting."

"Yes, sir," continued Al, a little more sure of himself after Mr. Able's remark. "The way I figure it is that with our two warehouses and three distributors, we could save money by rerouting our trucks. Our situation is very similar to a linear programming problem that I had in my course, Quantitative Factors in Administration. In fact, it is very similar to a sample problem, and I worked out our situation based on the model in the book; it looks like we can really save ourselves $100 a month and mileage costs."

"Oh, and how do you figure that?"

"Sir, I've laid it all out here on these pages if you'd like to go over it."

"No, no—I'll assume that your figures are right, but how do we make this saving?"

"Well, we change the shipping route so that all of our deliveries are not made to our nearest distributor. Instead there's a combination of units per truck per delivery."

"I see, but may I ask a question?"

"Yes, sir!"

"Would our drivers have to get used to different schedules and different routes?"

"Yes, sir, they would."

"Will this mean that the time of deliveries from our suppliers will be different?"

"Yes, sir."

"Have you checked with the distributors to see if this is agreeable with them?"

"Yes, sir, I've talked with one and he didn't seem to mind."

"Also, have you checked to see whether drivers will have to deliver to distributors they haven't known before?"

"Well, some would, sir, but . . ."

"Al, this might sound fine and look good on paper, but you know there's more involved than just figures. I think we better continue doing things the way we are. Is there anything else you want to discuss with me?"

"No, sir, Mr. Able, that's all."

"All right, Al, I suggest you get back to that receiving warehouse platform rearrangement. I'd like to have that by tomorrow afternoon."

"Yes, sir, Mr. Able," answered Al as he got up from his chair. "I'll have it for you tomorrow afternoon." With that he turned and left the office.

The next morning Jim was a little late taking his morning coffee break. As he entered the small lounge, he saw Al sitting at the far table looking a little dejected.

"Hey, Al, what happened?"

"Oh, you know, Jim. You told me you wouldn't say I told you so, but you were right. The old man gave me some excuses, said thank you, and told me to get back to work. I first thought he was going to be interested, but the more I explained it the less interested he seemed to be."

"Well, you know, Al," remarked Jim, "he doesn't like change. He thinks we've done it well enough over the past years, and he doesn't see any need to change. And besides, there are some awfully close ties that have been developed throughout the company."

"Yeah," said Al in a resigned manner, "I guess you're right. I better get back to the old drawing board and concentrate on what he wants me to do, but one of these days we've got to change."

"OK, Al," Jim shot back, "hold on a minute; why is it so important that we change?"

"Well, you know, Jim—to keep up with the times. We can't get by with our present costs forever. Some of the competition is coming down in price and we'll have to follow. It seems to me that this is a natural way to lower costs."

"It sure sounds logical, Al, but the old man's done pretty well up to now, and there's no reason why he won't continue doing all right from here on in. Why don't you forget about it?"

"Well, I guess I'll have to for now, but I hate to see this happening to our company."

Frustrating interaction

Situations similar to the one just described are familiar to many of us. Substitute another organization, replace the characters, attempt to solve another problem that requires a change by the other members of a group, and the reaction may be similar to that of Al's boss—resistance and perhaps outright rejection. Although this situation faces all age groups in industry, government, and service organizations, it probably occurs more often to the younger employee eager to see his organization utilize the latest practices of business administration. Having been exposed to the latest managerial thinking and armed with the most modern tools and techniques of the trade, he approaches his first after-graduation job intent upon putting his knowledge to use. It is then that the frustrating experiences begin—the resistance to change, the nonacceptance of new ideas, and perhaps the rejection of the new employee by the group.

Understanding people—the key to successful interaction

In view of this resistance and nonacceptance, how does one cope with the situation? How does one get along with the group and the boss? How does one become accepted and make a positive contribution to the efforts of the group? The answers to these questions lie with an understanding of people themselves—with an understanding of the fact that everyone's behavior is unique. In fact, not only is behavior unique, but events are also unique. Every event occurs at a certain place at a given time, to persons of a certain age and under specified conditions, under an arrangement of all that will never be repeated. Never again will the same thing happen to the same people at the same time at the same place under the same conditions; yet we attempt to categorize and assume that because something happened with a given outcome once, it will have the same outcome a second time. It is this very same uniqueness of people and events that causes conflicts and problems within organizations for, in the final analysis, perfect predictability is virtually impossible where people are concerned.

We all have to work with people

At every level of any organization, one is working for and with people. It is essential to know how to get along with people and to understand why they operate the way they do. Without the ability to understand, get along, and fit in if required, the chances for advancement are fairly slim. Although at higher-level supervisory positions some might not consider it as important to understand people because the prerogatives can be to tell employees what to do and not to worry about their desires or wishes, we now realize that this is not the way to interact with others. Unfortunately, this behavior pattern often provides a model for employees, who tend to emulate the characteristics of the boss and thus perpetuate interaction problems.

However, getting back to our original question, in order to cope with situations, to get along with the group, to be accepted, and to make positive contributions, it is necessary to understand people and the manner in which they operate. Only in this way will it be possible to predict the probable outcome of a suggested change, the correct timing for a course of action, or the chances of successful interpersonal actions.

The first step in the understanding of people in general is an understanding of the individual—the subject of the following chapter.

EXERCISE QUESTIONS

1. What knowledge would Jim Dee possess that Al Allen would not?
2. How would Jim have gained his knowledge?
3. Were Mr. Able's points valid?
4. Do you think Al was thoroughly prepared for his meeting with Mr. Able? Why or why not?
5. What could Al have done to better prepare himself for the meeting with Mr. Able?

DISCUSSION TOPICS

1. From your own experience, cite an example of successful interaction and explain why it was successful.
2. From your own experience, cite an example of a frustrating interaction and the reasons for its lack of success.

SCHOOL

2

The Individual

Each one of us is a unique individual. N. J. Moroney, explaining the multiplication law of statistics, considers the odds of a young man finding a young lady with a Grecian nose, platinum blonde hair, hazel eyes, and a first-class knowledge of statistics. Considering the probability of the nose as 1 in 100, the hair as 1 in 10, the eyes as 1 in 10, and the first-class knowledge of statistics as 1 in 1000, he calculates that a person with these characteristics would be 1 in 10,000,000. With additional input of a criterion for height, weight, vital statistics, and so forth, one more calculation might give odds of 1 to 1,000,000,000. Every person is unique when carefully compared point by point with another;[1] statistically or otherwise, everyone is unique. Everyone has an individual philosophy based upon his characteristic beliefs, attitudes, and value system. However, these, unlike the statistical example, which does not change, can change over time as they are exposed to different experiences.

Every individual is unique

In addition to our philosophy, each one of us has many needs (such as the need for love, recognition, esteem, and so forth) which we are attempting to satisfy at any particular time. The interaction of our philosophy and needs in a particular situation results in our behavior. Because we certainly would not expect everyone's behavior to be the same in similar situations, we are required to interact with others considering their philosophies, needs, and behaviors as well as our own. The degree of interaction depends upon each individual's behavior.

Unique needs affect interactions

With the expectation of unique behavior, a first step in learning how to interact would be to obtain an understanding of individual behavior—how one acquires his own beliefs, attitudes, values, and frame of reference. The attempt to understand the individual will also give insight into an understanding of oneself.

What is behavior?

To begin our understanding of the individual, we make certain assumptions: *Philosophy* (*P*) is a function of *beliefs* (*B*) and *attitudes* (*A*) as modified by *values* (*V*). *Behavior* (*BE*) is a function of *philosophy* as modified by *needs* (*N*) as affected by a *frame of reference* (*FR*), *past experience* (*PE*), *the present situation* (*PS*), *and future expectations* (*FE*).

For those with a mathematical inclination, we can say:

$$P = f\left(\frac{B + A}{V}\right) \tag{1}$$

$$BE = f\left(\frac{P}{N}\right) \leftarrow (FR + PE + PS + FE) \tag{2}$$

Next we must analyze each term in each of the above relationships. We'll begin with an exploration of the significance of the terms in Eq. (1).

What are beliefs?

Belief is "confidence in the truth or existence of something not immediately susceptible to rigorous proof." [2] Probably the most universally held belief is in God or a superior being. Certainly, by definition, this must be classified as a belief. Another belief is that the world is round. We know this is true, but it is not susceptible to rigorous proof. Other beliefs might be that honesty and right will triumph. Of course, all would concede that there are many more.

What are attitudes?

By definition, attitude is "manner, disposition, feeling, position, etc., with regard to a person or thing—orientation of the mind." [3] By this definition love and hate are attitudes, as are conservatism or liberalism. Respect for authority and punctuality are also attitudes. It is easy to see that arguments can develop as to whether a particular feeling or state of mind is an attitude or a belief. Consider stealing, for example. Would it be correct to say, "I do not believe one should steal," or "My attitude is that stealing is wrong"? Even the definition of stealing is a semantic problem. Actually, in the long run, what is important is to realize that beliefs and/or attitudes are modified by an individual's value system—that is, "the relative worth, merit or importance" that he gives to his attitudes and beliefs when they are in conflict with each other or with someone else's. Assume, for example, that we believe in honesty and have an attitude of respect for authority. If we find ourselves in a situation in which an immediate supervisor is a dishonest person, how should we react? Do we place a greater value on respect for authority, thereby overlooking dishonesty, or do we place a higher value on honesty, thereby losing respect for his authority? Similar situations face each of us many times. When conflict develops between different attitudes or beliefs, we must decide for ourselves which way to go or which attitude or belief must be ranked above the other in our value system. Thus, we have come full circle. Beliefs + attitudes, as modified by our value system, result in a philosophy—"a particular system of principles for the conduct of life." [4]

Value systems

Conflicts between attitudes and beliefs

To continue our analysis of terms, we next look to the relationships concerning behavior in Eq. (2). We said that behavior is the result of philosophy as modified by needs as affected by a frame of reference, past experiences, the present situation, and future expectations. The philosophy portion of the relationship was just examined, so now we must look at the remaining terms.

One very useful method of examining the needs referred to in the behavior equation is in the terms of: (1) physiological needs, (2) safety needs, (3) the need for love and belongingness, (4) the need for recognition and esteem, (5) the need for self-actualization (doing your own thing). These needs generally arrange themselves in a hierarchy of importance, with number 1 being the lowest-order need and number 5 the highest.[5] The hierarchy and importance of needs as motivators and reactors in the behavioral relationship will be discussed in greater detail later in the chapter. At the present time it should be obvious that needs affect behavior. For example, consider how behavior changes if danger is imminent, i.e., when one's safety need is threatened.

Maslow's hierarchy of needs modifies behavior

The behavioral relationship also tells us that frame of reference, past experiences, the present situation, and future expectations have a direct bearing on behavior.

Frames of reference affect behavior

Frame of reference is the summation of our own beliefs, attitudes, values, and cultural background. It provides a vantage point from which we may try to understand complex relationships. As one author puts it, it is our attempt to classify unique events into general classes or categories and then attach names or labels to each.[6] We might also say that it is a standard to which we try to compare a word, saying, or conduct. For example, examine the expression, "Let's rap." In one frame of reference rap means to tap lightly, like rapping on a door. It conjures up visions of tapping lightly on something or even of being invited to fight with the person making the statement, and it summons appropriate behavior. In another frame of reference rap means talk. When asked to rap, a reaction to the request would be acceptance or rejection of the idea of having a conversation. This is one example of how behavior is affected by frame of reference. This subject will be discussed in more detail when we explore how frames of reference are established.

Past experiences affect behavior

Past experiences can have a profound effect on behavior. We certainly know that behavior in animals can be conditioned by past experiences. What we are referring to in this case, however, is nonconditioned past experiences. Consider John Doe, who has been fired for really leveling with his boss when asked for an opinion about a certain occurrence or event. Do you think John will ever level again if placed in a similar situation? (The assumption is made that being fired is a nonacceptable occurrence.)

Present situations influence behavior

This example can be used with slight modification to illustrate how the present siutation can influence behavior. Assume that John is satisfied with his job, is not interested in a promotion, and really does not have to work (is independently wealthy). In his present situation he will probably level with his boss when asked for an opinion because he has nothing to lose—he does not have to "play it safe."

Future expectations influence behavior

The final term in the behavioral expression is that of future expectations. Although many people live only for the present and behave accordingly, some people are willing to endure many hardships today with the expectation of "making it" at a later date. The desire to act or behave belligerently in a current work situation might certainly be modified if the future expectations of such behavior would be loss of job—that is, if loss of job is important to the individual.

Having examined the rationale behind the terms in the equations concerning behavior, the next step in understanding the individual is realization of how philosophy—beliefs, attitudes, and value systems—develops.

PHILOSOPHY

External influences affect attitudes

At birth, all babies, regardless of their sex, are equal in the sense that they have no beliefs, attitudes, or values. Accordingly, attitudes that are developed about and by the child must, of necessity, be the result of the effects of outside influences interacting with the unique biological constitution and physiological maturation of the child. If external influences had no such effect, children could conceivably grow up together with physical appearances being the only thing different about them.

By time frame the first external source of influence for most children would be the family—mother, father, and other children; the second would be peer groups; the third would be the school and other institutions such as the church or social groupings, clubs, etc.; the fourth and last would be mass media. All of these influences are in turn affected by geographical regions.

FAMILY

The family as primary influence

In the family situation, usually the first, and probably the most important influence on a preschool child is exerted by the mother-figure, who passes on to her child preformed opinions and attitudes concerning the role of boys and girls—men and women—in society as she perceives it within her frame of reference. Frames of reference and value systems can change rapidly from place to place so that an understanding of the time frame and place in which an individual grew up is essential to an understanding of the individual. For example, how could an American who grew up in the early 1950s have an appreciation for the problems of an Englishman who as a child lived through the German bombings of London in the 1940s?

Mother influence

The mother, because of her own upbringing, will have preconceived and well-developed ideas concerning the role of a boy/girl in society. These ideas are passed on to her preschool child both consciously and unconsciously.

A girl child can be treated on the one hand as a "little lady," dressed in frilly clothes, given tea parties, encouraged to play with dolls and to "play house"—denied physical exercise and treated as a hothouse flower. On the other hand, a girl can be treated as a tomboy, allowed to play with boys, wear jeans, and be considered as "one of the guys" by her peers in the sandlot set.

Father influence

The father also plays an important role in the life of a girl. She sometimes has romantic notions about her father and sees herself as the rival of her mother for the father's attention. A domineering mother with a weak father or vice versa can have a considerable effect on the outlook of a girl.

Importance of sexual identity

Boys, in general, have different problems of identity than those experienced by girls in part because of the still-popular belief that man is the stronger sex. Statistically speaking, this may not be the case—males have a higher mortality rate at birth, die at a younger average age, have more incidents of high cholesterol, and record a higher suicide rate than females. Nevertheless, whether boy or girl, the child develops beliefs and attitudes in the early home situation based upon the roles played by the mother and the father.

Parental teachings

Religious beliefs and attitudes concerning morals, respect for authority, personal habits, work, conformity, obedience, race, color, and creed are acquired by the growing child either from parental teachings or inference from observation. Parental teaching in this case is not a direct form of teaching—it takes the form of attitudes relayed to children by such remarks as "No, no, don't touch" (respect for other people's property), "that's a naughty baby to take mother's thimble" (one should not steal), and statements such as "clean up your room, work hard, do what the policeman tells you, do what daddy tells you, don't interrupt, no, no." The constant repetition of such statements relays to the child the parents' feelings. The result is that the small child begins to acquire these feelings as his own attitudes.

Indirect influences

Less obvious than attitudes acquired from direct parental influence are the attitudes acquired from inference or observation. These include attitudes regarding fighting after listening to parents engage in name-calling contests when they specifically tell their children that it is not right to fight or swear; attitudes regarding race which can be formed by listening to the prejudicial talk of parents; attitudes concerning honesty after observing daddy staying home and enjoying himself while mother calls in to report that he is sick. Preschool children can sense the real feelings of their parents from these observations which many times belie verbalized teachings. In any case, the point to be made is that the early home situation results in the child's developing beliefs and attitudes which, if not changed at a later date, may stick with him for life.

Religious background as an influence

Parental teachings concerning morality, right and wrong, and attitudes toward work are often based on religious background. The Protestant Ethic is an example of such a background. According to Peter Blau, the Reformation resulted in a "disciplined devotion to hard work and the pursuit of one's vocation. The Protestant has no pope or priest to furnish spiritual guidance and absolve him for his sins, but must ultimately rely on his own conscience and faith; this encourages the emergence of self-imposed discipline . . ." Rational conduct geared toward saving man from his sins by conscience and methodical efforts in his everyday life and regular work was the rule. "Protestantism, therefore, has transplanted the aesthetic devotion to disciplined hard work from monastic life . . . to the mundane affairs of economic life." The result was a vigorous discipline and immersion in work as a way of relieving anxieties about self, family and community.[7]

The geographical region in which the parents were reared can also have an effect upon the development of their attitudes and beliefs which

Geographical region as an influence

in turn affect the child. Weber repeatedly emphasizes the industrial character and the hard-work attitude of the New England settlements as directly attributable to the cohesiveness of the congregations. The Church of England affiliation of many of the large planters of the South and the melting-pot characteristics of western communities gave rise to regional differences which have a bearing on the teaching of children of these localities. It is certainly not as true today as it was of the past generation, but we must consider that the past generation was the teacher of the present generation as discussed later.

Peer Groups

The second logical outside source of influence in the development of an individual's attitudes and beliefs is his peer group. Probably the most important and influential peer group in the experiences of the very young child would be that composed of the children in the neighborhood—most of the same age but some being younger and some older. A second peer group might be the members of a Sunday School class if the young child attends one. The third peer group might be the members of the child care center or nursery school that many small children attend.

Neighborhood peer group—a primary influence

In terms of exposure time, the neighborhood peer group often ranks first. The small child compares the attitude and feelings that have been relayed to him in one way or another from his immediate family to those of other members of the group who in turn relay their attitudes to him. It is in this kind of situation that the value systems continue to develop. Suppose, for example, the oldest members of the group might want to throw rocks at a passing car. Two or three of the others take up the idea, but Johnnie has been taught that it is wrong to throw rocks at cars. Although he has been taught by his parents that it is wrong, his desire is to join with the group and be accepted by being a rock-thrower. He must now choose between the alternative courses of action. In essence he is exercising a value judgment—that is, he is weighing the relative importance of an occurrence or of an event. Is his desire to be accepted by the group stronger than the teaching against throwing? If the answer is yes, he would value acceptance by the group (although he probably would not know that this was the real reason) as being more important than doing what his parents taught. Or would the influence of the parents outweigh the desire to join the group so that he would put a higher value on parental guidance? Each small child must really make such decisions—in doing so, he is developing a value system.

Religious group influence

The same reasoning and exposure takes place within the Sunday School or church group. The difference in this case is usually that many of the children may share some similar attitudes because their upbringing was influenced by parents of the same faith. However, in many cases this is not the case, and the same conflicts develop in this situation as those developed in the neighborhood, peer group, or social set.

Preschool care group influence

Finally, the most nonheterogeneous group would probably be found in the child care center or nursery school. In this situation children from different neighborhoods, different ethnic backgrounds, and different creeds may be thrown together. This may be a most disturbing situation for some small children who must now weigh an existing value system based upon exposure to new beliefs and perhaps ethnic prejudices. In many instances small children can indeed be very cruel, especially if they are echoing the sentiments of their parents. The desire to be accepted as a group member and considered as one of the gang can cause coalitions to form against weaker members of the group. Name-calling, the use of filthy expressions, and dysfunctional behavior are fairly typical at this stage of development, in both preschool and neighborhood situations.

Imitation

A common occurrence in many peer-group situations, particularly those in the neighborhood, is small children in a group trying to copy the behavior of a particularly esteemed or older member. The attempt to behave like the esteemed or older member and thus incur favor and perhaps a form of hero worship by the other members of the group can lead to behavior alien to most of the other teachings of a particular child. This phenomenon has been observed many times in the study of preschool children, gangs, and minority groups.

School and Other Institutions

Influence of formal learning institutions

The third outside source having an influence on the development of the individual is the school and other institutions. It is in the school situation in particular that many young children are first exposed to a structured teaching experience. It is here that beliefs and attitudes may be intensified or become less important. In fact some may even disappear. It is also here that definite attitudes concerning differences in males and females continue to develop. From the time they enter kindergarten, girls traditionally have been brainwashed to accept an inferior status in society. Kindergarten story books and first grade readers show little girls helping with the housework or baking cookies, not becoming involved with kites, chemistry sets, carpentry, or other active pursuits, which are left to the boys. The illustrations portray boys camping by themselves, getting jobs as delivery boys, or learning to do magic tricks and in general displaying a great deal of independence. Girls, on the other hand, are shown standing or sitting still in the background watching admiringly while the boys climb trees or play football or turn cartwheels.

"Boy" vs. "girl" roles

As the difficulty of reading progresses in the second and third grades, boys in the stories are told to be men and are shown driving busses, delivering mail, putting out fires, and so forth. Women, on the other hand, are shown working as teachers, librarians, and nurses, but not holding the so-called exciting jobs.

Influence of textbooks on female and male role learning

These facts, which can be verified by picking up any reading book in virtually any system, were brought to light by a group of New Jersey women calling themselves "Women on Words and Images." Their examination of 144 books making up 15 major reader series revealed that 881 stories contained boys as main characters, while only 344 portrayed girls. In addition, whereas 7 percent of the men in the stories are identified as fathers, grandfathers, uncles, or husbands, 69 percent of the women are known exclusively in terms of their relationships to others, and, in most cases, as being mothers.[8] When these facts were brought to the attention of the publishers, they agreed to listen to concerned parents and were willing to oblige by changing the image of women found in these books. However, we must remember that the mother who raised the 20-year-old woman of today was influenced in this manner more than three decades ago. Therefore, we must conclude that the literature that the average woman of today was exposed to as a little girl was probably biased and did nothing to instill in her a feeling of confidence that she had the ability and the brain power to compete with boys or men in many situations. In fact, the reverse would be true.

This image of course is likely to be intensified by the teacher who, herself, has been brought up with the same ideas and values. Traditionally, teachers of kindergarten, first, second, and third graders are female. In fact, over 90 percent of teachers at this grade level are women, according to the National Education Association. The Department of Labor, Bureau of Labor Statistics, also tells us that 70 percent of noncollege teachers for all grades are women. Because of their upbringing, these teachers intensify the biased image of little girls by attitudes and comments made in class concerning the roles of girls and boys. The stories teachers have children act out give the roles of breadwinner, head of family, judge, doctor, storekeeper, and so forth, to the boys while the girls play mother, nurse, teacher, clerk, and secretary.

Teachers' biases concerning traditional roles

Boy/girl roles at play

Not only do the teachers perpetuate this role-playing situation, but the children themselves often seek out the traditional boy/girl part in both spontaneous and planned play. This comes from their desire to emulate the actions and roles of their parents as they perceive them. The little girl dresses up in mother's clothes and attempts, by playing house, to act just like mommy. The boy, on the other hand, plays the heavy in the "house" game.

Think a few minutes about what you have just read about school. Think of your own upbringing. Can you now see why it is difficult for the male to believe in equality of the sexes?

Within the school system in general, certain attitudes are intensified, beliefs are examined, and value systems may be modified. Many times the philosophy acquired in the classroom or from classroom peers conflicts with the philosophy of the parents, thus causing the child to make additional adjustments in his own philosophy.

The role of religion

The church, as already mentioned, is another formal institution which can have an important influence upon the child. Although the influence of the Protestant Ethic has been discussed earlier, we must remember that its effects are strongest today in the "Bible Belt"—in general, those states which made up the confederacy. The Anglican and Scotch-Irish background of many people in this area, even today, results in church teachings that are very narrow concerning sin, goodness, right and wrong, the sacred-

Protestant

ness of the bible, and the position of the "preacher" in the community.

Catholic

The Catholic Church, on the other hand, teaches that the word of the priest is infallible, that the Church's word is law, and that the priest has the power to forgive sins. This attitude concerning sin does not appear to put as much strain on the child as does the Protestant "conscience."

Jewish

In the Jewish religion, the family attitudes and ties are very strong. The wife runs the home and has a profound influence on the Jewish child. The Orthodox Jew is strict in the interpretation of the law and considers education as being very important. This attitude is in turn instilled in the young child.

Organized activities alter values

In addition to the school and the church, other organized activities such as Boy Scouts, Girl Scouts, sports teams, and social clubs can influence beliefs, attitudes, and values. Attitudes concerning morals, ethics, fair play, and interaction with others are often acquired within the atmosphere of these organized activities.

Mass Media

Exposure to mass media

The final outside source having a direct bearing on the development of the beliefs, attitudes, and values of the child is mass media. Every day most children have opportunities to listen to the radio, watch television, listen to news, hear speeches, and read the newspaper, magazines, and books. These mass media outlets expose him to a variety of attitudes and value systems which he must weigh in developing or changing his own.

Influences of mass media

The messages relayed by the mass media are usually carefully screened and edited. According to Alvin Toffler, they "convey relatively nonrepetitive ideas. They tend to be more grammatically accurate than ordinary conversation; and if presented orally, they tend to be enunciated more clearly. Waste material is trimmed away." [9] Unfortunately, many are biased in the message they attempt to convey. Their persuasive power can be very effective if one is not exposed to all sides of the picture. Joyce Maynard brings this point out very clearly in her book *Looking Back: A Chronicle of Growing Up Old in the Sixties* (Garden City, N.Y.: Doubleday & Company, Inc., 1973) when she says, "Everyone's memories of growing up are different, of course, but those of us who grew up in the 1960's have something in common. It's partly because we are all media children—raised on television and *Life Magazine*."

Summary

In summary, we have seen that philosophy develops as a result of beliefs and attitudes as modified by values. Beliefs and attitudes are affected by outside influences upon the growing child, the first being the family, the second being peer groups, the third being the school and other institutions, the fourth being mass media. These four influences must also be set against geographical location, race of origin, cultural inheritance, religious background, and other subgroup identifications.

Analysis of philosophy

Any attempt to really understand the individual would, of necessity, involve an appreciation of the aforementioned influences. The degree of importance that one attributes to analysis of these factors in the attempt to explain a particular person's philosophy is of course entirely dependent upon the individual. Sometimes it might be most important; at other times it is of very little significance. At least an awareness of how philosophy develops and changes is essential because it can be useful in many problem situations.

Analyze your own philosophy

Having examined the manner in which an individual's philosophy develops and changes, it should be easier for us to analyze our own philosophies and how they developed. We should reflect upon our own upbringings, make a list of beliefs and attitudes, and consider the valuations placed on each. Are they really ours? Or have we taken them blindly because of certain background factors such as the area of the country where we grew up, the particular neighborhood, economic bracket, values of peer groups, school system attended, and the many other minute, subtle influencers of philosophy. In other words, we must get to know ourselves. Do

Are you your own person?

we as persons really want to live with the philosophies we have acquired, or do we want to change? How much are we willing to give and take in our interaction with other people? Are the value systems that we have acquired relevant to today's rapidly changing world? These things we must decide. Perhaps the information previously presented will assist in opening the closet and airing relevant factors.

BEHAVIOR

Referring back to our second equation, behavior is a function of philosophy, modified by needs as affected by frame of reference, past experience, present situation, and future expectations. Of the variables modifying or affecting behavior, one of the most important is the need variable.

Maslow's need hierarchy

We are indebted to Abraham Maslow for a theory of motivation which helps us to think systematically about man's basic needs. To review, he lists five such needs which he arranges in a hierarchy of importance in terms of the total life span of the individual. With the most important need at the top, they rank themselves as follows:

the need for self-actualization,
need for esteem,
need for belongingness and love,
safety needs,
physiological needs.

Physiological Needs

Physiological needs are basic

Physiological needs refer to such factors as food, sexual fulfillment, shelter, clothes for warmth, sleep and other needs dealing with the functions and vital processes of the living person. These are considered the basic needs because if many of them are not satisfied, man might die. Others profoundly affect behavior even though death does not result if they are unfulfilled. A man's behavior, for example, can change immensely if he is on the verge of starvation. Where, in a normal circumstance, he might place a high value on honesty and loyalty, if he were hungry to the point of starvation, his behavior might change so that he would hunt, kill, cheat, and steal just to get enough food to sustain life. Making someone extremely hungry, thirsty, or suffer from lack of sleep has been used quite effectively in war-time situations to break many prisoners who normally would have a high sense of honor and loyalty. In essence, this is the brainwashing technique which is sometimes most successful in forcing an individual to confess almost anything.

Safety Needs

Safety needs are important

The safety needs include "security, stability, dependency, protection, freedom from fear, from anxiety and chaos, the need for structure, order, law, limits, strength for the protector, etc." [10]

Many people in American society have most of the safety needs enumerated above satisfied. In many geographical areas one can feel relatively safe concerning tyranny, murder, chaos, criminal assault, continuation of a stable government, and so forth. However, when man receives threats to law and order and authority in his society this need readily comes to the surface.

The safety need of security may be what many people are attempting to indirectly satisfy when they first enter the job market. The majority of people who work do not thoroughly enjoy, look forward to, or get satisfaction out of each and every day of their occupation. However, the money gained from working makes it possible to satisfy the security as well as the physiological needs. A very amicable person in a work group can suddenly turn into a tyrant and back-stabber if he feels strongly that his job is being threatened and that this is the only course of action that will prevent his being fired. Thus, again, we see that behavior can be drastically altered by the attempt to satisfy a need.

Belongingness and Love Needs

The first social need

The belongingness and love needs can be considered social needs because the previously discussed needs center around the individual. These social needs explain the desire to be a member of a group, one of the gang, the desire to put down roots and be accepted, and the desire to make and keep friends. This particular belongingness need helps us understand the behavior of the small child in the group situation discussed earlier. We noted that becoming a member of the neighborhood peer group was sometimes more important to many small children than maintaining an attitude relayed to them by their parents concerning certain aspects of right and wrong.

Need satisfaction in knowledge worker

With the rapid changes taking place in our technology and society today, we may see these needs satisfied more and more in the "knowledge worker" by association with professional fraternities and societies rather than work organizations. The "knowledge worker" is Peter Drucker's term for "a man or woman who applies to productive work, ideas, concepts, and information rather than manual skill or brawn." [11] Drucker further points out that by 1980 the professional managerial and technical group will embrace the majority of Americans at work in the civilian labor force. Actually, we are already in a post-industrial society—that is over 50 percent of the civilian labor force is engaged in state and local government, services, professions, and communications. Specifically, the August 1973 Department of Labor Statistics report indicates that approximately two-thirds of the labor force is in this category.

The rise of the professional man is recognized by Bennis who states, "They seemingly derive their rewards from inward standards of excellence, from their professional societies and from the intrinsic satisfaction of their task. In fact, they are committed to the task, not the job: to their standards, not their boss. And because they have degrees, they travel. They are not good 'company men'; they are uncommitted except to the challenging environments where they can 'play with problems.' " [12] John Gardner also makes the same point. "The loyalty of the professional man is to his profession and not to the organizaiton that may house him at any given moment. Compare the chemist or electronics engineer in a local plant with the nonprofessional executives in the same plant. The men the chemist thinks of as his colleagues are not those who occupy neighboring offices but his fellow professionals wherever they may be throughout the company, even throughout the world. Because of his fraternal ties with widely dispersed contemporaries, he himself is highly mobile. But even if he stays in one place, his loyalty to the local organization is rarely of the same quality as that of the true organization man. He never quite believes in it." [13]

But whether a knowledge worker or a manual worker, each person selects a group which he joins to satisfy the need for belongingness.

Esteem Needs

Man needs recognition and esteem

Most people in our society desire self-respect and the esteem of others. The esteem need breaks down into two categories. The first is the desire for personal achievement or worth; the second is for "reputation or prestige, status, fame and glory, dominance, recognition, attentions, importance, dignity, or appreciation." [14] Without this recognition, esteem, and feeling of self-importance, man begins to feel inferior and sometimes helpless. In fact, his discouragement can be so great that his behavior can become much less effective, and he no longer gains satisfaction from many activities that were previously satisfying.

In some people this drive for the esteem need is so great that it can often affect their value system to the extent of reclassifying right and wrong to suit a particular desire. To get ahead, people have been known to falsify records, slightly warp the truth of a situation, give themselves credit for something done by someone else, and in general, act contrary to the attitudes and values that they have developed through the years.

Self-Actualization Needs

Man must do the best that he can

The final need, that for self-actualization, is probably the hardest to adequately define. In Maslow's own words, "The positive criterion for selection was positive evidence for self-actualization (SA), as yet a difficult syndrome to describe accurately. For the purposes of this discussion, it may be loosely described as the full use and exploitation of talents, capacities, potentialities, etc. Such people seem to be fulfilling themselves and to be doing the best that they are capable of doing." [15]

Recognition of the self-actualizing person can be accomplished by the observation of personal character traits enumerated by Maslow. Because relatively few people are self-actualized on the job, it is only necessary to note that more than one such person in the same group might cause problems. They tend to be "loners" often not committed to group goals and norms.

Hierarchy of needs varies with the individual

In discussing his needs hierarchy, Maslow makes certain points that must be kept in mind when we attempt to understand how needs affect philosophy and result in behavior. First, the hierarchy is not rigid. All people do not have the same hierarchy of needs. As far as Maslow was concerned, the two lowest-order needs appear to be of the same importance to all people; but once the social needs are experienced, relationships can be different depending upon the person and the situation. Esteem can be more important than love to some people, while to others self-actualization can be more important than either love or esteem. Second, a person will want the more basic of two needs if deprived of both, although there is no implication that he will act upon his desire. In other words, he may not change his behavior. In essence, there are more determinants to behavior than basic needs and desires. Third, once a need is satisfied it can no longer motivate behavior. This principle or maxim can be observed very clearly in the case of the small child. You can promise him a lollipop to be good, and he probably will be good if he wants a lollipop. But if he has just completed a big dinner with all the dessert that he could possibly want, a lollipop could not be used as a bribe to make him behave. The need for a lollipop has already been satisfied. Fourth, a lower-level need does not have to be completely satisfied before the next need becomes relevant in the behavioral relationship. One does not have to be completely gorged before he wants safety. He doesn't have to be completely satisfied before he looks for belongingness and love, and he doesn't have to have complete belongingness and love satisfaction before he looks for self-esteem. Maslow points out that most of us probably have all of our needs partially satisfied and partially unsatisfied at the same time. Need satisfaction overlaps as shown in Figure 1, which depicts the average person as being satisfied 80 percent in physiological needs, 70 percent in safety needs, 50 percent in love needs, 40 percent in self-esteem needs, and 10 percent in self-actualization needs.[16]

Behavior is more than needs

Needs overlap

The lines in Figure 1 are arbitrarily drawn to make a point—the composite of need satisfaction in a certain percentage of the population—

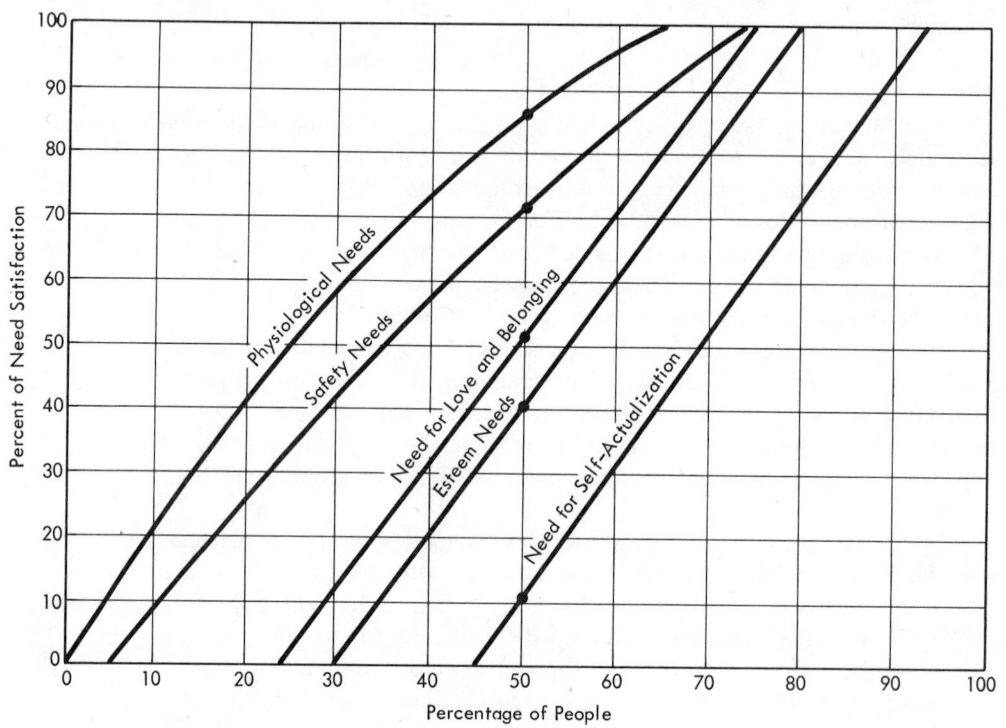

FIGURE 1
Need Satisfaction in People

because it is doubtful that sufficient research could be conducted to accurately pinpoint any one of them. Figure 1 does reveal that a need does not have to be completely satisfied before the next higher level need appears. Also, it is, in general terms, based upon total population. Different groups and different countries would have different profiles. It is important to remember that each individual's behavior at any given point in time is affected by a large number of needs in a hierarchical order, and that the needs and their hierarchical order are constantly changing as goals are reached, avoided, or supported.

Order of needs constantly changes

Frame of Reference

The next element of the behavioral relationship is the frame of reference—the standard by which we compare occurrences or events to help us determine how we might behave. Frame of reference is based upon word usage and meaning taught during our formal education as modified by social and political conditions existing at that time.

Frame of reference affects behavior and response

Consider the 1940s' frame of reference with banana splits, rationing coupons, DC 3s, trolley cars, model A Fords, Mickey Mouse, Albert Einstein, Lilly Marlene, Count Basey, Eddy Duchin, Glenn Miller, Scarlet O'Hara, Dale Carnegie, jukebox, k-rations, gardenias, bomb sites, saddle shoes. It was a swing era for the young. *Swinging* was dancing to the popular band music. *Gay* meant cheery and happy. *Far out* was a term applied to someone who did not fit in with the general group. *Dudes* referred to easterners who spent vacations on ranches in the West. *Bad* meant something distasteful. A *Rosie* referred to any woman working in a factory in war-time.

In the 1960s we had Twiggy, the Beatles, John Glenn, Billy Sol Estes, Bob Dylan, Jack Ruby, acid rock, pop and op art. Today, *swinging* means to swap mates in a sexual orgy. *Gay* refers to a homosexual. *Far out* means really good. *Dude* is the word for any man or guy. And if something is *bad,* it is very well-liked.

As reported by Toffler in *Future Shock,* at the level of slang, word usage turnover rate is so rapid that dictionary editors have had to change their criteria for word inclusions. The high turnover rate in all words reflects changes in times, processes, and qualities in the environment.

We interpret word meaning from frame of reference and behave accordingly. An innocent word in one person's frame of reference such as *gay* can be offensive to one with a different frame of reference and result in behavior which is completely contrary to what the first person might have expected.

Past Experience

Past experience conditions interaction patterns and modifies behavior

In addition to frame of reference, past experiences have a great effect as a modifier of behavior. Although closely akin to frame of reference, past experience involves situational conditioning—a learning process by which we attempt to predict outcome of a certain behavior or perhaps how we should behave based upon a similar past situation. If we smell wet paint, we know from past experience what will happen if we touch the newly painted surface. A baseball player learns from past experience not to pitch a fast ball to a certain batter. Past experience tells us not to joke about politics with a certain person in the office. All these past experiences have an effect on our behavior.

In reality our entire personality is based on a series of past experiences because that is the way our self developed. "People discover their self-concepts from the kinds of experiences they have had with life—not from telling, but from experience." [17]

What we are concerned with here, however, are past experiences in behavioral situations with other people. When we work with other people, we get to know what they are like, what really is behind some of their remarks and actions. Knowing this we may modify our behavior accordingly.

Sara Jane was insecure. Her parents had not given her any feelings of self-worth or importance as a person in her own right. She had no confidence in herself and felt that she could do nothing right. As a cover-up she always had some comment to make about other peoples' clothes as if she were the expert. This gave her a feeling of importance. Knowing this from past experience, other women in her office did not take offense at her remarks and behaved as they might have if the circumstances were not known.

Present Situation

Present situations can modify behavior

Just as frame of reference and past situations affect behavior, so does the present situation. We can all think of circumstances in which a certain situation altered the characteristic behavior of an individual. Servicemen in wartime situations have displayed courage and valor alien to their normal behavior.

General adaptation syndrome

In many individuals present situations cause frustration and stress, particularly when one thinks that he is not going to fulfill a need or achieve a goal. This reaction to the present situation stress has been called the general adaptation syndrome by Dr. Selye.[18] It is the reason why some people withdraw and some people use direct aggression in a stress situation —the fright, fight reaction. In both situations this is not "normal" behavior for the person concerned.

Although we behave in the present because of the past and in expectation of the future, many times our behavior is directly affected by the present situation.

Future Expectations

Influence of future expectations on behavior

The future expectations, the final portion of the behavioral relationship, more than anything else brings in general situational analysis.

J. P. was well-liked by all employees in the section. He had an open-door policy; he truly believed in participative management; and he delegated all authority possible. It was rumored throughout the group that he was being considered for promotion. Everyone was happy for him because to a man they agreed that this would give him the recognition that he deserved.

As J. P. was reading his morning mail one morning, his intercom buzzer rang and the pleasant voice of his secretary chirped, "Mr. Brown to see you, Mr. Evans."

"OK, Ellen, send him in."

About ten seconds later Ben Brown strode through the door. "J. P., I think we've got a problem!" exclaimed Ben.

"What's that?" queried J. P.

"You know Ed Lynch down in the proofreading section?"

"Yes, I know him."

"Well, he came in drunk again this morning."

"What do you mean, again?"

"To be truthful, this happens to be the third time. I mentioned it to him already and he knows very well that any mistakes in his particular section can cause us problems because it involves figures. And if you get a wrong decimal point or a wrong zero, you know what that can mean."

J. P. nodded, reflecting on the statement. He certainly did know what it could mean. Two or three wrong reports from his particular section could really louse up his chances for promotion. "Yes, Ben, I know exactly what it could mean. Do you think I should talk with him?"

"Yes, I think you ought to, J. P. I think I've been as lenient as I can. I think he needs a little shaking up on this one."

"OK, Ben, go back and tell him that I'd like to see him in about half an hour."

In half an hour Ed Lynch was standing in front of J. P.'s desk.

"Sit down, Ed," said J. P. "What's this about your coming in a little under the weather this morning?"

"You don't have to cloud it over, Mr. Evans. I wasn't under the weather; there wasn't a thing wrong with me."

"That isn't the way Mr. Brown put it."

"Well, Mr. Brown's wrong. Sure, maybe I smelled a little bit, but that doesn't affect the way I work at all."

"Ed, I'm afraid it does. On two occasions before you've come to work, as you say, smelling a little, and reports that you proofread were incorrect. Now this not only reflects on the group, but it reflects on this section and our whole operation."

"Well, if Ben Brown told you that, Mr. Evans, that's not true. No report that I ever did went out of this office incorrect. Furthermore, I don't think it's any of his business how I smell as long as the work gets done."

"Well, you might feel that way about it, Ed," shot back J. P. in a slightly annoyed tone of voice, "but we certainly don't feel that way about it! Now I think you're going to have to see that this occurrence doesn't happen again or else."

"Or else what, Mr. Evans?"

"Don't push it, Ed."

"I said or else what, Mr. Evans?"

"All right, Ed, I think with that attitude, I don't particularly want you working for this group. I'll give you two weeks' notice to look for another job. That's all."

The above is an example of a future expectation reaction on behavior. Normally, J. P. Evans was easy to get along with and liked by all of his employees. Yet here he was faced with a situation in which an employee had come to work in a slightly drunken condition twice before, causing mistakes to be made in a very precise proofreading job. J. P. was up for promotion and his rationale to himself was probably that if this happened one more time, he was really the one holding the bag. Therefore the future expectation of Lynch's being drunk again, making another mistake with the blame going to Evans, caused a blowup–firing episode that was completely out of character for J. P. Evans. His behavior was certainly modified by needs as well as by future expectations.

The future expectations concept comes into play in many behavioral situations. Its effects should thus be considered when analyzing the individual and his probable interaction behavior.

Summary

At this point we should have a pretty good idea of how a person's philosophy develops. We should also have an appreciation of how philosophy is affected by needs, to result in behavior that is in turn affected by frame of reference, past events, the present situation, and future expectations. We should furthermore be in a position to examine our own behavior.

Understanding self

What particular need are we trying to satisfy? Where are we on the hierarchy described by Maslow? What is the present hierarchical order of our needs? Is our frame of reference such that it is causing problems in our day-to-day relationships with other people? Are past experiences coloring our present actions to the extent that we cannot appreciate the present situation? Are our future expectations realistic—in fact, are we living too much for the future? In answering these questions the understanding of individual becomes the understanding of self.

Need to be a member

This analysis of self might also give us insight into why we join organizations other than the work group. In America today the great majority of us are not motivated by physiological or safety needs alone. We are also seeking belongingness, love, and self-esteem. If we can't satisfy these needs on the job, many of us join organizations such as lodges, fraternal organizations, civic groups, bridge clubs, sports clubs, or any activity in which people with the same interests as ours group together to satisfy the belongingness need and perhaps the self-esteem need. In these nonrelated groups we are looked up to by other people; we are recognized for our merit and we feel a sense of accomplishment. In fact some of us may find self-actualization in the nonpaid organizational grouping. However, we sometimes fail to realize that many of us in this type of organization are looking for the same thing. The result can often be a behavioral clash when more than one of us is trying to seek self-esteem the same way in the same situation—for example, three vying for a primary position of leadership in a very small informal group.

Uniqueness causes conflicts

In conclusion, then, we can see that each of us is unique in a wide range of factors—physiological constitution, behavior, philosophy, needs, past experiences, frames of reference, future expectations, beliefs, attitudes, and values. Is it any wonder that conflicts develop within the work organization as well as the other organizations to which many of us belong? Is it any wonder that successful interaction with other people is often difficult?

Now that we have an understanding of the individual and perhaps a better insight into how we ourselves operate, the next step in the understanding of people is knowledge of groups and how they operate, because almost everyone belongs to a group which affects each one's behavior accordingly. Part II will therefore explore the workings of groups.

EXERCISE QUESTIONS

1. Prepare a list of your beliefs. How did you acquire them? Are they valid today?

2. Prepare a list of your attitudes. How did you acquire them? Are they valid today?

3. Give an example from your own background of conflict between a belief and an attitude. What value system did you use to resolve the conflict? Why?

4. Cite an example of how a particular need has modified your behavior in a particular situation. Would you have behaved the same way in a different situation? Why or why not?

5. Considering frames of reference over the years, give examples of words that have changed their meaning from period to period. Give examples of how the different meanings could cause problems in interaction situations.

6. How has a past experience affected your behavior?

7. How has a present situation affected your behavior?

8. How has a future expectation affected your behavior?

9. Name the "Bible Belt" states and give the predominant religion in each state.

10. List the laws of Boy Scouts and Girl Scouts. Which ones refer to beliefs? Attitudes? Values?

11. Give an example of a television show that you feel has affected or modified one of your attitudes or values.

12. List some subgroup identifications that could influence beliefs, attitudes, and values. Explain each.

DISCUSSION TOPICS

1. What is your philosophy of life? How did it develop?

2. Considering changing frames of reference, what is your general frame of reference? Why is it as it is, and how did it develop?

3. How would it be possible for children to grow up with identical philosophies?

4. Give some examples of how value systems are different in different areas of the United States. Why are the value systems different?

5. Obtain a copy of a second or third grade reader. Discuss the roles played by girls and boys. Are the roles biased or are they fair in their interpretation?

6. How many people do you think are living under the "Protestant Ethic" today? How much of an influence do you think it has today? At what age level and in what groups?

7. Compare the development of at least three regionally separated states to see if you can predict what a person who grew up in the state might be like based on educational level, religion, race, national origin, and other factors that might influence beliefs, attitudes, and values.

8. From your own personal experience, how has your value system developed and changed over time? Do you think it is still changing?

9. How can church or Sunday School have an influence on the development of beliefs, atittudes, and values?

10. What are your attitudes toward members of the opposite sex in a work situation?

11. How do you feel about Women's Lib? Do you think men and women "play fair" in an interaction situation?

12. Do you think people have a need hierarchy as Maslow describes?

NOTES

1. N. J. Moroney, *Facts from Figures* (Baltimore: Penguin Books, Inc., 1956), p. 89.

2. *Webster's New Twentieth Century Dictionary,* Unabridged, 2nd ed. (Cleveland and New York: The World Publishing Company, 1968).
3. Ibid.
4. Ibid.
5. Abraham Maslow, *Motivation and Personality,* 2nd ed. (New York: Harper and Row, 1970).
6. Carrol Quigley, "Needed: Revolution in Thinking?" *NEA Journal* (May 1968), p. 8.
7. Peter M. Blau, *Bureaucracy in Modern Society* (New York: Random House, 1956), pp. 39–40. See also H. H. Gerth and C. Wright Mills, *From Max Weber: Essays in Sociology* (New York: Oxford University Press, 1958).
8. An analysis of this report with covering and enlightening comments was made in an article in March 1971 *Redbook* entitled "Harmful Lessons Little Girls Learn in School," by Betty Miles, p. 168.
9. Alvin Toffler, *Future Shock* (New York: Random House, 1970), pp. 147, 148.
10. Maslow, *Motivation and Personality,* p. 39.
11. Peter F. Drucker, *The Age of Discontinuity* (New York: Harper and Row Publishers, 1969).
12. Warren G. Bennis, *Changing Organizations* (New York: McGraw-Hill Book Co., 1966), p. 25.
13. John Gardner, *Self Renewal* (Evanston, Illinois: Harper, 1963), p. 83.
14. Maslow, *Motivation and Personality,* p. 45.
15. Ibid., p. 156.
16. Ibid., p. 54.
17. ASCD 1962 Yearbook Committee, *Perceiving, Behaving, Becoming* (Washington, D.C.: *NEA,* 1962), p. 84.
18. Hans Selye, *The Stress of Life* (New York: McGraw-Hill Book Co., 1956).

The following works were also reviewed in the development of Chapter 2.

E. James Anthony and Cyrille Koupernik, *The Child in His Family* (New York: Wiley-Interscience, A Division of John Wiley & Sons, 1970).

Erving Goffman, *The Presentation of Self in Everyday Life* (New York: Doubleday & Co., 1959).

Henry W. Maier, *Three Theories of Child Development* (New York: Harper & Row, Publishers, 1965).

Lewis R. Wolberg and John P. Kildahl, *The Dynamics of Personality* (New York: Grune & Stratton, Inc., 1970).

part II

UNDERSTANDING THE GROUP

The group is the backbone of any organization. Understanding of its make-up and operation is the second essential element in developing a plan for successful interpersonal relationships in organizations.

The objectives of this Part II are to enable you to

1. *identify* group characteristics;
2. *recognize* the manner in which group characteristics influence members and their interaction process;
3. *categorize* leadership styles;
4. *understand* the sources of power and influence within a group;
5. *appreciate* problems that may be encountered between individuals in a group —group interaction;
6. *anticipate* problems that may be encountered when joining a group.

3

The Group

Why understand groups?

With an understanding of the individual and, hopefully, of one's self, the next step in the attempt to develop a modus operandi for successful interaction with people both outward and upward is an understanding of the group; because, to be accepted and get along, we may have to change our behavior, adjust our values, modify our philosophies, or defer gratification of a particular need.

Group memberships

All of us belong to groups—"assemblages of people" [1]—many of which are classified as an organization—"a body of persons established for some specific purpose." [2] The first group of which most of us become a member is the family. This group, which can be classified as an organization because it has many specific purposes, one of which is to satisfy man's need for belongingness and love, we join involuntarily because we are born into it. The family and the school system, which most of us are required to attend by law, are often the only two groups or organizations of which we are members on an involuntary basis. Most other groups and organizations to which we belong, such as the one for which we work, social clubs, religious groups, fraternal organizations, and miscellaneous clubs, are joined on a voluntary basis to satisfy many different needs or desires.

Limit to small group theory

Because the majority of us have left the parental family group and are beyond the legal age of enforceable school attendance, further discussion will be limited to voluntary group membership. Also, because we are most frequently interacting in small groups, usually less than ten people, even though we belong to a large organization, our discussion will be limited to small-group theory.

Available literature

The abundance of literature available concerning small-group theory is staggering. According to the handbook of small-group research, over 1,350 articles and books are available on the subject.[3] Most of these have been published since 1950. However, most of us do not have time or would not even want to read all the literature in order to become experts. We just want to know enough about groups to be able to get along, be accepted, be productive, and perhaps gain some recognition. To do this, we have to understand groups and how they operate; because as an entity, they are as unique as individuals.

Characteristics of small groups

Small groups have characteristics attributable to the results of group performance that could not be determined entirely by an analysis of the individual members. Although different authors develop different characteristics, at least four appear to be more common than others:

1. Norms or rules governing behavior
2. Role relationships or patterns of activity
3. Power and influence
4. Cohesion or degree of attachment.

NORMS

Norms—ideas about what to do

Norms are ideas in the minds of members about what should and should not be done by a specific member under specific circumstances.[4] Some situational examples are: classmates refuse to tell who threw the spitball at the blackboard; girls in the secretarial pool in a given organization do not rat on one of their members who takes longer than the normal lunch break (as long as she doesn't do it too often); in another organization, older members of the group may come to work later than younger members; in still another organization, one is never too eager to do more than asked; never volunteer; don't make suggestions.

Consider the situation in, let's say, a government office consisting of secretaries, clerks, and typists. Most of the women in the office are in their late forties. None wear excessive make-up and skirts are worn at about knee level. The husband of one of the women is transferred, so she leaves this particular work group. Her replacement is a young lady in her early 20's who reports for her first day of work wearing a micro-mini-skirt, long artificial eyelashes, and excessive make-up. She wonders why she gets the cold shoulder from the other group members and why she is not accepted into the group as the rest apparently are. The answer is obvious. She doesn't fit in. This particular group has a norm that skirts should be worn at knee level and make-up should not be excessive. To be accepted, the new young lady will probably have to adjust her philosophy system in order to accept the form of appearance required to get along with this particular group. In other words, she may have to learn to conform.

Norms influence behavior

It has been found that the rejection that follows not conforming to group norms can be a powerful factor in motivating behavior of individuals. In fact, these pressures to conform form part of the internal structure of most small groups and often have a tremendous influence as behavior modifiers.

What is a small group?

Before continuing our discussion, it might be well to give a definition of small groups. In the context of our discussions, we are defining groups as "two or more persons who are interacting with one another in such a manner that each person influences and is influenced by each other person." [5] By this definition, interaction between individuals must exist. Shaw points this out by noting that if a person is standing looking up at the top of a tall building and some other people come by, see him looking up, stop and look up also, the resultant gathering of people does not constitute a group because no interaction exists. If now, however, they begin talking among themselves about the object they are looking at, then the gathering becomes a group, because of the interaction aspect. Another example might be in the management situation in which the leader who is very authoritarian always tells the followers what to do. The followers are never given a chance to talk or participate whatsoever. A gathering of these people would not be a group by Shaw's definition, because interaction does not take place.

ROLE RELATIONSHIPS

Roles—status and prestige

The next characteristic of the group is role relationships—characteristic patterns of influence. Roles refer to the relative status and prestige of members and their rights and duties as members of the group.[6] The role specifically consists of the behavior expected of the various occupants of each specific position.[7]

An office manager, for example, might be expected to assign housecleaning tasks within the office, insure that the switchboard is manned, and parcel out work to the secretarial pool. The supervisor of the secretarial pool is expected to farm out work to the various secretaries depending upon their experience and work load at the time. The bookkeeper keeps the books and records. These we might call the overt roles associated with each position within a group. In most instances the overt role originates from job titles and job descriptions which are expected to result in a predicted behavior of the position incumbent.

Overt roles

There are other roles in small groups, however, which are not as obvious because of their subtle overtones. These we could name the covert roles. One member of a certain group may be a practical joker, another plays the straight man; one always accepts the scapegoat role, while another plays the jester. The covert roles are only known to the members of the group and might be difficult or impossible to identify if one were not a member of the group.

Covert roles

Of the various roles within groups, the one most discussed in management literature is that of the group leader and his leadership style. Keep in mind that leadership style is usually best known to members of the leader's group.

Leadership role

Likert examines four basic styles of leadership and relates them to group and organizational variables. Although he lists them as systems of organizations, each could be characterized as a leadership style. They are: (1) exploitive-authoritative, (2) benevolent-authoritative, (3) consultative, (4) participative-group.[8] These leadership styles can be found in any group and influence the group considerably.

Leadership types

The exploitive-authoritative (type 1) leader would create a group climate in which the members would not feel free to communicate with the leader and wherein the leader would dictate what needs to be done and expect immediate compliance and commitment. A very strong reward/

Exploitive-authoritative

punishment system would undoubtedly exist. Any new ideas by members of the group would very likely not be accepted. This type of leader probably believes that human beings have a dislike for work, and that because of this they must be controlled, directed, and threatened with punishment to put forth adequate effort. And, finally, he also believes that they prefer to be directed and wish to avoid responsibility, probably have little ambition and want security above all.[9] Life in a group with such a leader would certainly not be the most pleasant experience.

Benevolent-authoritative

The benevolent-authoritative (type 2) leader probably has the same attitude toward people as the type 1 leader, with the exception that he probably doesn't let it show. He tries to be the good guy all the time, with the open-door policy. He plays the fatherly or motherly role and takes an interest in people because he thinks he should. Besides, he thinks that if he has happy workers, he will have satisfied workers. The type 2 leader still does not want participation and doesn't care to know how the people in the group feel about decisions and actions. Consequently, he gives the orders based upon what *he* wants but in a manner he feels will create cooperative compliance.

Consultative

The consultative (type 3) leader is really interested in knowing what the members of the group feel about matters that must be decided. He consults them for their opinion and very likely weighs what they have to say when he makes the decisions. He probably has an attitude toward people such that he assumes that (1) people probably enjoy working, (2) the threat of punishment is not the only way to get people to cooperate—man will exercise self control if he is committed to an objective, (3) commitment to objectives is a function of the rewards associated with their achievement, (4) most people under proper conditions will seek responsibility, (5) most people have more brains than you give them credit for and are capable of assisting in the solution of organizational or group problems, (6) the intellectual capacities of most people are not being used to their fullest.[10] This is not to say that he believes this wholeheartedly, but he believes it to be true in most cases and, as a result, uses the consultative approach in his leadership activities.

Participative-group

Finally, we have the participative-group (type 4) leader, who is truly committed to the assumptions of the type 3 leader and desires the group not only to participate in the decision-making process of the group but if possible have a consensus so that the group arrives at solutions and thus is completely committed to their execution.

Linking-pin concept

Likert also points out that within an organization members of one group often are members of a second group. In fact, under his linking-pin concept, he points out that the leader of one particular group always is a member of the next higher group and as such has an interaction-influence relationship between groups.[11] Actually, *all* of us belong to more than one group. We belong to the work group, the family group, perhaps a social group, and as such are influenced differently by the norms, roles, values, attitudes, power, influence, and cohesion of each particular group that we belong to.

In considering the foregoing discussion, it should be apparent that role relationships are one of the most important characteristics of small groups. Further, although the overt role might be readily identifiable, the covert roles certainly are not. Also, specific leadership styles can often not be identified until one joins the groups.

Importance of roles

POWER AND INFLUENCE

Control of members

Power and influence *within* a group refers to the kind and amount of control that members have over each other. Power and influence *of* the group would determine its relationships to other organizational units or groups within the overall company. However, we are not interested at this time in outside influences of groups, only with internal influences affecting members. Members of a group exert power and influence over other members of the group based upon a wide range of factors including strategic position, leadership style, personality, outside relationships, specific skills and abilities, money and information.

Formal strategic position

That the group leader or supervisor has power by virtue of strategic position is obvious. Whether one likes him or not, whether he has strong or weak personality traits, or whether he has essential skills often may not matter if the organizational structure places him in the supervisory position. His power, in this case, emanates from his position. On the other hand, consider the close friend of the supervisor who always is placed in charge of the group when the supervisor is absent. In this case the friend is in a strategic position which gives him power derived from a source different from organizational position. If his behavior can be vindictive, the members of the group will certainly not ruffle his feathers—because they all realize that if the supervisor is absent, this particular person will be in charge of the group.

Informal strategic position

Strategic location

Another example of power from strategic position or location might be the power exercised in the group by a receptionist. In her position, she gets to meet visitors and receive telephone calls that can or cannot be routed to the proper individuals. She could, if she cared to, conveniently forget to inform the member of the group that a certain person had called; or she could delay delivering a message, thus creating problems for the particular member involved. Thus, the person in this particular position enjoys power based upon strategic position.

The informal leader

Power and influence based upon leadership style is obvious. But consider that we are not always talking about the formal (organization chart) leader. Many groups develop an informal leader who is not the organizationally designated leader. He is the one that the group members look to for approval of their actions and guidance if their particular goals are not in agreement with the goals of the group. Because the members of the group like and admire this particular individual, they will often seek his advice and act accordingly. Thus, he has power and influence based upon this leadership style. Also, different group members may assume the leadership role because of a particular situation, kind of problem to be solved, change in interpersonal relationships, and other factors.

Personality can also be a source of power and influence within a

Personality power

group. Although a good personality and leadership effectiveness sometimes go hand in hand, it is possible to have good characteristic behavior without displaying leadership ability. A person with pleasant behavior characteristics can often influence a group, because the group would not want to make a decision that they feel would hurt this particular individual. The influence is more passive than active, but it still can be felt within the group. Consider the case of a "real nice guy" whom everyone gets along with but who is rather slow in performing his duties. In this particular group, this doesn't disturb the others too much, and the job usually gets done. If a crash project had to be completed, other members of the group might eliminate this particular person from their planning in order to accomplish the desired results. Thus he influences the group in a subtle way. No one really wants to get mad at him, so they work around him. In this matter, he certainly influences the action of the group.

Outside relationships as a source of power

Outside relationships can also be a source of power and influence for a group member. A member who has a friend in another unit of the organization so situated that he can affect a favorable consideration for the group certainly has power and influence. As an example, consider John Brown in Group A. John has a buddy in the accounting department who can influence the budget allocation to Group A. As a result of a favor done by John for his buddy, he is able to have Group A's budget increased more than other groups when the year-end surplus is split. Because the members undoubtedly know of his influence in the accounting department, they certainly are going to see that he gets along well within the group.

Power based on ability

Possession of specific skills and abilities can give an individual power and influence within a group. Consider the group member who has a particular flair for turning proper words and phrases. His talents are often called for if the group is task-oriented and achievement of the goal calls for preparation of a delicately worded piece of correspondence. Another example might be in technical information-gathering groups wherein the member with a specific technical expertise can often influence the work of other less knowledgable members.

Money as a source of power

Money can also be a factor in the power and influence of a member of a group. If any group member is in a position in which he really doesn't have to work—that is, he is independently wealthy and is only working to satisfy a need for belonging—he is in a position to influence other members of the group. This influence can take the form of being always available to lend money, pay the lunch and dinner check, throw plush parties for the group, and in other ways lavish presents and favors that only money can buy. Although this might be a rare situation, it is certainly possible. Enough money certainly can give a member of a group power and influence.

Information as a source of power

Finally, information itself can be an important source of power. The man who possesses the relevant important information can shape the destiny or the outcome of the situation. This becomes obvious if we consider that decisions affecting a situation can only be based upon information that is the best and most complete available at the time. Furthermore, the gaining of an objective must always be based upon the decision of someone else if we do not have the power to make the decision ourselves. Therefore, if a decision must be made by someone else, the person supplying information for that decision really possesses a considerable amount of power. The secretary of Group A who is a good friend of the big boss's secretary and often has lunch with her can have a great influence on the members of Group A, because she gets the hot information directly from the big boss's secretary that can affect the members of her group. The young design engineer who rides to work in a carpool with one of the members of the advertising department and always has the latest information on design changes that the advertising people feel will be essential for promotional purposes certainly can influence the rest of the members of his group in their thinking toward design changes. Many other examples could be used to show how information can be a source of influence and power within a group.

COHESION

Cohesion—degree of attachment

The final characteristic of the group is cohesion, which refers to the degree of attachment or involvement that the members have for the group. People often develop many common points of view when they work closely together. Constant association and socializing between members of the group result sometimes in common ways of thinking and acting. The strong member reinforces the weak member and the weak member gains strength from the strong, thus developing group attitudes and values. This, in turn, develops the cohesion that members have for the group. "Cohesive groups are internally consistent in their measures of status and are more likely to act in unison when their expectations are violated either by management, by one of their own members or even by another group." [12]

Does cohesion vary with age?

In considering cohesion, the age of the group is most important. In this case we are speaking not about the average age of the group but the approximate range of ages of most of the members—that is, a group whose members are in the 20 to 30 age bracket as compared to a group whose members are in the 40 to 50 age bracket. In general, the younger the group, the less cohesive and the easier it is for the group to change. The older the group, the more set it becomes in its ways and the harder it is to change. In general, somewhere between the ages of 30 and 45 the greatest shift in ideas and opinions comes in people and also in groups. These general relationships were published in chart form by Dr. Roger Gould in November 1972.[13] Figure 1 shows some phases of adult life changes in particular age periods. The charts are based upon ranking, which shows relative importance of the different items; or looking at it another way, how strongly the person believes in the particular statement at the particular time period. Looking at the general age of any group against the chart, results clearly show that younger groups are more receptive to change and not as set in their ways as older groups.

GENERAL COMMENTS

Groups are a social system

In general, we have to remember that a small group is really a social system. In addition to its norms, roles, power and influence, and cohesion,

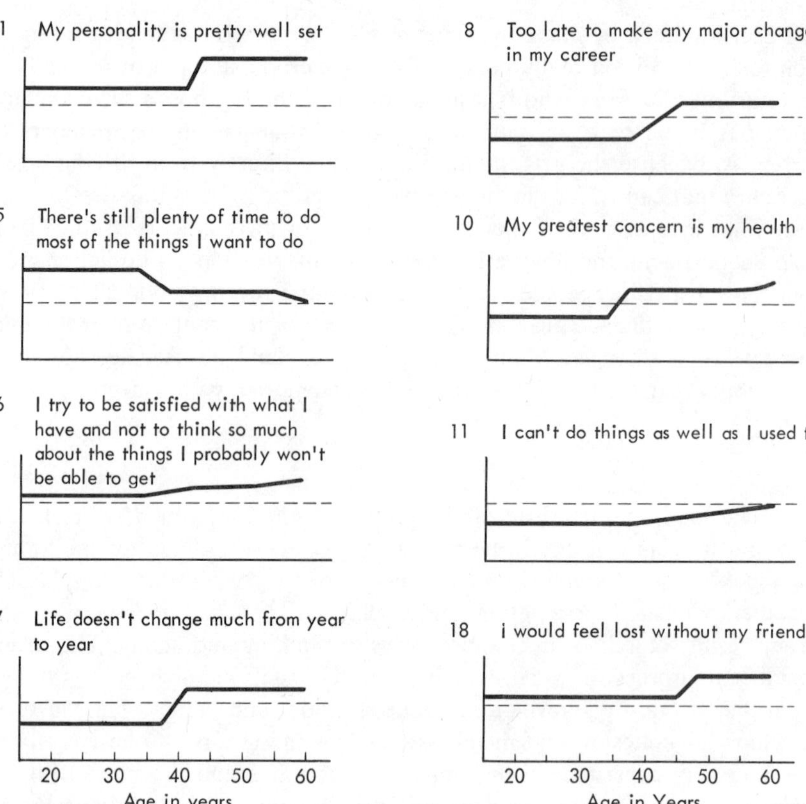

FIGURE 1

Adult Life Changes

Charts reprinted with permission from Roger L. Gould, M.D., "The Phases of Adult Life: A Study in Developmental Psychology," *American Journal of Psychiatry,* Vol. 129 (1972) p. 528.

it develops membership criteria, communications patterns, consensus, and adaptations. It expects certain behavior from its members and, in turn, will strongly support the member in most of his activities. Many times, the group characteristics have developed over a long period of time and are, figuratively speaking, set in concrete. These groups are usually unwilling to change. If they do change, it may not be at a rapid pace. Remember, what must be changed is the combined attitudes, value systems, and beliefs of the group members acting in consensus—indeed, a most difficult undertaking.

Change is difficult

Multiple group membership

In considering small groups, it must be kept in mind that people in an organization belong to more than one group. According to Kurt Lewin, these groups are the framework for our perceptions, felings, and actions.[14] Jerry Jones is a member of the accounting department and officially belongs to the group labeled cost accountants on the organizational charts. He eats lunch each day with a salesman, a draftsman, and a production inspector. The four eat their sandwiches in a hurry and then have a couple games of pinochle before going back to work at one o'clock. He also belongs to the company's Section A softball team and with other members of the comptrollers department belongs to the Association of Professional Accountants. Thus, he belongs to at least four groups within the company, each of which influences his behavior at different times. Of course, he really only has to belong to the one group, that in which he works in the organizational chart; but for reasons of friendship, companionship, identification, or other reasons, he chose to belong to three additional groups. In any of these groups, he might find that he could be accepted for himself and that his needs, values, attitudes, beliefs, behavior, and other factors would be acceptable to all of the members of the various groups. However, this is usually the exception. Somewhere along the line he will probably, if the desire to belong is important enough, have to modify a philosophy, adjust a value, or defer gratification of a need. In fact, he might find that he must change much of his overt behavior:

Group interaction

Pinch, probe, poke—
Humanity, like a giant internist,
Hacks away at one lone man
It tests the eyes—what does it see?
Can it know what lies behind the liquid film?
It takes the pulse, but does it hear the steady beat of a battle drum?
Will Humanity diagnose the ills of one of its parts
Or, knowing the whole is greater, will it sweep him in? [15]

RETROSPECT

This chapter on understanding groups—their characteristics and philosophy—gives us the second element in developing our modus operandi for successful IOU: interaction outward with our work peers, upward with our supervisor. Part I gave us an understanding of self, while Part III will give us an understanding of changing frames of managerial reference or frames of managerial philosophy. Finally, Part IV will develop a plan of action for interaction.

EXERCISE QUESTIONS

1. Give your definition of "small group." Does it agree with that cited by the author?
2. List some group characteristics other than the four discussed in the chapter. Define each and give an example that shows your understanding.
3. Prepare a list of group norms and give an example of how each can affect—in both a positive and negative manner—a new group member.
4. From your personal experience, give an example, if possible, of each of the four leadership types discussed in the chapter. What criteria did you use for your selection? In essence, how did you type each one and why?
5. Prepare a list of five strategic locations that could give a person power and influence within a group.
6. Give some examples of outside relationships as a source of power.
7. Give some examples of money as a source of power.

8. How can information outside an organization be a source of power and influence?

DISCUSSION TOPICS

1. Can you think of leadership styles other than those discussed in the text? If so, what would they be and what would be their characteristics?

2. Think of some situations wherein the informal leadership role could shift within a small group. Why does this happen?

3. Do you believe that a special ability can be a source of power and influence? Defend your answer.

4. What are your views concerning the change of cohesion over a period of time?

ASSIGNMENT QUESTIONS

1. Prepare a chart depicting Likert's linking-pin concept and explain its importance in the interaction process within an organzation.

2. Observe a group to which you belong and identify the roles played by its members.

NOTES

1. *The Random House Dictionary of the English Language,* unabridged ed. (New York: Random House, 1966).
2. Ibid.
3. A. Paul Hare, *Handbook of Small Group Research* (New York: The Free Press of Glencoe, 1962).
4. Theodore M. Mills, *The Sociology of Small Groups* (Englewood Cliffs, N.J.: Prentice-Hall, Inc., 1967).
5. Marvin E. Shaw, *Group Dynamics* (New York: McGraw-Hill Book Co., 1971), p. 10.
6. Clovis R. Shepherd, *Small Groups* (Scranton, Pennsylvania: Chander Publishing Co., 1964), p. 25.
7. Shaw, *Group Dynamics,* p. 244.
8. Rensis Likert, *The Human Organization* (New York: McGraw-Hill Book Co., 1967).
9. These are the assumptions about human nature or human behavior that Douglas McGregor labels as Theory X. See Douglas McGregor, *The Human Side of Enterprise* (New York: McGraw-Hill Book Co., 1960), pp. 33–34.
10. McGregor's Theory Y assumptions. Ibid., pp. 47–48.
11. Likert, *The Human Organization.*
12. Leonard R. Sayles and George Strauss, *Human Behavior in Organizations* (Englewood Cliffs, N.J.: Prentice-Hall, Inc., 1960–1966), p. 101.
13. Roger L. Gould, "The Phases of Adult Life," *The American Journal of Psychiatry* (November 1972), Vol. 129, p. 528.

14. Kurt Lewin, *Resolving Social Conflicts,* Selected Papers on Group Dynamics (New York: Harper & Row Publishers, 1948).
15. Angie Sedwick, "The Physician," *SYNERGY* (Peterborough, New Hampshire: Windy Row Press, 1972), with permission.

part III

UNDERSTANDING MANAGERIAL PHILOSOPHY

Managerial philosophy, as developed within a certain time frame of reference, determines the communication characteristics of an organization and that organization's receptiveness to innovation and change. An understanding of managerial philosophies with time frames of reference is the third and final essential element in developing a plan for successful interpersonal relationships in organizations.

The overall objectives of Part III are to enable you to

1. *understand* the managerial philosophy that was taught in a particular time frame of reference;
2. *appreciate* the fact that managerial philosophy and thinking has changed through time as a result of economic, social, and political influences;
3. *learn* to identify the managerial philosophy of a co-worker or supervisor;
4. *recognize* that knowledge of managerial frame of reference is essential in the achievement of successful interaction—both outward with co-workers and upward with supervisors;
5. *trace* the development of human relations and behavioral science in management thinking;
6. *Develop* your own managerial philosophy;
7. *Decide* how you *really* feel about other people.

The chapters in Part III are presented as lectures that might have been given to students studying business administration at the time indicated. As such, the only reference material used is that which would have been available to a professor at the time indicated. The presentation style and word usage is also as it might have been at that time.

THINK
MY WAY III
SALES AVERAGES
OLD SALES
MY WAY I
MY WAY II
OUT
IN

4

Appreciation of Managerial Philosophy

The next step in the process of learning how to interact successfully with work group equals and immediate supervisors is to develop an understanding of different managerial philosophies or frames of reference.

As we saw in Chapter 2, each person is a unique individual with a personal philosophy of life and a characteristic behavior pattern. In addition, each person has a managerial philosophy made up of beliefs, attitudes, and values concerning work, people, and the functions of management. However, the two philosophies are different in many respects.

Managerial philosophy

First, though the development of a personal philosophy begins with the small child, the development of managerial philosophy begins with the first exposure to management training—either in the classroom or in the school of hard knocks on the first job.

Learned

Second, managerial philosophies are not necessarily unique. People who grow up together in the same geographical area and go to the same school at the same time very often have similar managerial philosophies.

Not unique

Third, managerial philosophies have been changing over time based upon economic, social, technological, and political forces at work in specific time frames. Furthermore, in retrospect, events that took place in past time frames can be identified to give an insight into possible frames of reference and to reveal the managerial philosophies that were being taught as well as practiced at that particular time. Based upon this identification and knowing the age of our peers and supervisors, we might be able to predict what their managerial philosophies and frames of reference would be.

Changes over time

Predictable

Figure 1 shows how this prediction can be accomplished. If we strike a line across the chart from a man's age parallel to the year axis, we can determine when he undertook his training. The beginning and ending dates should pinpoint the years in which his managerial philosophy developed. This figure also gives the time frame in which the teacher's managerial philosophy developed. For example, let's take a person who is forty years old today. Figure 1 shows us that his business education would have taken place in the years 1954 to 1957. His teacher, on the other hand, would

Method to determine

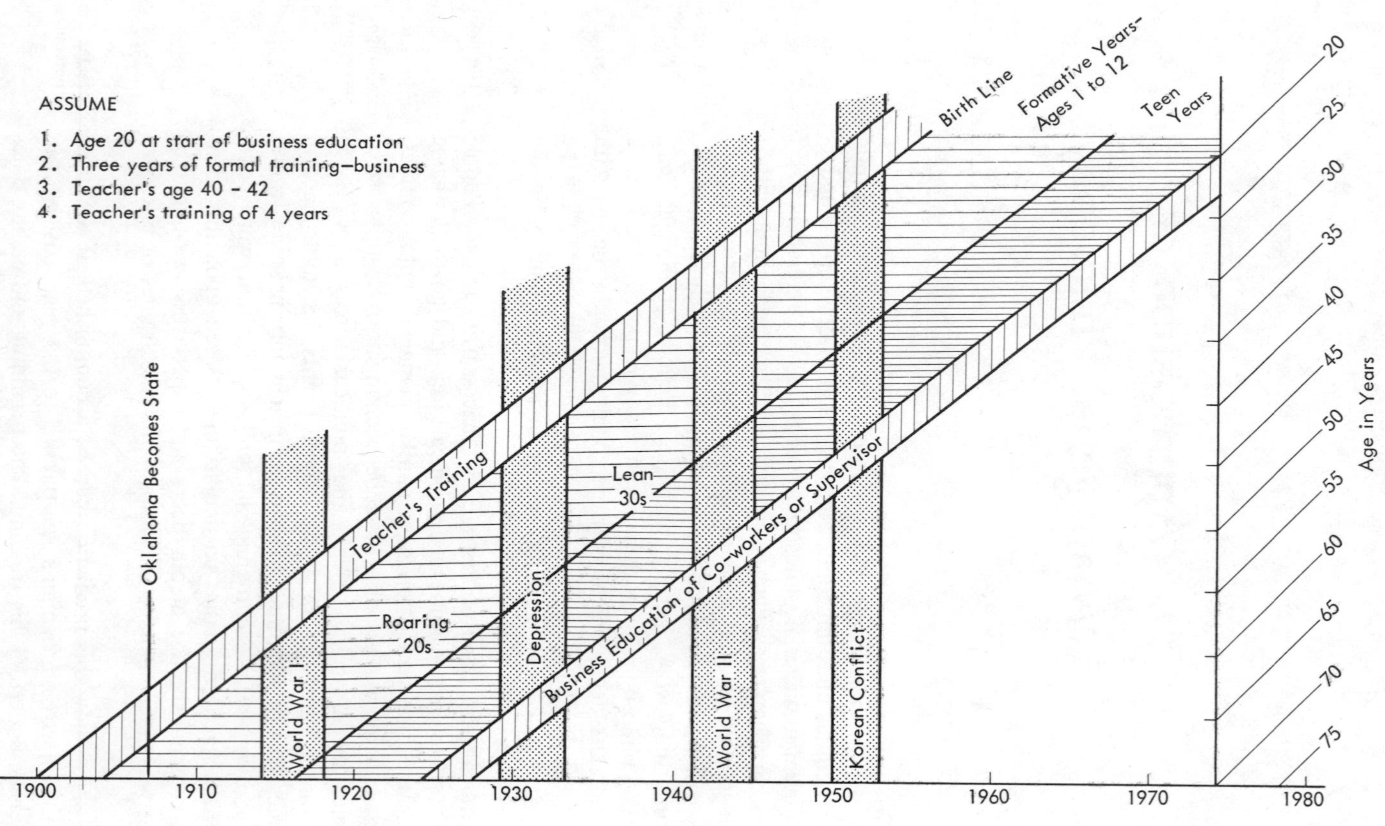

FIGURE 1
Managerial Philosophy Development

have acquired his business education during the years 1930 to 1934 and might still be influenced by that training.

Based upon the above reasoning, we will examine the managerial philosophies taught at ten-year intervals beginning in 1910. In this way, we can complete Figure 1 to indicate what particular philosophy might have been developed by our co-worker or supervisor based upon when he received his education, and more importantly, when his teacher received his.

To accomplish our purpose, the following chapters are lectures as they might have been given in a final course in management at the end of the indicated decade. In reviewing each lecture, we should be able to develop a feeling for the managerial philosophy being taught as well as the conditions prevalent during the time frame of reference of the professor as well as the student.

5

The Age of Confidence 1900-1910

The objectives of this chapter are to enable you to

1. *understand* the managerial philosophy taught in 1910;
2. *realize* that the 1910 managerial philosophy would very likely be taught in later years by a professor who received his management training in the 1910 era;
3. *appreciate* that very likely today's sixty-year-old manager would have been taught by a professor who gained his initial managerial philosophy against a 1910 frame of reference.

PROLOGUE

What was it like?

It was a decade of confidence—confidence in the fact that we knew all the anwers. "Truth has been established. Our job then is to pass it along to the young." Father was the head of the household and there was no questioning of parental authority. Rigid class distinctions, race distinctions, and extreme prejudice were in evidence in most areas of the country. The poor were poor; the rich were rich; and there was no large middle class.

At the turn of the century, 60 percent of the population lived on farms or in communities of less than 2,500 inhabitants. Forty percent of employed persons worked in agricultural activities; about 25 percent worked in manufacturing; and the rest were employed by service industries.

The horse and buggy, streetcar, and train were the main means of transportation at the beginning of the decade; yet by 1910, 460,000 cars had been sold and the airplane was an actuality.

The ice cream store and the nickelodeon were popular with all ages; song hits included "Anchors Away," "Take Me Out to the Ball Game," "By the Light of the Silvery Moon," "Meet Me in St. Louis, Louis," and "In the Good Ol' Summer Time." The best seller of the period was *The Jungle* by Upton Sinclair.

Ziegfeld and Valentino were household names, and the big picture of

1907 was Ben Hur in sixteen scenes. "Cleanliness is next to godliness," and "Man earns his bread by the sweat of his brow" were imprinted on the young mind. Many mothers kept house by gaslight, coal stove, and wood-burning cook stove. The pace of life—in general—was slow.

Against this background we meet Dr. Brown in January of 1910.

Professor Jonathan Brown adjusted the shade on the electric lamp so that it cast more light on the top of his paper. As he did, he thought to himself that he was fortunate to work in a university that had the funds to modernize its buildings and install electricity rather than continue with the old gaslights. He shivered a little and got up and moved over to the pot-bellied coal stove that stood in the middle of the room. "Well," he thought, "you can't have everything, although the new central heat would be nice. If I had my choice, I'd rather have electricity." His eye moved to the calendar hanging on the wall—January 12, 1910. "My, my," he thought to himself, "how time flies—it seems like just yesterday that it was the beginning of the fall term and here it is the beginning of the spring term. My boys will be ready to graduate, and this is the last chance I'll have to get my point across." He went back to his desk, pulled out the chair, sat down, and began to think about this final class in industrial organization.

He knew that his students had completed the standard course in production, sales, accounting, and finance. Now he wanted to tie the picture together for them and give them some background on actually getting the job done—the chance to see how theory was actually applied by a manager.

"Rather than beginning with a discussion of modern management techniques, I'll give them a little bit of background of the labor movement and an appreciation of how different things are now from what they were as little as twenty years ago." With this thought in mind he worked late into the night preparing the next week's lecture.

Promptly at nine o'clock the following Monday morning Professor Brown entered the lecture hall. The class snapped to attention as the distinguished professor moved across the platform and finally stood in front of the podium.

"Please be seated, gentlemen!"

He waited until the class was comfortably seated—or at least until they stopped squirming in their seats—then began.

"To set the stage for our course in industrial organization, I feel it is essential that you have a brief understanding of how business in general has developed since the time of the Industrial Revolution. I know it isn't as startling or fascinating to you as it is to me, since you are of the modern generation; but consider that when I was a boy, there was no such thing as the automobile, the airplane, or even these electric lights that we take for granted. But that's beside the point. Let's briefly review the period from, say, the start of the Industrial Revolution in England until the present time—that is, January 1910. It feel that it's essential that we cover this period of time because it was during this period that our present wage system developed—and as you were told in your political science course, the wage system is one of the factors that causes the labor problem as we know it today. The other facet of the general labor problem of course is the highly capitalized form of modern industry which is a direct result of the Industrial Revolution.

Development of the laboring class

"Before continuing, let me digress for a moment and consider the development of the laboring class. As we know, almost the first laboring class that history records was composed of slaves. Over the years, slavery turned into serfdom and serfdom into the modern wage system. But remember that the last serf did not disappear from England until the eighteenth century; and in other countries of the world, serfdom lasted well into the nineteenth century. Actually, there were three major reasons that caused slavery to evolve into a wage system. In the first place, slavery is not compatible with the deepest instincts of the human race. The simple animal instinct for freedom played an important role in the abolition of slavery, aided of course by the teachings of the church and the common law whose teachings in England were always toward the side of liberty.

"Second, the bondage system became socially wasteful and uneconomical. Freedom gave man the incentive of self-interest, thus causing him to work harder. You all are willing to work harder for yourself than you are for someone else. Finally, the people who owned the land to which many of the serfs were bonded found it impossible to provide the services to the serfs that they were required to perform. So, instead of the services, they gave money, so that they would not have the responsibility for the welfare of the serfs. The money, then, became the equivalent of the old feudal obligations.

Wage system emerged

"So as the feudal system more or less disintegrated, industry began to develop in the free cities and the chartered towns. However, until about 1750, the start of the Industrial Revolution in England, most people were still farmers except, as I have already said, for the small, independent craftsmen that developed in the cities and towns. In these locations, trade and industry were regulated by the guilds. The master manufacturer worked out of his own house and was assisted by apprentices who usually lived with the employer's family on terms of equality. In fact, many of them married into the family after they learned their trade. These guilds were, in fact, monopolies, and no man could practice a trade in any city unless he belonged to the guild. Their advantage was that they prevented conflicts of interest, guaranteed the quality of goods, stimulated the organization and the division of labor, and trained skilled workers. Most historians will agree that the guilds were beneficial. They were moral and educational. They served the society of the Middle Ages by promoting thrift and developing in their members the qualities of good workmanship and active citizenship.

Small independent craftsmen

Development of guilds

"As time went on, though, the guilds became closed corporations jealous of their rights and privileges. Membership to mastership became hereditary. Dues were raised; production was limited to keep up prices; and regulations were introduced which hindered progress in production and exchange. It sounds a little bit like some of the practices carried on in industry today, doesn't it, gentlemen? Well, to continue, after the guilds became aristocratic, the old transition up the line from apprenticeship to journeymanship to mastership, which in the beginning had been easy and accepted universally, became extremely difficult. A class of permanent journeymen was created which became large and relatively numerous in western Europe during the sixteenth and seventeenth centuries. Master craftsmen of course engineered this chain of events because they desired to keep their numbers small. In other words, they liked their social superiority and wished to protect it by the erection of class barriers. When a few of these master craftsmen accumulated much wealth, they began to copy the manners of the nobility and aristocracy. They began to intermingle and marry within their own or a higher class and thus move up the social ladder of the times. In the guilds the richer and more powerful masters separated into distinct classes while the guild government came under the control of the still smaller group whose regulation of industry became monopolistic. Thus the laboring class developed, and the stage was set for the appearance of a capitalistic class. In fact, it developed long before the Industrial Revolution.

"On the continent the class of wealthy craftsmen and the wealthy merchant clothiers appeared in the woolen industry as early as the thirteenth century. In certain parts of England, that industry had passed beyond the domestic stages as early as the beginning of the sixteenth century.

The Industrial Revolution

"The Industrial Revolution came gradually and thoughtful men were expecting it. It just so happened by 1750 that the socioeconomic conditions for the Industrial Revolution were right in England. Expanded trade over the years had made many merchants rich. Enclosure of the land for sheep-raising purposes had driven many people off the land—in other words, a floating population had developed. The combination of this floating population and the wealthy merchants (the men and money required for management) were responsible for the start of the Industrial Revolution.

"The men and money combination coupled with people's desire to keep up with the Joneses, the abundance of coal and brick and the requirement for cotton to clothe salves, led to industrialization first in the textile industry. It began by businessmen taking yarn into the homes where cotton was spun by the women. Because cotton must be spun under special conditions of relative humidity and low atmospheric static conditions, Lancashire and Cheshire were the only counties in England capable of sustaining the cotton industry. Because hand-spinning of cotton was a slow and laborious process, the merchants advertised prizes for any individual who would come up with a successful spinning machine. As a result, between 1764 and 1767, James Hargrave invented the spinning jenny. In 1769 Arkright developed the first water frame, and in 1778 Crompton combined the jenny and the frame into a device for spinning fine yarn.

Beginning of the textile industry

"Because of these inventions the businessmen found that it would be cheaper to start a factory where all the machines could be put together. Now, instead of taking the yarn to the cottage, the workers came to the factory. Accordingly, the factory system developed as the inevitable result of the increasing effort to cut the cost of production.

The development of factory system

"As a result of the factory system, we find the complete transition from the guild society to a wage-earner society and the present day-wage system. Under this wage system, the laborer is responsible for securing work and supporting himself and his family. He does this by selling his services to the capitalist. He becomes not only a producer but a merchant. He must acquire a certain strength or skill and sell it to the best advantage. As a result, he has combined with others of his class in trade unions in which the standards are more consciously fixed and maintained and where he can bargain through agents. Underlying all the problems of course is the system which makes the laborer responsible for his own maintenance, which makes him merchant as well as producer, and which compels him to take his chances and stake his welfare upon successful bargaining in the labor market.

The wage-earner society

"So much for the development of the factory system. In summary, it was the logical transition from slavery into the free agent worker. It was caused by the Industrial Revolution, which provided the machinery that produced more things cheaper. It became possible because many people found that they could earn more money in the factory than they could on the farm even though the hours of work were long, tedious, and exhausting. But it is here to stay.

"To work successfully today in most lines of industry, men must own or control large capital in order to build and equip complex mechanical plants. And the plan under which production is carried out in these plants is still called the factory system. We know it is directly responsible in a large degree for many labor problems. Child labor, industrial accidents, factory regulations, the unemployment resulting from the labor-saving machinery, and other things are directly attributable to the factory system. It is responsible for the strikingly unequal distribution of wealth because the great majority of men do not possess the abilities or the opportunities to secure the capital necessary to begin a business. For most people, the principle of "once a wage earner always a wage earner" is certainly true. The laborer feels that he is permanently held within a class whose interests are antagonistic to those of the employers with whom he bargains and haggles over wages. But, in any case, we are where we are, and this brief introduction should give you an appreciation of how we got there."

Evils of the factory system

At this point, Professor Brown adjusted the glasses that had slipped down toward the end of his nose, cleared his throat, and took a sip from the water glass sitting on the table next to the platform. He looked over the audience and noted that most of the students were still awake.

"Gentlemen, in case any of you have any questions as the lecture proceeds, please feel free to ask." With these words, he turned the page of his notes and continued.

"As far as America goes, the Industrial Revolution did not start until after the Civil War. Fifty percent or more of the total work force was engaged in pure agricultural work until about 1878. In fact, if we add forestry and fishing, it wasn't until 1880 that the percentage of all workers in these two combined industry classifications dropped below 50 percent. If you'll turn to Chart 1 which I gave you during the last week

The Industrial Revolution comes to America

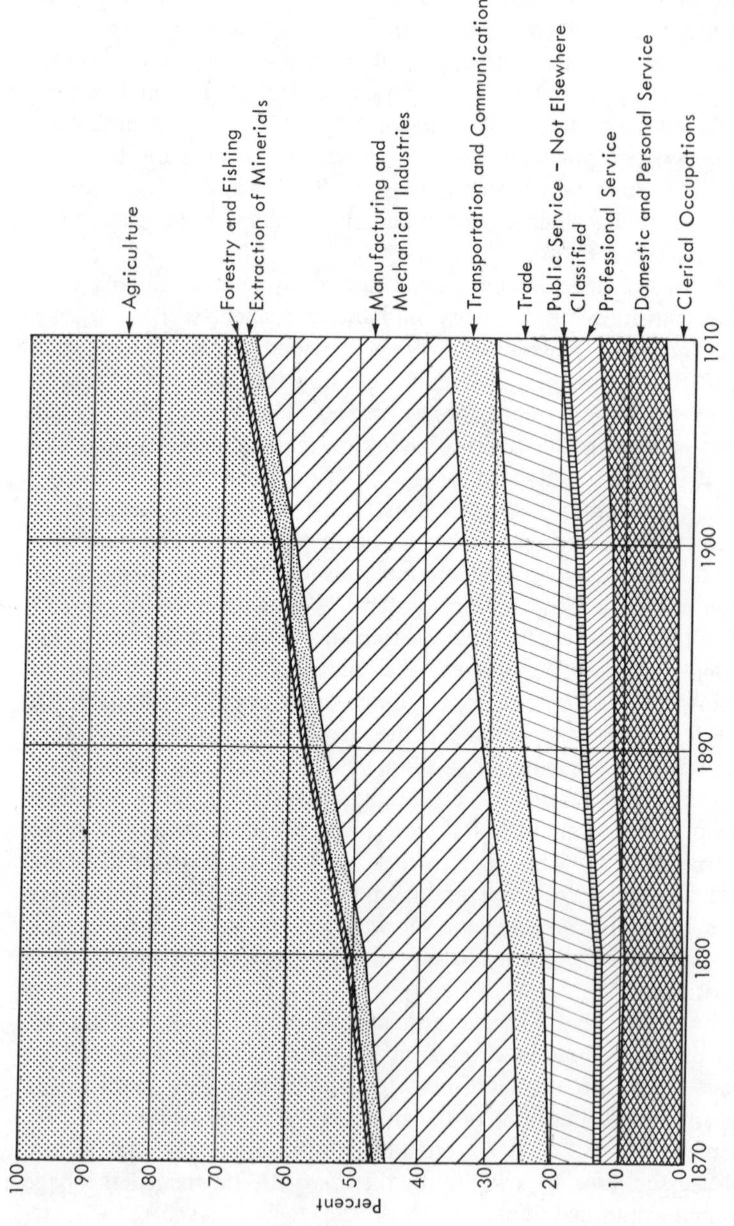

CHART 1
Percent Distribution of Gainful Workers by General Divisions of Occupations for the United States: 1870 to 1910

of our first semester, you'll notice the shift in gainful employment from 1870 through 1905. Certainly, I would expect this trend to continue. I would expect that agriculture would continue to be a smaller portion of the work force as other industry grows."

Professor Brown looked up from his notes momentarily before continuing and saw a hand raised halfway up the tiers of the lecture hall. "Yes, sir," he replied.

"Professor Brown, do you mean that agriculture will be a smaller proportion percentagewise or a smaller proportion in actual numbers?"

Without a moment's hesitation, the professor answered, "Both. As the work force grows, which it must because of our increased population, the percentage of workers in agriculture will diminish because of the development of machinery which will enable the farmers to turn out more produce with fewer people. Does that answer your question?"

"Yes, sir, thank you very much."

"All right," continued the professor, "as I was mentioning, industry is certainly going to grow. We know that the motor car industry is here to stay. Ford built 10,660 Model Ts during the 1908–1909 season. He's already started branch manufacturing assembly plants and his Highland plant should be set up sometime this year. Most of you might not remember, but the automobile industry was the first to develop the assembly line. It was completed in early 1902 by Ransom E. Olds. As a result, his production went up from 425 cars in 1901 to 2,500 in 1902."

At this point, Professor Brown noticed another hand raised. "Yes, sir?"

"Dr. Brown, could you describe the assembly line. I've seen quite a few factories, but each one worked under a system where the work was carried from location to location either by crane or by push cart; and I just don't exactly see how the assembly line works."

Early assembly lines

"Certainly, young man," answered the professor. "First let me describe the normal method of production. Let's take, for example, the Pullman works in Butler, Pennsylvania. The sleeping car division assembles cars in one location. All the workmen are there and parts are brought in by crane or by dolly and assembled in one spot. Olds' assembly line, on the other hand, uses a different process. He uses a wooden platform supported by rolling casters. On this he puts the body frame of the car. The workmen are all stationed in a long line, each one with a certain task to perform. The car frame on the wooden platform is then hauled down the line and each workman, in turn, performs his particular operation until the car is finally assembled at the end of the line. As you can see, this is the most efficient method of production because each worker can become skilled in his particular job, he does not get in the way of other workers, and the material flow can be very easily laid out."

"Thank you, sir, that explains it to me. It seems to me, though, that the workers might find the job monotonous."

"Perhaps they do, but there are always others to take their place if they don't like the work."

Notice the attitude of the professor concerning the feelings of the worker as a human being.

"Now," continued the professor, "as for our other new industries, take that of the airplane. We've seen it grow from that first flight of twelve seconds and 120 feet in December of 1903 to its present status of night flights, a nonstop, round-trip flight across the English Channel, and an attained height of 3,000 feet altitude. In fact, when we look around at all the things being made, we can't help but realize that at the present moment, conditions and methods are changing more rapidly in the workshop and the factory than anywhere else. The application of new methods, the invention of new tools, the use of new combinations of cutting steel are some of the things that are, in themselves, revolutionizing not only factory practice but the character and skill of the laborer employed. Vast increases in output per man hour are being realized through Dr. Taylor's scientific management techniques. Factories are being run less and less by the authority of experience and more and more by the authority of figures and facts.

"Older workers and supervisors who are using rule-of-thumb techniques are going to be replaced by younger men trained in scientific management—trained as you have been over the last few years. You will be taking your place in industry prepared to question everything that is being done and with an appreciation for cost techniques and modern production practices.

Early systems management

"Gentlemen, your challenge is staggering. The factory must be considered as a thing by itself, as a living, breathing, moving, being which has an anatomy particular to itself, of course, but which can nevertheless be analyzed in its every function. You must look at the factory as a system. Consider proper organization of all departments and the flow of material throughout the plant. Where the old accounting system would have taken an existing condition in factory practice and applied a method of rendering accounts for it, the new system must develop an accounting system that forces each and every one of the organizational units to function properly and render a correct accounting of itself."

It would appear that the systems management approach is not new. In fact, is anything in management really new—or has it just been rediscovered?

"But, gentlemen, I'm getting ahead of myself; I get too excited when I think of our modern management techniques, and I forget that the purpose of this particular course is to tie together the loose ends for you so that you can see the factory as a system, so that you can see the need for the improved accounting methods, so that you can see the relationship between men, machines, materials, and methods, the relationship between the latest theories in line and staff organization and an appreciation for factory organization itself which today is certainly a far cry from the one-owner, small-factory system of less than twenty or thirty years ago.

"The appreciation of why you must practice modern management techniques can be gained from considering how the superviser of many of our larger manufacturing shops rose to his position. The typical superintendent came up from the ranks. He usually started as a workman and rose up through the various ranks until he became manager of the whole establishment. He knew the area in which he worked for the most time, for example, manufacturing, accounting, or sales, but he had little appreciation of what went on in the remaining departments. We often find that the department of the works in which he started out is run very efficiently while the other departments have a far piece to go. This is because the manager who rises through the ranks does not have an appreciation of the overall operation. This, unfortunately, is true in many cases today where management is looked at in relation to the man and not upon methods.

Predict and plan

"Today, management practices must concentrate on the methods and the overall plan and stress the fact that industrial engineering, of which shop management is an integral part, implies not merely the making of a given product but the making of that product at the lowest cost consistent with the maintenance of the intended standard of quality. Furthermore, that the lowest cost can only be attained by considering the overall organization of each alternate plan and the best method of operating each consistent with the objective. Modern management practices can tell us how to produce at the lowest cost consistent with the intended standard of quality.

"In prior courses, you have considered the economic theory of factory location, the planning of factory buildings, the influence of design in the production capacity, departmental reports, general office arrangement, the order department, bills and material, the drafting department, the pattern department, the purchasing department, stores and stock, the production department, foundry systems, the machine shop, the tool department, shipping and receiving, time-taking, cost allocations, inventory analysis, special methods, employment of labor and labor policies, wage systems, piece rates, and time studies—these are all essential parts of the running of a factory. The one thing missing is how the various departments and functions are pulled together into an organization with a smoothly running set of operating principles and efficient managerial staff. This being the case, let's consider the situation. Any more questions to this point?" There being no hands raised, he continued.

"Gentlemen, the most important element or principle of modern management is a strong central executive control with clear cut lines of authority. This can only be accomplished by prior planning and a proper organizational structure. Think of the factory as you might an intricate machine. If you wanted to design a machine, you would probably sit down and decide what you wanted it to do. You must figure out what the machine is to do and what parts are going to be needed to enable it to do this. You break each part down into its smallest element and compare and analyze what each part should do in relation to the overall purpose. You decide what each part must do, the practical conditions under which it has to work, and you set an obtainable commercial standard for each operation. Next you determine how to meet this standard involving both quantity and quality and then how to interlock or assemble all these prime elements into the well-arranged, well-built, smooth-running machine.

Organization and functions

"Think of an organization this same way. You have to decide what the output or purpose must be. You must list all the functions that must be performed; you must decide how each will be done again involving quantity and this time perhaps the number of men and quality as to your control standards. Then you have to see how each function fits together in an interlocking assembly which we can call the physical organization. And, finally, you have comparison—usually in the form of your accounts of planned output against projected output. It's rather obvious that thinking along these lines involves knowledge and ability in science and engineering as well as training in accounting and commerce. The industrial engineer today, then, must acquire these additional skills, which is exactly what I hope you gentlemen have gained during your course of instruction at this university. You must be competent to give good business advice to your corporation. In fact, this sound business judgment and good advice can sometimes be responsible for the making or losing of large amounts of money. We might call this new concept production engineering. Production engineering must consider the output of men and machines; it must require a knowledge of both and it must involve the knowledge of modern management practices.

Production engineering

"As a final parallelism between the machine and factory, I might point out that the greatest advancements and improvements in the construction of engines have depended on precise observations and research which brought to light conditions existing during the smallest fraction of a second representing any instance in the single stroke of the piston. Thus, it should appear obvious that only by observing and recording the running conditions of our industrial engine, the factory, and analyzing each part as it relates to the whole, will we be able to improve the efficiency and thus the output of the factory. Therefore, not only must you understand manufacturing processing, but you must be able to make precise observations and to record systematically the results of these observations. Continuous records of everything that goes on in the factory are essential in developing a proper organization which will permit efficient factory management.

Importance of observations

"The first step in the planning of the organization should be the preparation of a functional list, without the names of any people, showing the duties of each department and of each man in each department.

"Are there any questions as to how this would be done?" Professor

Brown looked up from his notes and caught the hand raised in the second row. "Yes, Mr. Fine."

"Professor, you say that we make a functional list without showing names of individuals, showing the duties of each department and each man in each department. It would seem to me that this means that all we're doing is showing what the existing organization does. I don't see how this helps in a process of organization."

"I see what's bothering you, Mr. Fine," replied Professor Brown, "but let me continue for a minute. After we have made a list of the functions that are now performed, we then can rearrange and regroup these functions into logical groupings. These logical groupings could lead to the establishment of a department with a distinctive function.

"You see, the next step after our listing of functions would be to make up a chart if possible of the organization as it now exists and then, secondly, of the improved, or we could say the ideal, organization that we would hope to achieve."

"Oh, I see, Professor," remarked Mr. Fine. "This, in other words, is the scientific analysis to develop the best organization."

"That's correct, Mr. Fine. Then, you see, the next step, as I just mentioned, would be to chart the organization.

Charting organizations

"Probably the best method of charting might be circles connected by lines or arrows where each circle might represent a department or a particular function. The lines or arrows could represent subordination or some type of relationship. The one thing, of course, that is most important is that we have a clear-cut line of authority so that we would know which department reports to which other department and how the overall organizational picture looks.

Early organizational charts

"Mr. C. E. Woods of the International Harvester Company has had considerable experience in charting organizations. In his latest work on organizing a factory, he tells us that, 'Charts can express more on one page than is sometimes expressed in several chapters in writing.' It is necessary as a first step for analytical and other purposes to make a chart expressing all of the relations governing the organization of a business so as to show the very foundation upon which all authorities, accounting and business transactions are based and conducted. There have been more failures, both personally and financially, for the lack of these very elements in a business than by reason of any other one thing. With his permission, I have copied and will now hand out to you three charts depicting how we might think of a business as being organized and showing the direct lines of responsibility and authority. Before explaining his chart, I'd like to point out his definiton of an organzation, because you should keep this in mind as we look at the chart. 'An organization is a system to unite individuals into a body proposed to work together for a common end, to show reciprocal and concrete relationships and duties, to show the connection and cooperation of the parts of the whole and to show how officers, both elected and appointed, committees and authorities are divided and subdivided so that the duties correlate and cooperate with all.'

"Now Chart 2 shows the prime elements of the industrial body. This chart shows that the stockholders are elements belonging to the public who elect the directors. The directors then elect their executive officers who, in turn, with the advice of an auditor or controller, appoint a general manager who is responsible for the manufacturing and commercial side of the organization.

"Chart 3 shows the authorities governing different departments and their relation to the industrial body as a whole. Note that the outer perimeter covers the stockholders and the entire organization. Then we have the next inner oval headed by the directors, the next oval shows the executive officers, the position of the controller and, finally, the general manager. The general manager, of course, has responsibility for the commercial section and the manufacturing section. In the manufacturing section, as a further example, we see that the purchasing agent works directly under the general manager, as does the office of superintendent. The chief of storage is under the purchasing agent, while the chief cost clerk, the chief engineer, assistant superintendent, and chief shipping clerk would be under the superintendent. Then, finally, under the chief engineer would come departments 5, 6, and 7; under the assistant superintendent would come 8, 9, 10, 11, 12, and 13; and under the chief shipping clerk would come 14 and 15.

"Finally, Chart 4 is the other way of looking at the organizational structure. It is the circle method that I indicated earlier that I prefer, giving a detailed circular representation of what might happen in each particular nonproductive as well as productive department.

"I've tossed out two words that are most important, gentlemen, that is, productive and nonproductive. This, in essence, is the line/staff relationship within the production plant that sometimes leads to many of the problems we have today.

Explanation of charts

"However, before getting off on this discussion, you'll notice that the charts presented by Mr. Woods show the executive authority and clearly define departmental lines with a responsible head or assistant head for each department. The charts show the factory departments so organized that each department head is responsible to the superintendent or, as he is sometimes called, the works manager, without any intervening bosses. This, to me, is essential for successful factory organization and for prompt and efficient management or administration. It is the form of control characteristic of the most successful manufacturing organization. Let me stress that there must be no paths whereby company officers or other departments may deal with departments responsible to the superintendent except through his office.

Line and staff operations

"Now, back to my comment about line and staff. The line departments of the previously passed out organizational charts would be numbers 8, 9, 10, 11, and 12. In essence, these are the departments responsible for getting

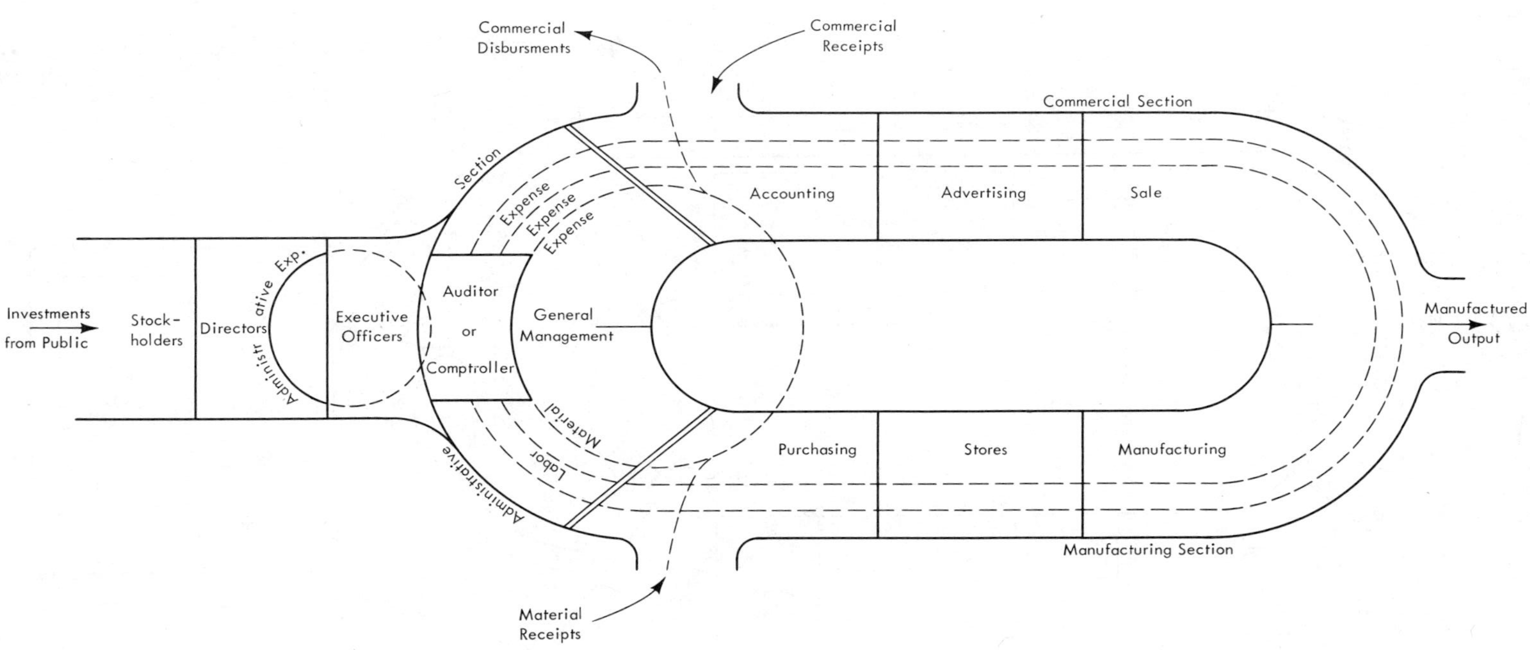

CHART 2
The Prime Organization Element of an Industrial Body

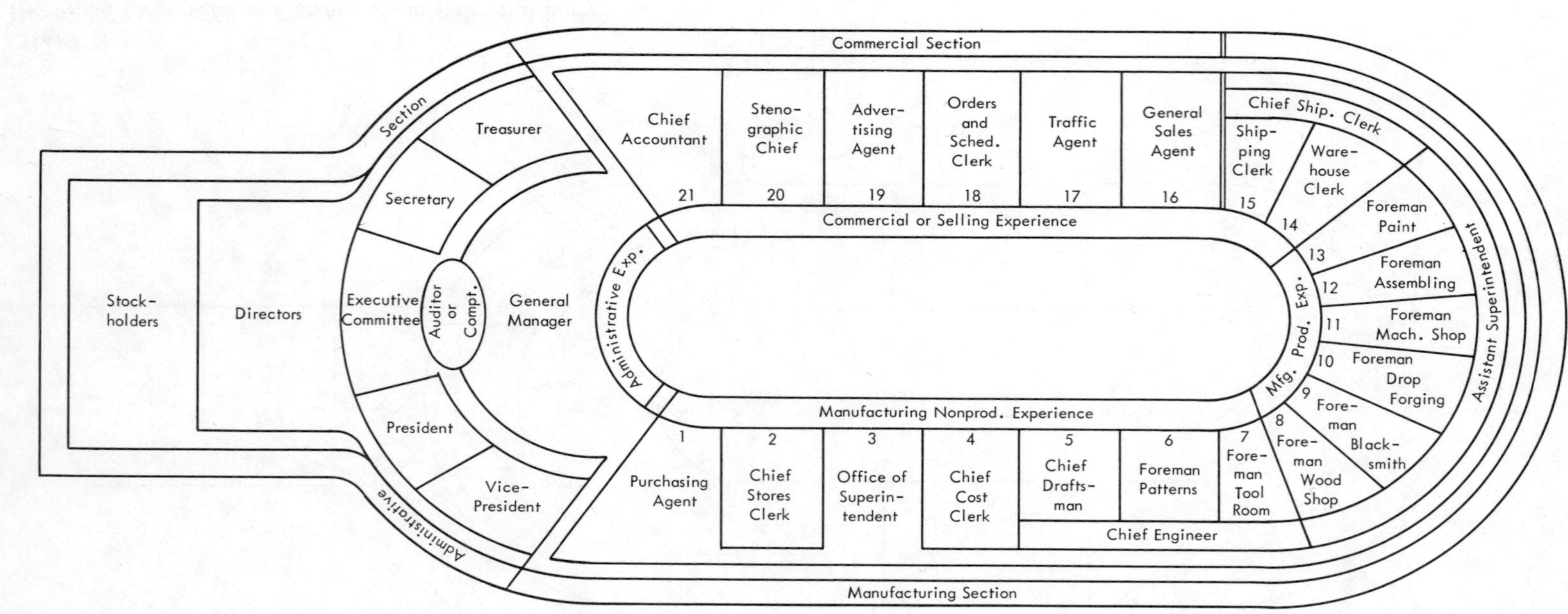

CHART 3
The Prime and Working Authorities of an Industrial Body

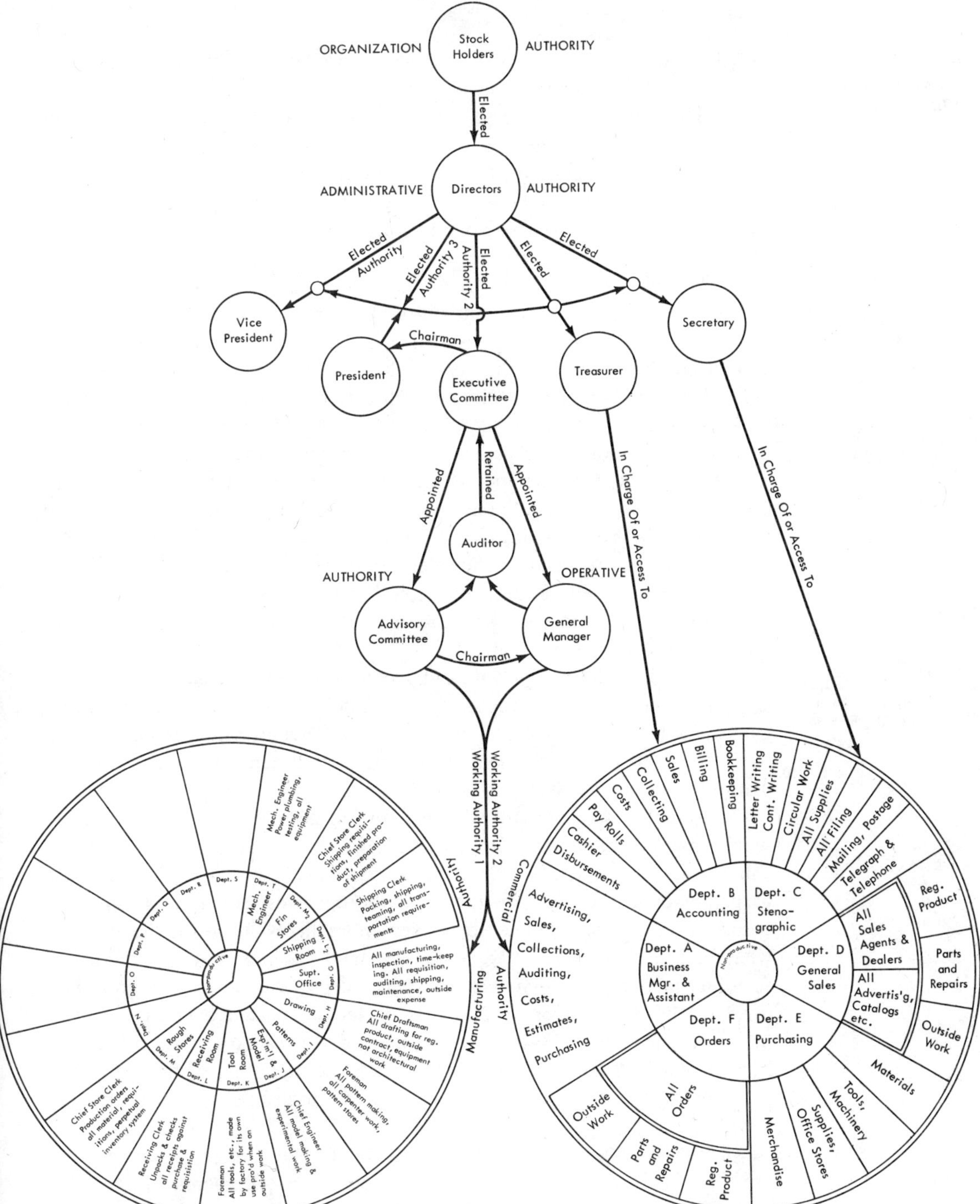

CHART 4 **The Segregation of an Industrial Body into Authorities and Departments**

This chart shows the absolute division between commercial and manufacturing ends of the business emphasized in the accompanying discussion and the authority lines connect the various departments in these two divisions with the governing authorities. In each case the number and formal name of each department is in the apex of its triangle, the various detailed duties that come under it are grouped beyond; the productive departments in the manufacturing section are left empty, because their work will vary with the kind of factory under consideration—each factory carries the same non-productive departments.

out the product. The strength of the line organization, of course, is in its indestructibility. There is always someone in authority if someone isn't there. The weakness of course is that no one man knows much more than any other and that promotion is very often by seniority and not by merit. Because no one man in the line can possibly know or be an expert in all operations of the company, the staff are there as experts in their particular field to give advice and assistance to the line when required or when called upon.

Is the staff as important today?

"Mr. Harrington Emerson, in his latest book, *Efficiency as a Basis for Operation and Wages,* points out that the man down the line is the one who needs staff assistance most for a special case. He is the one who should be able to call on the very highest special talent to solve his difficulty. He is not supposed to know all the answers, but he should certainly have the assistance of a highly trained staff to guide him. Emerson tells us that what is needed in organization is complete parallelism between line and staff so that every member of the line can, at any time, have the benefit of staff knowledge and staff assistance. He wisely points out that any modern company, whether railroad, industrial, or other, is organized for a specific purpose which is realized by the interplay of men, machines, materials, and methods. For myself, I think he should have added money to make the picture complete, and even perhaps management, but, of course, management is what we're talking about.

Management is the fifth M

"Mr. Emerson points out, and I believe wisely so, that because each step of the line from the top to the bottom involves men, materials, machines, and methods, there should be a staff department for each which would develop the latest scientific techniques for handling *m*en, *m*aterials, *m*ethods, and *m*achines.

"Actually, men are still selected, not on account of the qualities that would make them good on any particular job but because they, themselves, call themselves something. That is, a man calls himself a plumber or a carpenter or a bricklayer or a turret lathe operator, etc. If he's done this before in some other plant, he is even more likely hired on the basis of what he calls himself. Dr. Taylor has certainly pointed out that there is a scientific method of assigning at least industrial workers to their job. This involves the time-motion studies that he has advocated over the years as first published in 1903 under the auspices of the American Society of Mechanical Engineers. I understand that the compilation of this particular shop-management technique is going to be published next year by Dr. Taylor.

"But, to continue, the staff departments Mr. Emerson recommends are also based upon scientific analysis of the requirements of machine, material requirements, and a detailed listing of the methods to operate the overall plan.

The Gantt chart is still being used!

"Once we've developed proper methods of matching men, materials, and machines, Mr. Gantt, in his latest book on *Work, Wages, and Profits,* gives us a method to analyze what's been going on. This charting system as developed by Mr. Gantt gives time on the bottom line and workers' names on the side with different colored blocks to indicate at a glance how each is doing on a particular piecework or bonus system. I strongly suggest that all of you read the particular pages in Mr. Gantt's book, because the charting technique is certainly an easy way to show the interrelationship between parts on a time scale.

"Under the system of having staff responsible for methods, it would be hoped that everyone, or nearly everyone, in the organization would know exactly what his duties were and the limits of his authority. This might be accomplished in the true spirit of honesty and trust. As you all know, there has been suspicion on the part of many workmen toward the employer and his representatives. In the beginning, Dr. Taylor's scientific shop management technique was played up on the part of the unions as causing men to work harder without telling the whole story that when their output increased, their wages also increased. One other staff department that should be established is advocated by Dr. Taylor and is certainly one that I would agree with—the planning department. Dr. Taylor tells us that as far as possible, the workmen, the gang bosses, and the foremen should be relieved as much as possible from the work of planning. The planning department would lay out the work for the entire factory using an order of work and route clerk, a time and cost clerk, a method of instruction cards, speed bosses, inspectors, repair bosses, shop disciplinarians, and other men to do functions for the entire establishment. This, in essence, is the staff function I mentioned earlier. It's called functional foremanship by Dr. Taylor. But, in this case, it is divided down into the lowest possible functional area so that there is always an expert on call and always someone to tell the direct line workers specifically what to do and when to do it.

The planning department

Functional foremanship

"In summation, then, gentlemen, we see that modern management practices today dictate that we have a sound organization set down on paper showing the relationship between all individuals with clear-cut lines of authority. We need staff departments, to be experts in different fields, that can provide guidance for our line organization. And we need a strong, central planning department which coordinates and plans the operations of line and staff departments and specifically makes plans for following the work through the plant. Finally, and most important, this is all accomplished by a scientific study of all operations, setting down observations, attempting to determine what goes on, and scientifically, if possible by means of time-motion studies and a stop watch, determine the best possible way of doing all things. In this manner, more goods can be produced by the company that brings in more money, which increases the amount left to pay the worker. Wages can therefore be higher, making workers happier.

Sound organization for 1910

"For the remainder of the course, we will go into detail on the methods and items covered in this first lecture so that you will be thoroughly grounded in the latest literature in the subject and the techniques for achieving and carrying out these modern management practices."

With that final statement, Professor Jonathan Brown looked up from his notes and over the top of his glasses at the students, closed his notebook with a snap, and stepped from the podium. Immediately, the class jumped to attention, the dapper professor turned to his right, and strode out of the lecture hall.

As he walked along the hallway, he heard footsteps running behind him and a voice calling, "Professor Brown." He stopped and turned his head to see one of his students pounding up the hall.

"Yes, Mr. Mikeson?"

"Professor Brown, something bothers me a little bit about the lecture you just gave us concerning modern management techniques."

"What is it, Mr. Mikeson?"

"Well, you mentioned Dr. Taylor, and I have read his works, of course, and I understand the fact that he wants to apply scientific time studies so that he can find out just exactly what a man can do and then set that as a standard and pay him extra if he exceeds that standard. But it seems to me if we can get labor so cheaply now and we can afford to pay the wages, why are we worrying about a man turning out more? I remember reading just last week that 30 percent of the labor force is made up of immigrants and 20 percent by women and children, both of whom are paid very low wages."

"Perhaps so," nodded the professor, "but do you think your attitude is a good one to have concerning your fellow man?"

Biased value system

"Well, I don't know, Professor, but my father says that a lot of these foreigners are better off than they ever were anywhere else and that they just take the wages away from native-born Americans. And he says why should we try to up their wages so they can take more wages away from us."

"Well, I'm sorry your father feels that way, and I certainly hope that you don't. Let's look at it another way. If you'll remember, I said that manufacturing is going to, at least by my predictions, employ more and more and more people. In fact, I venture to say that the demand for labor will be greater than the supply. And you certainly know from your economics class what happens in that case. If we don't improve the output of the worker and raise his wages now, we most certainly are going to have to raise wages at a later date without any increase in output, and you know what that means—higher wages, higher prices, higher wages, higher prices—and no one is any better off than they were before."

The wage-price spiral

"I hear what you say, Professor, but I just can't grasp it."

"All right, let's go into this empty classroom here, and let me show you an example on the board."

They both went into the small classroom and Professor Brown put the following illustration on the board.

PRODUCTION COST PER DAY

Old System		*Differential Rate System*	
Wage	$2.50	Wage	$3.50
Machine cost	$3.62	Machine cost	$3.87
Total cost/day	$6.12	Total cost/day	$7.37
5 pieces produced cost per piece	$1.224	8 pieces produced cost per piece	$0.92125

"You'll note from the example I just put on the board, Mr. Mikeson, that the worker's wage has gone up $1.00 per day under the differential rate system. Production has gone up by three units and cost per piece has come down to $.92. The beauty of this is that the prices on the market can be lowered while the wages of the employee are raised."

Frustrating interaction upward

"All right, Professor, I see the point. In fact, it's very clear. You know, I've mentioned this to my dad. He works down at the steel plant—and he thought it wasn't a bad idea. In fact, he kind of liked it and he mentioned it to a couple of the other workmen and one of them got up enough nerve to mention it to the strawboss, but boy-oh-boy, it just didn't go across at all. How come if it's so logical the boss wouldn't have gone along with it?"

"Well, Mr. Mikeson, this is one of the problems of Dr. Taylor's new scientific method. The men are normally very willing to go along with it, but the superintendent and the foreman can't find any reason for changing their methods. They've been successful as far as they're concerned, and most of them owe their position to their force of character and the fact they're able to rule over men and get things done."

"Thank you, Professor Brown, I think that explains it to me pretty well. But I just hope I can convince my plant superintendent when I get my first job."

"I certainly hope so, too," remarked the professor. With that he continued his walk along the hall thinking to himself, "Yes, I certainly hope he can. Unfortunately, many of the men who graduate from our program find strong opposition to new techniques when they get their first jobs. I guess it's just human nature; people don't want to change." At the end of the corridor, he turned, walked down the stairway, and out the path to the street. Luckily the streetcar was just rounding the corner, and he was able to get a ride. "It sure will be nice when I make full professor," thought Brown as he sank into the webbed seat. "Then I'll rate a place to tie my horse at the backyard of our building. In fact, I might even have enough money to buy one of those new-fangled cars Mr. Ford is turning out. Wouldn't that be something! But why change? Horses were good enough for Dad and they are certainly good enough for me."

Typical 1910 Frame of reference

EPILOGUE

What are they like?

They are managers approaching 65 years of age today who probably received their business training in the late 1920s from a professor who received his business training in the latter half of the 1900 to 1910 period.

The professor's formal training would probably have included courses covering principles of accounting, commercial contracts, economic resources of the United States, banking and finance, foreign investment, corporate finance, railroad organization finance, railroad accounting, and industrial organization (Frederick Taylor taught a few sessions of industrial organization at Harvard during its first few years). There was still not too much science in management, so the professor's training would have been along the lines of how to perpetuate the business as far as the optimum use of men, money, and materials was concerned. His industrial organization background would have stressed authority and rigid hierarchy and the fact that man was an interchangeable part who had to be controlled and closely supervised.

Exposed to a professor with this background, we might expect these senior statesmen of the working population, in general, to be set in their ways, to resist change, to favor the formal organizational hierarchy, and to think of employees in terms of mistrust—as people who have to be closely watched and controlled. As members of the board and senior management personnel, their ruling considerations might be the profit motive (if in industry) or the power motive (if in government or service).

DISCUSSION QUESTIONS

1. What economic factors would have influenced a teacher of management who received his training in the latter half of the 1900 to 1910 period?
2. What political factors would have influenced the teacher referred to in question 1?
3. Analyze and arrive at a solution to a modern management problem based upon a 1910 managerial frame of reference.
4. What, in your opinion, did management really think about the worker in the 1910 time period?
5. What would a typical interaction situation between worker and supervisor have been like in a 1910 industrial setting? In a service industry setting?

NOTES

Books available for use during this period included:

Charles Babbage, *On the Economy of Machinery and Manufactures* (London: Charles Knight, 1832).

Hugo Diemer, *Factory Organization and Administration* (New York: McGraw-Hill Book Co., 1910).

Harrington Emerson, *Efficiency as a Basis for Operation and Wages* (New York: The Engineering Magazine Co., 1900).

Lee Galloway, *Organization and Management* (New York: McGraw-Hill Book Co., 1910).

Henry Laurence Gantt, *Work, Wages and Profits* (New York: The Engineering Magazine Co., 1910).

Frank B. Gilbreth, *Bricklaying System* (New York: The Myron C. Clark Publishing Co., 1909).

Alfred Marshall, *Elements of Economics of Industry* (London: Macmillan & Co., Ltd., 1892).

Henry Metcalfe, *The Cost of Manufactures and the Administration of Workshops Public and Private* (New York: John Wiley & Sons, Inc., 1885).

Frederic Smith, *Workshop Management: A Manual for Masters and Men,* 3rd ed. (London: Wyman and Son, 1832).

Frederick Taylor, *Shop Management* (New York: Harper & Bros., 1903).

Andrew Ure, *The Philosophy of Manufactures* (London: Charles Knight, 1835).

C. E. Woods, *Organizing a Factory* (New York: The System Company, 1905).

US MAIL
US
US
TITANIC
VOTE TO WOMEN
STRIKE
STRIKE

6

The Age of Innocence 1910-1920

The objectives of this chapter are to enable you to

1. *understand* the managerial philosophy taught in 1920;
2. *realize* that the 1920 managerial philosophy would very likely be taught in later years by a professor who received his management training in the 1920 era;
3. *appreciate* that a supervisor or co-worker in his early fifties today would very likely have been taught by a professor who developed his personal philosophy in an 1895 to 1915 frame of reference and his managerial philosophy in a 1916 to 1920 frame of reference;
4. *recognize* that today's 54- to 64-year-old supervisor or co-worker developed his early personal philosophy during this decade;
5. *identify* the changes, if any, in managerial philosophy from 1910 to 1920;
6. *comprehend* the reasons for changes in managerial philosophy from 1910 to 1920;
7. *note* any changes that may have developed in managerial thinking about human nature in the 1910 to 1920 decade.

PROLOGUE

What was it like?

The second decade in the twentieth century—the teens—the age of innocence. Labor unrest could no longer be ignored during this period. It was the period of the Great World War and unrest caused by women's suffrage, birth control, advancement for colored people, progress, education, and prohibition. One English visitor stated that "America became a nation sitting in judgment of itself." The age-old battle between the sexes took on a new and unsettling turn. The new kind of female smoked cigarettes, drove autos, bobbed her hair, discarded pinched-in corsettes and cumbersome petticoats, earned her own living, and commanded the right to vote, finally won in 1919 with the nineteenth amendment. Ford, the master builder in the business, was fast becoming the biggest automobile manufacturer in the world. In 1914, he turned out 240,700 cars, almost as many as all other auto companies combined, and during the war the airplane came of age. The entertainment capital of the world was Broadway, with Vernon and Irene Castle the toast of the town.

Hooverizing was a belt-tightening program, and the daily dozen was a system of fitness exercises. *Quo Vadis* and *Birth of a Nation* were the major movie hits.

"Down By the Old Mill Stream," "Alexander's Ragtime Band," and "Hail, Hail, the Gang's All Here" were songs of the period. Some of the best-sellers were *Seventeen* by Booth Tarkington, Zane Grey's *The W. P. Trail,* and the first book on contract bridge. The radio outgrew the experimental stage at the same time the camera became reliable, understandable, and compact. Chautauquas or tent shows were called by Teddy Roosevelt "the most American thing in America."

Although the young were kicking up their heels, the family was still the center of the home. The father was the all-important character even though the war had caused women to take over as auto mechanics, telegraph messengers, elevator operators, and street conductors. The guiding thought seemed to be that man, through his rationality, could solve all problems—that only emotion and feeling got in the way.

Against this background we again renew our acquaintance with Dr. Brown in February of 1920.

"It certainly doesn't seem like ten years since I gave the final lecture in the principles of management class at the university," thought Professor Brown. "So much has changed in the past ten years, but I must admit I was flattered when the Dean called me and asked me to give a final lecture to the present class. I can see why he asked, though. Since I left the university in 1915, I've had a chance to study industry at first hand and to find out that everything we taught in the early days of the business school is certainly not practiced in industry. In fact, I'm welcoming the opportunity to tell the students what it's like on the inside. Most of them have only seen a factory from the outside. Very few have ever been inside.

"One thing I'm glad to see is that the curriculum has changed over the past ten years. Factory management has replaced the old industrial organization course. The social factors in business are now being taught as well as business statistics. It was most interesting also to note in the Dean's letter that the Taylor system of management was actually given as a course for a couple of years.

"Well, I guess as a first step, I'd better review my notes from that class ten years ago, because my lecture will be entitled, 'A Decade of Management, 1910–1920.' My old 1910 notes will give me a starting place."

He rummaged through his briefcase and finally came up with his notes. "I certainly am glad I kept these," he thought. "Now, let's see what I said." With these thoughts, he reviewed his notes for the next hour or so before drafting his lecture.

"It certainly appears that I was stressing the scientific management aspect, but that was what was in vogue at the time; and I went into organizational types. It's interesting to see, though, how things have changed in the last ten years. In reading over my notes, I certainly wasn't thinking too much of the individual—the emphasis was mainly for the good of management. And now I see that things have changed—at least a little bit. So, in essence, I think I'll cover five points in my lecture.

"First of all, I'll review Taylor briefly and point out how his theories are not all they're cracked up to be based on my experience. Then I think I'll review organizational types. This I didn't mention before, and things have changed in light of Professor Duncan's latest book. Then I'm going to expose the students, if they haven't been already exposed, to the human side of management and give them an appreciation for the worker. Next I'll cover some of the newer tools of management analysis, such as statistics, and lastly a little review of the problem of the ability of the executive." With those thoughts, Professor Brown began to fill in his outline.

It was the last Friday in February of 1920, a surprisingly warm day for the area of western Pennsylvania. Jonathan Brown, in the familiar lecture hall of the university, found the rows of chairs the same; central heating, of course, had been added, but the room had changed very little. The only unusual thing was that this time he found himself sitting on the end chair in the front row rather than walking into the large lecture hall. He really did miss the academic life, but compared to the salary he was making as a consultant and management specialist with the Link Belt Company, academic life just wasn't that lucrative. His thoughts were interrupted by the shuffle of feet as the class, as had been the custom when he was teaching, snapped to attention as Dean Johnson entered the door and crossed to the podium.

"Gentlemen, we are fortunate to have with us today a former colleague and professor of this august institution who has consented to take two days off from his busy activities at the Link Belt Company of Philadelphia, drive westward to our area, and give us the introductory lecture in this last course of your curriculum—factory management.

"To briefly review, Professor Brown was one of the first members of the faculty of the business school and was the first instructor in the old industrial organization course which is now called "Factory Management." Unfortunately, he left the university in 1914 to go with the Link Belt Company where he has become famous as a professional manager and consultant of high regard. He is going to review today changes in management concepts in the last decade, with particular emphasis on modern management practices. Gentlemen, I give you Professor Brown."

Jonathan Brown stood to the ovation of the class, shook hands with Dean Johnson, moved to the podium, and looked out over the audience.

"Gentlemen, I must admit something. In all the years I taught at the university, I never before realized how easy it must have been to sneak in and out of the lecture hall until I sat behind the partition this morning. All you can see is one head, and I'm sure, in fact I'm positive now, that many times I must have played to less than a full house. Yes, gentlemen, I think I certainly was naive at that time. But that's a perfect example of seeing things from the other side. Only in my case, instead of the other side being from the students, the other side is from industry. As a professor during the early years of the school, my training was entirely academic. I relied on books, magazines, articles, and discussions with my colleagues and industrial managers to put together notes for my lectures in industrial organization, and tried to impart to my students the modern management practices of the times.

"Since leaving the university, I find that as my students saw things differently from the other side of the barrier, I now see management in a slightly different light, having actually worked with a large company for the past six years. Also, I have been acting as a consultant during the last two years to other manufacturing establishments in the Philadelphia area, specifically, the Taber Manufacturing Company, the Standard Roller Bearing Company, George Oldham and Sons Company, and Smith and Ferbush Machine Company.

"Now I can talk to you about modern management practices, as well as changes in the last decade, from a practical as well as an academic viewpoint.

"In preparing for today's talk, I reviewed my notes from a previous lecture—that given in the spring of 1910. I used this as the base lecture in the attempt to sum up changes in the past decade. In that lecture, I mentioned the Taylor system of scientific management, the importance of line/staff relationships, the functional approach to management, the logical, clear-cut lines of authority, and the overall systems planning needed to run an organization. Of course, these are points you have undoubtedly already covered in prior courses in your present curriculum. However, you must remember that my remarks at the time were based upon conditions at the time. Most of you were mere boys, 10 or 11 years old in 1910. I dare say that many of you had never seen an automobile, much less an airplane, or even used a telephone. And at the age of 10 or 11, you probably hadn't made one major trip of more than 25 or 30 miles. However, as you know, things are certainly different now. The airplane came of age during the war, many people use an automobile and even own one. Means of marketing, distribution, and transportation have improved so that we no longer have to worry about supplying only the needs of a small geographical area. Electricity and central heating are found in almost all buildings, and many of us think very little about 100-mile or more motor trips. More people work in manufacturing now than ever before. In fact, in comparing statistics prior to this lecture, I noted that the increase from 1900 to 1920 was 5.8 million people in the manufacturing industry and 2.4 million people in the clerical industries, while the agricultural workers in pure numbers remained almost the same yet decreased 10 percent in the total employment picture. Forty percent of the population is engaged in service industries as compared to 34 percent in 1900. If this trend increases, I rather suspect that within the next 10 to 15 years the service industries will amount to more than 50 percent of employment, truly a remarkable situation when you consider that over half of the employment was in agriculture as late as 1878. But, the point is, gentlemen, that the industrial age is here to stay and we certainly need to consider changes that have taken place in size, complexity, and make-up of manufacturing plants and industry in general.

"But, to begin the review of trends, let's go back and consider the points of scientific management as taught by Mr. Taylor as a starting point for our general review. In general, scientific management was to be a system applied to the entire organization. It was to employ the scientific method of time and motion study to review the job of each employee to determine the best way to do each job and to establish a standard for payment—a standard which the worker would or should be able to meet and exceed, thus gaining more money for himself. In addition, the entire plant had to be studied as a system so that the flow of goods could be traced and all the necessary steps pinpointed. A planning department consisting of eight functional foremen would be established to handle order of work, routing, time and cost, instruction cards, speed, inspection, repair, and disciplinary measures. Law instead of rule of force was to be established. Actually, it was a line/staff ultimate set-up wherein a core of specialists had a duty to instruct and train the worker and to assist him whenever difficulties arose. If carried out in accordance with Dr. Taylor's ideas, it rewards the men for suggestions and improvements; it requires the workers to perform not one but several operations or tasks and trains them so that each can become a "first-class man"; it energizes them and stimulates them intellectually and promotes their self-reliance and individuality; it insures just treatment of individual workers; it guarantees the worker against the arbitrary high task setting, rate cutting, and elimination of earnings; it raises his wages and shortens his hours; it increases the security and continuity of employment; it promotes friendly feelings; and it tends to prevent strikes.

Taylorism in review

The Taylor system was introduced in Chapter 5. It is emphasized again here and on later pages because in the time period being considered it was controversial and would have been discussed again and again.

"This, in essence, is what Dr. Taylor says is the logical outcome of scientific management. It sounds utopian, doesn't it?

"Unfortunately, gentlemen, I must say that the functional-foreman idea and the complete changeover emphasized by Dr. Taylor is not working, as I have found out during my practical experiences in the last six years.

Taylor system not working

"First, I could not find one single shop in which all of Dr. Taylor's system was put into effect. Now I realize that I have only visited shops around the Philadelphia area, but during a few of the ASME conventions that I attended I talked to other industrial engineers, professors, and consultants who are familiar with manufacturing institutions in New York, Pennsylvania, Massachusetts, and, in general, in the industrial northeast. They had all found, as I did, that there was no factory or plant that represented fully and faithfully Dr. Taylor's system.

Not a complete system

"Secondly, apparently no one could find uniformity in the process of the completeness of the installation. What I'm getting at is that the various

Nonuniformity in practice

shops took pieces of the overall system to fit their needs. Some applied scientific management practices of rate setting to certain specific groups of workers without considering all workers as a whole. Some tried the disciplinarian functional foreman and the instruction functional foreman alone without incorporating all functional foremen. Some used a portion of a planning department in some particular shops and not in others. In other words, each one only used parts with the result that overall efficiency was improved in some departments but not in others."

Looking up from his notes at this point, the professor noticed a hand waving in the second row. "Yes, young man?" he asked, looking at the face underneath the hand.

"Professor Brown, why do you think that situation is so? Why don't plants completely adopt the Taylor system, because it seems so logical and leads to such wonderful results?"

"Young man, you have two questions in one, and you made an assumption which I did not make. To start with your second point, I did not say that the Taylor system leads to wonderful results. I only said it was purported that it would.

Complete changeover is costly

"Now, back to your first question. I think the reason that plants do not adopt the system in total is strictly a matter of economics. It costs money to install the Taylor system completely. You must study your plant, hire people to make time-motion studies, rearrange facilities and, in general, make a capital outlay which is going to reduce profits. Too often, businessmen appear to be short-sighted and only consider short-run profits. That is probably why no one plant adopted the whole system. However, in adopting pieces of the system, they felt they could increase the profit picture in certain areas of the plant. You see, unfortunately, this does not tend to achieve the overall results envisioned by Dr. Taylor. In fact, it leads directly to the criticism by the unions that the scientific management method is only a method to exploit the worker. Does that answer your question?"

"Yes, sir, I see what you mean now. In other words, if it's going to cost them money, a plant isn't going to do it."

"Yes—that, in general, is correct. You see, scientific management has to be a complete change in thought. Dr. Taylor brought this out very well at the congressional hearings at which he testified; because as you will remember in one of your earlier courses, his system was envisioned by some as a method of forcing laborers to work harder. As a result, the strength of unions caused the particular investigation. But, as I was saying, Dr. Taylor said during his testimony that scientific management involves a complete rethinking by management. Let's look at it this way. The total cost of producing a product is the sum of the costs of material, overhead, and labor. The selling price includes producing costs plus profit. Now, if both management and workers agree that material costs are fairly well-known or can be determined, and that overhead is a more or less fixed total cost, then what's left over when these two cost factors are subtracted from sales income is a residual that can be split between the workers as wages and management as profit."

What the professor is saying is that: selling cost − (material cost + overhead) = wages + profit (the residual).

"Now, if we can make this residual as large as possible, profits can go up dollarwise and certainly wages can also. This, then, is the reasoning behind scientific management. If we can make the worker more productive, he can earn more money and profits can be higher. In fact, the product could perhaps be sold at a lower price. This very same subject came up during a question after my lecture ten years ago. I remember it well because that young man went on to be a successful businessman. At that time, I used the following little example that I'll repeat for you on the blackboard. You'll notice that this shows the economics of the situation I described above. But without the mental revolution, unfortunately, results are not going to be achieved and, in fact, have not been achieved because of what I mentioned about businesses not employing the system in total."

PRODUCTION COST PER DAY

Old System		*Differential Rate System*	
Wage	$2.50	Wage	$3.50
Machine cost	$3.62	Machine cost	$3.87
Total cost/day	$6.12	Total cost/day	$7.37
5 pieces produced cost per piece	$1.224	8 pieces produced cost per piece	$0.92125

"Does that explain it, sir?"

"Yes, thank you, Professor Brown."

"Well, to continue with my findings from the practical side of the academic fence, very few of the plants had uniformity in the method of selecting and hiring workers. In this sense, I could find no record of any justification for the claim that scientific management makes possible the scientific selection of the workers. In almost every case, workers were hired as they had been in the past. In other words, if they were available to work, looked strong and willing, they were hired. After they were placed on the payroll, though, they were given training specifically in the job they were hired to do. Thus, Harrington Emerson's claim—I'm sure you all were required to read this book, *Efficiency as a Basis for Operation and Wages*—that a manpower staff be set up to insure proper selection of workers for the jobs certainly appears to be valid.

No standards for time studies

"Another glaring discrepancy in actual practice is that of time study and task-setting. There is apparently no exact rule as to how time and motion studies are to be set up. The allowance for rest period is strictly and arbitrarily made on the basis of a foreman who has a tendency to distrust the worker and thus assume that he is always soldiering. Very often the results of the studies are inaccurate and subject to all the errors that can arise from human ignorance and prejudice.

No standards

"One of my main objections to time and motion study for the purpose of setting wage rates is that the rate established after the study for the actual wage payment is the rate that was prevailing in the industry in general in the area or in the particular plant. No consideration whatsoever seems to be given to the accuracy and justice of the rate once it is established."

At this point, another hand was raised. "Professor Brown, would you explain that one, please?"

Rates not fair

"Well, yes—what I mean is that the time and motion studies establish how much a man can do or how fast he can turn out a particular job—let's say how fast he can shovel a ton of coal. The study sets a standard rate which is then taken as the hourly rate that should have been in effect before the time-motion study. The new rate is set as the wage rate in existence in the area or at that particular mill. Now, it would seem to me much more fair to compare rates over a statewide or two or three statewide systems to see what the going wage rate is in the whole area—wider area, that is—for this particular job. Next establish the average of all wages paid throughout a general area as the hourly rate. Then base the premium on this wage rate. I think this would be a much fairer way and would cause workers to grumble much less than they do. And, believe me, gentlemen, even under the Taylor system, there is still a lot of grumbling about work. Does that answer your question?"

"Yes, sir, I see what you mean. In other words, if a low wage is paid in the beginning, it isn't fair to establish that low wage as a piece rate."

Initiative is stifled

"That is correct, sir. Now, as I mentioned earlier, because no adequate allowance for rest and other purposes is established, the system actually does not protect the worker from over-exertion and exhaustion. But this is not the main thing. My main observation and thus my main objection to scientific management as advocated by Dr. Taylor is that it does not provide opportunities for advancement and promotion. Actually, it takes all initiative from the worker. He's told what to do, how to do it, how to set his machine, what piece to work on, when he's supposed to get it finished, and in what particular amount of time. All iniative is taken away, and in actuality, all he becomes is a machine tender. A first-class man in this case is, in my mind, simply one who can turn out the most pieces per day. I certainly will admit that the modes of discipline are better than the old methods and that all men are treated more equally. However, many of the plants neglect to incorporate this particular functional foremanship responsibility because of the objections of the old-line bosses."

Does Professor Brown's discussion give you any clues as to what Taylor really thought about workers as human beings?

"Lastly, I would say that as to methods of discharge and length of service, there isn't anything unique about the Taylor system. In fact, if a man doesn't come up to standards, he sometimes is fired where he wouldn't have been before. Apparently, though, more attention is now given to the man's production record than the whims of the foreman. We must remember that one of the great assets of the wage worker in the past was his craftsmanship—in other words, his ability to see what had to be done, set his machine as a skilled machine operator, and, based upon his own practical knowledge, come up with a solution. Unfortunately, under scientific management, there is really no real craftsmanship left because, as I stated before, everything is planned by someone else, and all the man has to do is tend the machine. So, gentlemen, you can see in summary that there is quite a gulf between scientific management principles in total as prescribed by Dr. Taylor and the actual practice in industry today. Although many of his points are valid and well-taken, they cannot be used indiscriminately without considering the plant as a system. And it would appear from my studies that this practice of systems analysis is what is lacking more and more in our manufacturing establishment.

Taylorism does not allow for self-growth

"It's obvious, then, that another step must be taken in the organizational process. Taylor took the military form of organization, which obviously was not able to keep up the pace as plants got larger and larger and evolved the functional foremanship type of organization. With the functional plan, of course, it is possible to train enough men to carry out functional duties. Unfortunately, many times it is virtually impossible to finely define the lines of authority and responsibility so that there isn't some overlapping, which causes conflicts and, at times, bad feelings in the factory situation. As a result, many plants today use a departmental system along with the staff functions as outlined by Mr. Emerson, so that we have what we might call a line and staff organization. The departmental system divides the plant into a number of clearly defined departments and puts the department heads in charge of the various operations.

Beginning of departmental system

"Dr. John C. Duncan was discussing this with me the other day. In fact, he will soon incorporate a discussion of the departmental system in his forthcoming book, *Principles of Industrial Management*. As he puts it and as I can state from my own experiences, the department system puts each department under a general foreman and then breaks down that department into a line organization under the control of gang bosses.

"If you'll follow me, gentlemen, I'll draw a typical organizational chart on the board so that you can see the relationship between the parts of the organization. Now, observing the chart, in the machine shop, for example, there is a man to look after the large machine tools, such as the lathes, planers, and milling machines. There is another foreman appointed to look after the erection of the large parts of the engine. Another is given a valve-setting gang, still another is given charge of the toolroom, while another looks after stores. The riggers and crane men are under a subforeman who would also keep all the machines supplied with work. In addition, the repair department is in the hands of one man, the toolmaking and grinding department in the hands of another, and the storage department in the hands of another. Each man is thus held responsible for the output of his machine or his particular area of work."

This is a more detailed picture of the general organizational philosophy attributed to C. E. Woods in Chapter 5.

"The system works similar to this. When a set of drawings comes into the shop, the head foreman gathers all his gang bosses or subforemen together, and they all look over the drawing. Each man then clearly understands from either written or oral instructions his particular job. It is then his duty to keep his machines going and his men employed on the particular tasks.

How much departmentalization exists today?

"The main advantage of the departmental system is that it divides the work up into small departments, each under the absolute control of one man. And the departments are so related to each other that no individual workman will have to obey two bosses. As an example, in the functional system, the workmen would be under a certain foreman who was at the mercy of half a dozen functional foremen. In the department system, on the other hand, the workmen learn from their boss, who is responsible only to his head foreman. Thus, it is possible to fix responsibility and further to train men for advancement. In addition, it is impossible to have any shifting of responsibility, because the men must show results in output and not prove, as they do under functional foremanship organization, that they have given or followed instructions.

"Actually, gentlemen, the line and staff situation leading to departmentalization of work is not a new principle. It has probably been practiced in many, many locations, but it has probably never been scientifically explored. Thus, in setting up such a system, we should probably remember basic principles of organization and the twelve principles of efficiency so clearly stated by Harrington Emerson in his book published in 1912. I am sure that you have studied these particular points, but to reiterate, let's keep in mind that

Are these principles applicable today?

1. we need clearly defined ideas
2. we need to use common sense
3. we need competent counsel
4. we need discipline
5. we must practice a fair deal
6. it is essential to have reliable, immediate, and adequate records
7. dispatching is essential in any organization
8. there must be standards and schedules
9. we must achieve standard conditions
10. we must standardize operations
11. we must have written standard practice instructions, and
12. there are needs to reward for efficiency.

"One of these principles, in particular, is gaining more and more emphasis today, and that is events associated with principle 5—regarding a fair deal. This, gentlemen, gets us into the labor side of management and into considering man as a human being and not just a product or a tool of industry as expressed by some of the political economists of the nineteenth century. In other words, we apply psychology.

"Lillian Gilbreth makes the point of the use of psychology in management in her recent book, *The Psychology of Management.* She stresses the individuality of scientific management in treating each worker individually, recording his output separately, including his tasks, his work, his instructions, his teachings, his incentives, and his welfare. Personally, I think she means well, but I do not feel that the individuality treatment under Dr. Taylor's system was entirely motivated by the desire to have a happy, satisfied worker. However, we do see that efforts are being made to truly consider the welfare of the worker and his working conditions. I must say that I have found this to be the case in some of the factories where I have been called to consult.

"Personally, I have found from practice over the past few years that some of the statements made by Dr. Briscoe of the City College of New York accurately reflect practices that are being carried out in industry today in relation to the worker. These are so different from the attitudes developed during the first part of the century that I think they should be shared with you and carefully explored.

The human problem is recognized

"First, and unfortunately so in the past, too little thought was given to the cooperation, loyalty, and enthusiasm of the working man. I firmly believe that the most important element in the business enterprise and the most important problem facing business is the human problem. Co-operation between management and the worker is the strength of any business enterprise. To encourage mutual interests and support of the workers is one of the most important tasks of management. Furthermore, success very often hinges upon its solution; the best physical plant organized along the latest scientific line, staff, and functional relationships with all departments supposedly doing their job can really not function without the support of the workers. Thus, to obtain their cooperation, men must be given a square deal, proper treatment, and reward for services. Furthermore, they should have a share in developing the methods in the plant, so that they can feel that they really are an important part of the organization. They should be consulted concerning difficulties and encouraged to suggest ways of overcoming these difficulties. As Dr. Briscoe so aptly states, 'Working together with the interest of the enterprise at heart is the proper spirit of workers and should be sought by every management. Cooperation has two sides, but management frequently sees but one.' "

The above statement reflects the teachings of many current behavioral scientists. Unfortunately, the advice was not taken to heart by the majority of managers.

Suggestion systems are not new

"It's interesting to note that this philosophy is certainly not new. Professor Diemer of Penn State discussed the very same aspects in his book *Factory Organization and Administration,* published in 1910. In that work, the professor discussed the need for cooperation, for a suggestion system with prizes, the forming of committees to solve problems, encouragement of ideas from the rank and file; and he further stated that the ability to get along with people was more important than technical ability.

"Another thing I pass on to you, gentlemen, is that personality is one of the strongest links between men and management."

"What do you mean by that, Professor Brown?" asked a first-row student.

"What I mean is that a man's personality is sometimes more important than other things. In other words, two people get along well because their personalities are compatible. If this is true between a worker and a boss, then the relationship is a good one. If their personalities clash, then the relationship is bad. That's what I mean by the statement that personality is one of the strongest links between men and management. I should have continued by saying, too, that knowing this, you can sometimes change your personality to get along better with the worker if you really want his cooperation."

This is the first hint at the recognition that successful interaction involves a give and take between people.

Good human relations advocated

"Along these same lines, I would say or advise a policy of keeping an open door so that you can be in touch with your men at all times and be ready to discuss any differences or grievances that they might have. Men can sense attitudes; and these attitudes of yours are soon learned by the men who, in turn, have strong feelings toward you as a manager. In fact, the way you behave toward them very often will be the way they behave toward you. I will go further and tell you that loyalty to business develops from loyalty to bosses. Another important aspect of getting along or treating your workers well is to have sympathy. If, for example, the head or superintendent of a works knows that the board of directors appreciates his efforts and will back him up in a crisis, his enthusiasm for the success of the enterprise will be ever-present; also, if a foreman and a superintendent know that management is watching their efforts, they also should be enthusiastic. In other words, if men are recognized, patted on the back, sympathized with, and told that they are doing a good job or that you are willing to help them in any way, they certainly are more willing to work harder and put their hearts into their work.

Praise and recognition are important to productivity and loyalty

"In this regard, gentlemen, I am talking to you from actual practice. Although some of my thoughts are scattered throughout some of the management texts, they are not strongly emphasized; but they should be. Because relationships with the men are, from my practical experience, much stronger than supposed in creating a good work atmosphere and in the long run greater profits for the business enterprise.

"Finally, we need to be fair and impartial in all our dealings with our subordinates. We should have a system of promotion within the ranks to show men that we reward their efforts, and we should most certainly have a grievance system so that they can tell us when we are wrong. In essence, gentlemen, get to know your workers. They are the lifeblood of the organization. Be truly interested in them, show them that you are interested, and help them in any way. This will give you a far better and surer way to be a successful manager than all the prior planning and organization in the world.

"As mentioned earlier, I would direct your efforts toward the study of psychology, because much has been written lately about psychology and industrial efficiency and industrial psychology in general.

"Now, in addition to a slightly—I should say more than slightly—a drastically different way of thinking about workers in general, there are new tools being added to the manager's toolbox. One of these is statistics.

"As businesses grow larger and larger and can no longer be managed by one man—that is, one man cannot possibly know what is going on in each part of his business—we have seen the development of new and expanded accounts. As a result, the men who keep the books have seen the advantage of constructing figures that tell the operating manager what he needs to know about all the areas of his business. In fact, I would categorically state that no business can operate successfully unless someone constantly analyzes accounts and presents the results in a clear and concise statement. Certainly, this is a different task than the bookkeeper of yesterday performed. Although the bookkeeper records only known facts, the accountant, by scientific analysis, must learn the facts to be recorded and direct the bookkeeper so that the analysis presented to management is clear and concise and all-inclusive. Accounting data in the traditional form is no longer adequate. We now need figures on materials, causes of waste, standards and indicators, all scientifically analyzed and carefully presented in a clear, concise manner to top management. Charts and graphs should be used, so that at a glance, the manager can tell where he stands and compare planned output with actual operating results.

Tools of management

"Statistics applied in a logical manner can sometimes reveal problems which otherwise could not be identified.

"Another area of statistics," continued Professor Brown, glancing up from his paper for a moment, "is in the area . . ." At this point a waving hand caught his eye and he stopped to find out the reason. "Yes, sir, you have a question?"

"Yes, Professor Brown—could you give an example in which statistics can uncover the real reason? You just mentioned it in your last sentence, but I don't exactly see what you mean. I've had the courses in accounting and statistical measurement, but I don't remember seeing how analysis of some statistics could uncover a problem I didn't even know I had. Could you help me out?"

"Certainly," said Professor Brown. "May I ask your name?"

"Yes, sir, it's Jack Smith."

Statistical analysis can pinpoint problem areas

"Well, Mr. Smith, let's look at it this way. Suppose as the functional foreman of a drill-press operation, you found out that the output of the men in your section was not as great as you would wish. Or, as another way of putting it, let's say that jobs were taking longer than the planning department had anticipated. From your direct observations, you note that the men apparently are working at their normal rate, but you just don't seem to be getting as much done. All right, let's further suppose that you keep records on power consumption within your particular area of operations or that you can get figures on power cost. Power consumption,

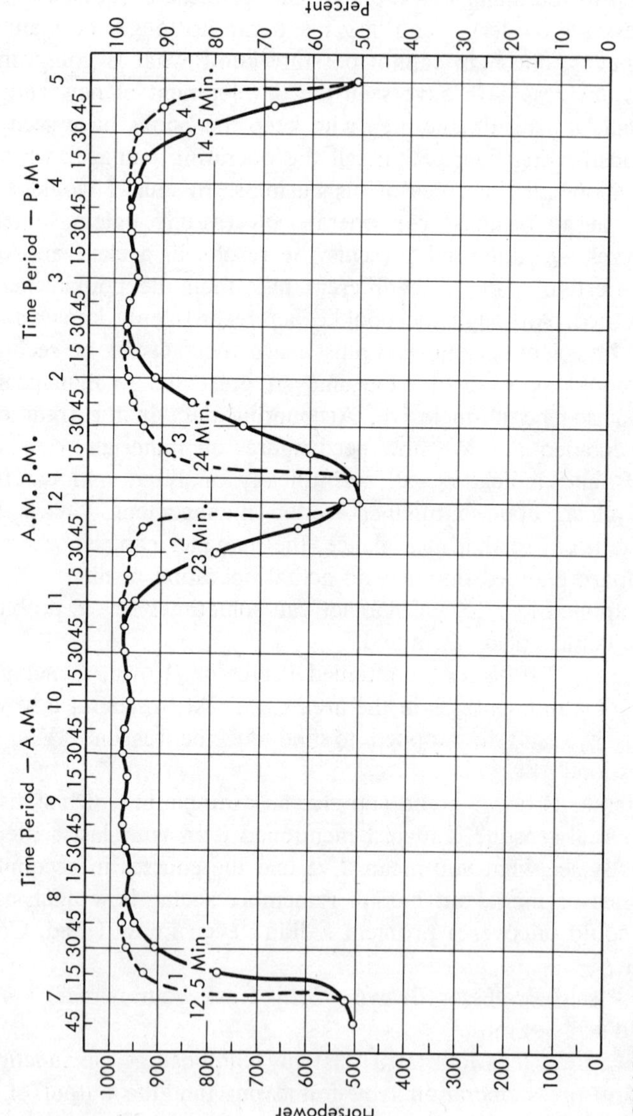

CHART 1
Power Consumption over Time

of course, will give you utilization of machine time. All right, now let's plot power consumption over time." At this point Professor Brown turned and put the preceding chart on the blackboard. Turning around to the class, he continued. "It's obvious from this, Mr. Smith, that power consumption is following a pattern. You'll note that within the first fifteen to twenty minutes of the time the day shift starts, the power goes up on a slope not reaching peak output until approximately half an hour after the shift starts; then you'll note it dips a little in the morning, falls off a little before lunch period, builds up after lunch, and slows down prior to the end of the shift. This certainly indicates that all work is not set up and ready to go the minute the men report to work in the morning. It also appears that there is a slacking-off before lunch and after lunch and that the men are not working at peak output until the whistle blows. Thus, you see that the examination of statistics plotted against an appropriate time frame reveals a situation that leads to the real problem of inefficiency in the production area which could not be seen by observation alone. Now, is that clear to you?"

"Yes, Professor, it certainly is. I also see that if statistics were not available, I would not have been able to find out what the real reason was."

"Well, Mr. Smith, this is a very good example of how statistics can be used to pinpoint a real problem when, without statistics, only symptoms would be available—very much like the doctor when he analyzes a sick person; all he knows are the symptoms—he has to make tests and comparisons to determine the real disease that must be cured."

With that Professor Brown turned back to his notes and continued his lecture.

"Now, gentlemen, as I was stating before Mr. Smith's question, there is another use of statistics in modern organizations—that is, the use or projections of future requirements. In this case, we analyze what has gone on in the past as far as sales, market projections, plans versus outcomes, and then we project these to determine what is likely to happen in the future. Thus, we have a more scientific way than mere seat-of-the-pants estimation as to what our plans must be for the next accounting period.

"Now, gentlemen, before concluding, I'd like to look back over some of the things we've covered. I've tried to point out that scientific management as Taylor envisioned it certainly isn't working the way he planned. I next reviewed for you some of the organizational types and some of my own experiences. I mentioned Mr. Emerson's efficiency. Next we discussed how the human element in administration is being brought into play more and more and lastly the new tools of management, specifically statistics.

"At this point, I'd like to bring up two more thoughts. The first is that there is a complete change in philosophy today toward executive duties and abilities. In fact, Professor Gowin of the New York University has devoted an entire book to developing executive abilities. And, last but not least, the new terminology for the work of the executive as well as most managers and foremen is *administration*. Administration, of course, refers to the work carried out by the various managers while *executive ability* refers to the top manager in his thinking concerning his entire business organization.

"First, let's look at administration. Probably no one has summed up administration better than Dr. Edward D. Jones, one of my prior colleagues at the University of Michigan. In essence, Dr. Jones recommends certain principles of administration which I am sure you must have covered in some of your other courses; but if not, I will repeat them because this is a summing-up lecture trying to relate to you management principles as applied in actual practice. I will also state that I agree with each one of his principles, because they are carried out in practice more or less as he states. These principles are:

Do these principles remind you of any we use today?

1. Clearly established lines of responsibility and authority. No one person should report to two others in the same responsibility, and we should avoid undue concentration of authority at any one point. Certainly, this is a true principle of administration. As mentioned, this was the fallacy of the functional foremanship developed by Dr. Taylor. It did place responsibility, or I should say it had the worker reporting to more than one boss.
2. The division of functions. The division of labor and functions is most essential. The best-qualified men should be placed where they can do the most good for the company, and similar functions should be grouped together. Again, I find this to be the case in industry and certainly in its practice as well as sound theory.
3. Talents and functions should be in harmony. In simple words, this means that we must have the right man in the right job.
4. Coordination. The administrator is responsible for coordination of work so that each functional unit is able to perform as much of its kind of work as is possible within the relationship of other departments.
5. Cooperation. The power of any organization is a result of its constructive and aggressive forces, and cooperation is essential between departments.
6. A system of orders. Performance should be in response to orders only, the order being a communication of necessary authority.
7. We should have a system of reports to determine what is going on and adequate information flow so that adequate authority can flow down through the organization.

"Finally, gentlemen, I leave you with a couple of other thoughts which have developed over the last decade and were probably unheard of twenty years ago. I believe that the old system of management with the slogan of "the public be damned" has developed into a new system in which the public is served. I certainly agree with Dr. Gowin in this regard. I also believe as he does that the corporation has discovered its soul. The best methods of financing, production, and marketing depend upon high standards of truth and fairness of service—and these, I sincerely believe, when practiced, have resulted in a profit-producing power far in excess of interest and replacement of return on tanglible assets. I also

Social responsibility

believe that business has a social consciousness. As Dr. Gowin states, 'The development of a more vivid, social consciousness constitutes for most men perhaps as difficult a task as any.' In reality, however, it calls only for the inclusion of more persons and more territory within the scope of the relations which men usually exercise in narrow circles, such as the family, the club, or the neighborhood. This means that a man is to recognize his wider obligations and perform them with something of the flesh-and-blood interest that closer obligations have always received.

"Gentlemen, I thank you."

EPILOGUE

What are they like?

They are supervisors and co-workers in their early fifties today who probably received their business training in the late 1930s from a professor who received his academic training and developed his managerial philosophy during the latter part of the teens.

Our professor's training would have stressed the rigid hierarchy, authoritarian management principles of efficiency, productivity by scientific methods, and the importance of organization. The seed of human relations might have been planted in his mind through exposure to Hugo Musterberg's theories. However, the space devoted to human relations in his time in most texts was minimal and probably would not have made too much of an impression. Remember, this man's personal philosophy developed in the 1895 to 1915 time frame.

Exposed to a professor with this background and with a personal philosophy strongly influenced by the Depression, we might expect these supervisors or coworkers in their fifties to believe in hard work, to be interested in having the right man in the right job, and to realize that man may be important but that a good job, money, and material objects might, in the final analysis, be more important than doing "one's own thing." Most would have seen service in World War II and many would have had the attitude of living through their children the life they had missed. In general, the contemporary terms "square" and "Establishment" could be used to describe them.

DISCUSSION QUESTIONS

1. What effect did World War I have on the development of human relations in management?
2. What would managers' attitudes toward workers have been during this period?
3. What major changes in managerial thinking developed during the 1910 to 1920 period?
4. What human relationship/behavioral science seeds of thought were planted during the period?

5. What political activities would have influenced the management teacher who received his training in the 1910 to 1920 period?

6. What economic conditions would have affected the thinking of the management teacher who received his training during the 1910 to 1920 period?

7. Analyze and prepare a solution for a current management problem based upon a 1920 managerial frame of reference.

NOTES

In addition to the books available in the 1910 period the following books would have been available:

Norris A. Brisco, *Economics of Efficiency* (New York: The Macmillan Co., 1914).

Alexander Hamilton Church, *The Science and Practice of Management* (New York: The Engineering Magazine Co., 1914).

Hugo Diemer, *Factory Organization and Administration* (New York: McGraw-Hill Book Co., 1914).

John C. Duncan, *The Principles of Industrial Management* (New York: D. Appleton and Co., 1911).

Harrington Emerson, *Efficiency as a Basis for Operation and Wages* (New York: The Engineering Magazine Co., 1911).

Frank B. Gilbreth, *Motion Study* (New York: D. Van Nostrand Co., Inc., 1911).

———, *Primer of Scientific Management* (New York: D. Van Nostrand Co., Inc., 1912).

L. M. Gilbreth, *The Psychology of Management* (New York: Sturgis and Walton Co., 1914).

C. B. Going, *Principles of Industrial Engineering* (New York: McGraw-Hill Book Co., 1911).

Enoch B. Gowin, *Developing Executive Ability* (New York: Ronald Press Co., 1919).

R. F. Hoxie, *Scientific Management and Labor* (New York: D. Appleton and Co., 1915).

E. D. Jones, *The Administration of Industrial Enterprises* (New York: Longmans, Green & Co., Ltd., 1916.

D. S. Kimball, *Principles of Industrial Organization* (New York: Graw-Hill Book Co., 1911).

Hugo Munsterberg, *Psychology and Industrial Efficiency* (Boston: Houghton Mifflin and Co., 1913).

Frederick W. Taylor, *The Principles of Scientific Management* (New York: Harper & Bros., 1911).

Frederick W. Taylor and S. E. Thompson, *Concrete Costs* (New York: John Wiley & Sons, 1912).

Ordway Tead, *Instincts in Industry* (Boston: Houghton Mifflin Co., 1918).

Bertrand C. Thompson, *Scientific Management* (London: Oxford University Press, 1914).

Sidney Webb, *The Works Manager Today* (London: Longmans, Green & Co., Ltd., 1917).

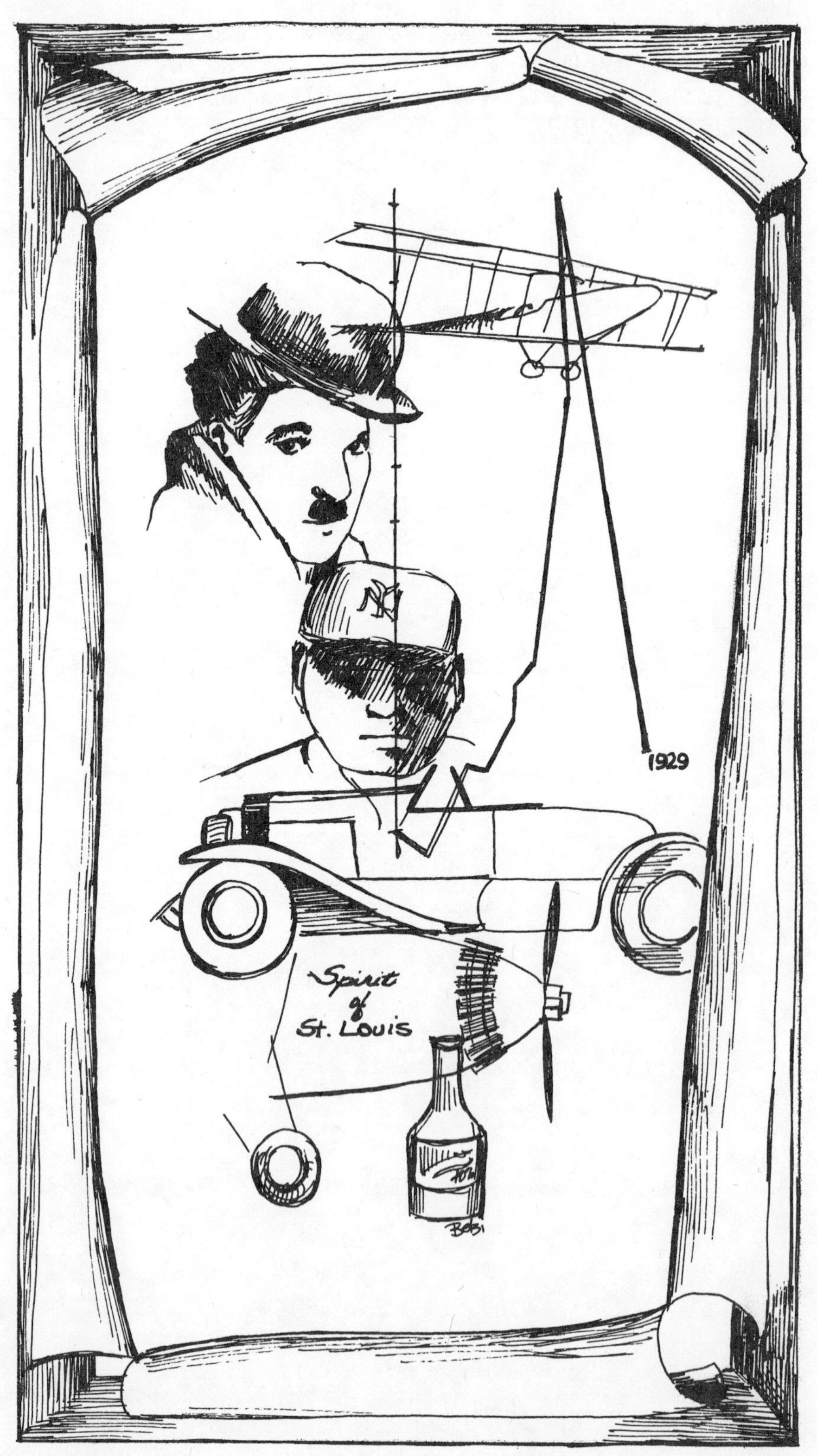
1929
Spirit of St. Louis

7

The Roaring Twenties 1920-1930

The objectives of this chapter are to enable you to

1. *understand* the managerial philosophy taught in 1929;
2. *identify* the changes in managerial philosophy that occurred during the 1920s;
3. *note* any changes that may have developed in managerial thinking about human relations from 1920 to 1929;
4. *comprehend* the reasons for changes in managerial philosophy during the period;
5. *realize* that the 1920s would be the time frame of reference for a professor who would have been the teacher of the businessman who is in his forties today;
6. *appreciate* that senior members of today's work force received their managerial training in the 1928 to 1929 period;
7. *recognize* that today's fifty-year-old supervisor or co-worker developed his personal philosophy during this period.

PROLOGUE

What was it like?

The roaring twenties—an exciting and perhaps frightening time to be young. It was the era of the first youth rebellion: girls smoked and wore shorter skirts, silk stockings, fake jewelry, and bobbed hair; the college man had his ukelele and hip flask. His hair was slicked down to look like Rudolph Valentino's—he liked to be called "sheik" and called his girl "Sheba." Slang terms included "hooch," "giggle water," "applesauce," "blind date," "bull session," "carry the torch," "dumb Dora," "flapper," "gold-digger," "necking," and "sob sister." The Charleston was the dance of the era. Radio and electric refrigerator sales zoomed, and credit buying was paramount. Between 1922 and 1930, there were 13 million radios in the U.S. Chain stores emerged; business was considered a cult with legions of high priests and thousands of boosters who belonged to Rotary, Chamber of Commerce, Kiwanis, Lions, and Elks.

In advertising, the decade's dominant trend was the increasing use of psychology—the deepening appeal to the secret emotions that motivated people to buy. Racketeering and gangsters came of age. Flagpole sitting, Mah Jongg, and marathon dances were the rage. The first Miss America contest was established in 1921 and the speakeasy (illegal liquor salesplace) was "the" gathering spot.

This was the period when Amos and Andy started their radio career, and, believe it or not, the first color television was demonstrated at Bell Laboratories. The handset telephone replaced the wallset, and the first transatlantic radio telephone was established between New York and London. Lindbergh flew the Atlantic; Byrd flew over the North Pole; the first sound motion picture was *Don Juan*.

Song hits included "I'll Get By as Long as I Have You," "Girl of My Dreams," "One Alone," "Dinah," and "California, Here I Come." Influential books included *Main Street* and *Elmer Gantry* by Sinclair Lewis and of course *The Great Gatsby* by F. Scott Fitzgerald.

Parents still had an influence in the home situation but to a lesser extent than in the past. The automobile increased mobility, privacy, and sexual freedom, while radio broke provisional restraints on information. Life was risqué and had a direct effect in shaping lives. In general, the belief was that America had the answer to just about anything if a man was willing to work hard enough for it. It was a land of milk and honey emphasizing the philosophy of the self-made man.

Yet with all this, the era closed as the darkest period of our economic history with the stock market crash of 1929.

Against this background we first meet Professor Mikeson in February 1929—luckily, before the "crash."

Professor Mikeson reluctantly laid down his copy of Thornton Wilder's *The Bridge of San Luis Rey,* knowing full well that he wouldn't get back to it for at least two days. He hated preparing lectures, but at times they were necessary—all classes could not be seminars or case studies. He turned off the radio in the middle of the song hit "I'll Get By As Long As I Have You" and forced himself to think about school.

"Professor Brown was certainly right," he thought as he began to prepare his notes. "Manufacturing certainly has been employing more and more people. It's been twenty years since I sat in his class in Industrial Organization. I guess his statement sticks in my mind because of what he was comparing it to when he said 'more and more' and I guess because of that little example he put on the board about how you could make more money for the company and make more money for the worker by increasing output.

"Yes, the world has come a long way since I graduated that summer. We've gone through a war and emerged one of the leading manufacturing countries of the world. I am a professor at the university—something beyond my wildest dreams twenty years ago. At that time my aspirations were only to be a works manager, but things certainly changed."

He thought for a few more minutes. "I know why I thought about that lecture. I am in a similar position today almost twenty years later. Today I am giving the wind-up course in a business school and introductory lecture, just as Professor Brown was doing with me. That must be the reason.

"Well, back to the present! Along with today's modern management practice, I should cover the significance of some of the events that have taken place over the last decade. However, I don't want to bore them. They've certainly read Dr. Taylor's work, because it's required reading. I'm sure they are familiar with it, but there are still just a few points that I want to make. I'm not sure that they know what the actual criticisms of his system were because their average age is only about twenty-one. No, they wouldn't have remembered it. In fact they're lucky if they remember the war. The main criticisms were made just prior to the war; and, certainly, if their fathers were in industry, they wouldn't have been exposed to them. So I think I'll give them some background about the war's effect on scientific management; then certainly we need to cover the emergence of the different ways of looking at people. Actually, when I went to school, there was little, if any emphasis on human management, social responsibility of business, resistance to change, or a man's instincts. I've got to get these things across because this is probably where we stand today. And, of course, I want to tell them about my trip to the International Management Institute at Geneva where I learned about the works of Henri Fayol. I would predict that his work will go down as one of the classics of management. It's just a shame that his work hasn't been translated for general distribution to the United States. But I am sure that will come. Now I'd better review my references and fill in the detail."

Promptly at ten o'clock on the first Monday of February 1929, Professor Mikeson entered the classroom as scheduled to give the first lecture in the last term of the senior level course in Organization and Management.

"Gentlemen, I certainly am pleased to see so many of you in this class. It speaks well of your efforts to date, because many of your original group have not been fortunate enough to make it this far in the program.

"As you are aware, this course will attempt to tie the rest of your courses together so that you will have a grasp of the big picture and present managerial philosophy.

"To review, one of your assigned texts last term was the *Taylor Society Papers on Scientific Management.* As we know, Taylor's was the great breakthrough in thinking in the management field. His desire to improve the wages of the worker by causing a mental revolution in the thinking of management was exemplary. However, as you note in your readings, much criticism has been leveled at Dr. Taylor. Specifically, the Hoxey Report and the congressional investigations as well as problems with the labor unions did little to encourage more widespread use of scientific management. However, the Hoxey Report and the investigation and labor unrest occurred in the period between 1910 and the start of the war.

"But because of the war, the status of scientific management has been

Is scientific management being confused with science in management?

greatly affected. During the war it was necessary to increase production in order to supply our allies and our own armies. It was essential to turn out products in mass as rapidly as possible. Under these conditions scientific management principles were the only answer. As a result, labor was able to see that men could turn out more and make more money without being exploited by management. Not only did we appreciate the principles of scientific management here in America during the war, but as some of you may have remembered from overhearing conversations at home, the French were so impressed with our scientific management that they adopted it for many of their army operations. The war seems to have eliminated some of the prejudice and the misunderstandings concerning scientific management, and paved the way for better relationships between management and labor.

Resistance to change is not new

"But, gentlemen, even though scientific management has come of age, it is still not practiced in total in many organizations. I certainly believe, also, that the understanding of *why* is important in our present managerial philosophy because it directly concerns the natural tendency of people to be reluctant to change—and believe me, scientific management does cause changes. The changes must be made based on harmony and understanding within groups. This is probably exactly why there are so few complete adaptations of scientific management. By complete, I mean 100 percent change to all of the Taylor techniques. First, many managers and workers are reluctant, except when directly ordered or coerced, to undertake drastic improvements. Second, because American industry has prospered, there isn't any real felt need to make a radical departure from the ordinary ways of doing things. At least, this is the impression one gets when talking to industrial workers and leaders.

"This resistance to change or fear of change has been in existence and probably will remain in existence for all times. However, I would say that it is just coming to the front as an important factor to be realized by management.

"Resistance to change is not so hard to understand if we remember some basic facts about people. Everyone develops a different mass of experience. Everyone assimilates and uses information according to his own particular frame of reference. You must realize this when you want to get any particular idea over to different people."

Again we see that successful interpersonal relationships require work and an appreciation of differences between people's background and philosophy.

Remember Chapter 21

"It isn't the things the working people stand for or object to at any one time that matter; it's that they have certain attitudes which they get from certain situations that they happen to be in, and when these things are changed, their policies and beliefs also must change; this makes them unhappy. It is important for the manager to understand that this change in attitude is constantly taking place either because of the unions, shortage of labor, rising prices, or any number of things. Further, the manager who doesn't see these things changing and thinks that he can follow one set policy in managing human beings is bound to have trouble with his employees.

"Questions, of course, which arise concerning the workers, are varied and numerous. In recent years we've seen increasing emphasis being placed on the social significance of the problems involved and relationships of the company to the workers as human beings. The manager who doesn't realize this will probably not do as well as the manager who does. Although attention to the human element is essential, we must not forget that workers are one of the factors of production. If they are not efficient, the company will not prosper. As a result, it is sometimes difficult to reconcile conflicting interests of the workers and the company; but this is a task that cannot be avoided. It's the task of management—the task that you are being trained for in your present curriculum.

The human element again

"What I am saying is certainly not new. One of my colleagues from the University of London, Sidney Webb, gave an address for a series of private gatherings of work managers in which he reminded us that what the manager has principally to handle is not wood or metal, but human nature—not machinery, but health. And remember, gentlemen, this speech was given in 1917."

At this point Professor Mikeson noticed a hand raised at the back of the class.

"Professor, if all this influence on the human element is so important and you're telling us that we have to consider the workers as human beings and consider the group in ideas, why haven't we heard more about this before? Why don't we see it being practiced in industry? I was talking to my dad the other night and he said that at the plant where he works, you sure don't get treated as an individual. If you can't do the work, you still get fired. No one really cares why you can't do the work."

Theory vs. practice

"Well, I'm afraid this is true," remarked the professor. "You see, there's often a big difference between theory and practice. Theories are what certain people believe, based upon some of the experiences they have had. When enough of them believe the same way, then we have a body of theory that we attempt, by scientific method if possible, to practice in the field. Unfortunately, many people, because of the basic fear of change, do not wish to change. They take the attitude that if something was good enough before, it's good enough now. So I'm afraid you are always going to see a difference between theory and practice. Furthermore, theory will always come before practice, and practice will not catch up unless it is forced to. It's just human nature to want to continue in ways of the past because they're known and they're easier. To make changes requires thinking and a journey into the unknown, which for many people is uncomfortable. Basically, we are creatures of habit and it is difficult to change."

"Thank you, Professor—I guess that explains why, but I'm certainly interested in this new philosophy."

"Well," said Professor Mikeson, "it's really not that new. Let's say that it really hasn't been picked up too much until now, but it's not that new."

Remember the 1920 lecture, in which Professor Brown discussed the value of considering the human side of management at that time?

Tead—the forerunner of many modern concepts

"Now, because we are discussing the art of handling men, or human relations, let's review. As I just mentioned to you, this idea is not that new. An appreciation of instincts and the reasons why people do things was brought out by Tead in 1918. His book, *Instincts in Industry,* was actually a study of working-class psychology. I think it's essential that we examine his theories in detail, because they are very applicable to our understanding of the worker, which, after all, is one of our prime responsibilities as managers—that is, to understand the worker and to insure the success of our organization. Tead listed ten basic instincts:

1. Paternal instinct
2. Sex instinct
3. The instinct of workmanship, contrivance, or constructiveness
4. The instinct of possession, ownership, property, or acquisiteveness
4. The instinct of possession, ownership, property, or acquisitiveness or 'give-a-lead'
6. The instinct of submissiveness or self-abasement
7. The instinct of the herd
8. The instinct of pugnacity
9. The play impulse
10. The instinct of curiosity, trial and error, or thought.

"Instincts as defined by Tead are those forces in our mental life which appear to have a deep-rooted basis in the nervous structure of the individual and the race. He further defines an instinct as an inherited or innate psychophysical disposition which determines its possessor to perceive and to pay attention to objects of a certain class, to experience an emotional excitement of a particular quality upon perceiving such an object, and to act in regard to it in a particular manner, or, at least, to experience an impulse to such action.

"I'm going to recommend to you, gentlemen, that if you haven't read Ordway Tead, you certainly should before the end of this course. And on the assumption that you will, I would like to make the following points that should affect your thinking as managers. These points come from his comments concerning the ten instincts.

"From the paternal instinct he concludes that the desire for pay which covers more than the comfortable minimum stems from the desire to attain status, permanent security, and respectability for the family. He also cites the paternal instinct as the reason that families in many working-class neighborhoods try to keep their standards of living on a par with and preferably superior to those of their neighbors. Thorstein Veblen's leisure class apparently doesn't have a corner on conspicuous consumption."

This particular instinct survives strongly today in many people.

"The sex instinct, Tead points out, is obviously behind much of the advertising technique of today. If you'll look around, you'll notice that most advertising involves pictures of women often in enticing poses.

"Tead's third instinct, that of workmanship, I believe is most important to us, because as he points out, there is no true joy in work and no true workmanship apart from an appreciable degree of self-direction and self-control. This, of course, was one of the criticisms of the Taylor system—that there was no more pride in workmanship. As a result, Tead tells us that if there is no machine work which offers an outlet for creative energy, perhaps we can vary the work. We can even shorten the work day to a point where a compensatory leisure can offer the time needed to engage in some other activity which is interesting and can give a sense of workmanship."

Tead's ideas sound like Maslow's esteem needs, and a forerunner of the 4-day, 40-hour week.

"The instinct of possession probably explains the fear of change or the apparent fear of change that many people possess. He cites the example of shop girls who cried because their old sewing machines had been taken away even though the new machines were identical. Consequently, he feels that a profit-sharing plan wherein the workers have a sense of belonging or ownership in the factory will give them a much more secure feeling than strictly a bonus system.

"Concerning the instinct of self-assertion, he makes the point that this gives impulse to an individual's attempt to rise above the level of humanity and to become an individual."

Again, shades of Maslow.

"The instinct of submission explains the fact that more than 50 percent of individuals have a tendency to submit rather than to be self-assertive; in other words, they will go along with a group in causing changes or overcoming fear of change. This fact is most important to you as managers.

The group influence (see Chapter 3)

"The next instinct, that of the herd, is also a grouping instinct, for it explains the reason that so many people stay with those of their own kind. He uses this idea to explain why groups get together and live in one particular area and do not want to intermingle with other groups. This also explains why some people don't like to work by themselves and prefer to work in a group. He makes the point, which should not be ignored when we are considering the structure of an organization, that people are more sensitive and submissive to the voice of the group than to any individual voice. He further points out that in every gathering of human beings called together for whatever purpose, the evidence of suggestibility will be abundantly in evidence.

"The instinct of pugnacity or violence of course is self-explanatory. The play impulse explains the fact that no matter how serious the situation, somebody somewhere will find something to laugh at and that it is necessary for a manager to go along with some horseplay. He recommends recreational events for the business as a means of satisfying the play impulse.

"His final category, curiosity, is a basis for advocating that people should have some time to think.

Of what importance are instincts today?

"In summary, gentlemen, we find that an appreciation of instincts gives us an appreciation of the conduct of groups in industry. Furthermore, groups are more easily understood when we know a little more about the instincts or moving energies of the people within the group. We must insure that the instincts are allowed to find expression, because they cannot be suppressed forever. Finally, we can come up with definite conclusions: first, that perhaps the cause of conduct of individuals can be predicted; second, that perhaps human nature can be analyzed and found subject to law, and that if subject to law, can be controlled.

The topdown viewpoint

"Appreciation of the instincts is essential, gentlemen, for our practicing of the art of handling of men. We have to realize that a man is moved to action by something that arouses an impulse or causes one of his instincts to guide his actions. And in turn, actions result from the interplay of all the impulses or instincts. Often there is conflict between the impulses created by the instincts which thus find themselves in opposition. Sometimes a prolonged and irreconcilable conflict leads to a sort of splitting of the personality—the individual in his home may be a model of kindness, for example, while in business he shows another side of his character. Of course none of us knows all the depths and reaches of the human mind—in fact we probably know the least about our own minds. But if we examine the conduct of others and our own feelings and actions, we should come to learn something of the actions of others, which as leaders, we have the ability to influence. Of course, there is a distinction between learning in this case and the skill to apply the learning. Psychologists can analyze the motives underlying human action, but may sometimes be completely helpless in influencing these motives."

Professor Mikeson is again referring to interpersonal relationships—in this case the need to understand self and the other individual.

Still applicable today

"Along these lines I would give you certain guidelines that I feel have developed from the fields of psychology, and, in general, have been applied to leadership principles during the past few years. The first prerequisite to understanding other men is the *ability to listen.* Second is to learn *the use of praise*—to use it without cheapening or making it appear an insincere effort to curry favor. Show a genuine interest in people. Third, *be enthusiastic.* Many leaders owe their leadership ability not to cultivated powers of personality but to a contagious, genuine enthusiasm. Fourth, *act as you would have your men act.* Finally, of course, you must *have an appreciation of the group as a unit,* as I have previously mentioned.

Mary Parker Follett's theory of integrative work

"Before leaving our discussion of the human element, I'd like to share with you the content of a few lectures given recently by Mary Parker Follett. Miss Follett has made a name for herself in industrial circles by applying political and social philosophies to the management of business. Her approach is to analyze the nature of the consent on which any democratic group is based by examining the psychological factors underlying it. This consent, she says, is not static, but is a continuous process generating new and living group ideas through the interpenetration of individual ideas. Noting that conflict exists in all organizations, she advocates that the most beneficial way of resolving it is not compromise but integration, in which both parties examine different ways of achieving the conflicting objective. She also says that authority—that is, the traditional kind of subordinate-boss relationship—offends human beings and really is not a good foundation for an organization; actually authority should be a function in which each person is responsible for what he's doing and that personal power gives place to what she calls the law of the situation. According to this law, a decision, although it might appear to be the act of the boss, is really only what she calls a moment in a process which may have started with an office boy. Leadership, therefore, is not a matter of dominating personality. Coordination is all-important in organization.

"These are certainly interesting ideas and I understand that some businessmen have testified to their usefulness. We'll discuss Follett's ideas more fully in later sections of the course. I think they're going to have a profound influence on the way we think of authority in the future and in our relationships between superiors and subordinates—what we might call the interaction situation.

"Are there any questions about this point?" Looking around the room and not seeing any raised hands, Professor Mikeson continued. "Next, gentlemen, we need to have an appreciation for the latest in organizational thinking; for, in the last analysis, management is practiced within an organization.

What is organization?

"Organization is the spelling out of the scope and limits of action of the various individuals and groups of individuals whose work is required for carrying on the objectives of the establishment. It consists further of the uniting of the individuals and groups of individuals in such a way as to insure cooperation for the common good. Furthermore, organization is distinct from system and management. We organize to manage and we manage through system. We also organize, of course, in order to exercise control."

Organization has been discussed in earlier chapters. It is covered again because the 1929 professor wished to stress its importance and the changes in managerial thinking about organizations.

"Organization may be based on the principle of military authority as exemplified by the line officers, on specialization, on functionalization, or on a combination of different degrees of two or more of the principles. With this in mind let's consider each one in turn.

"First, in the strict military or as it is sometimes called, numerical type of organization, men are divided into groups in such a manner that each group receives its orders and instructions from one man only. The typical organization chart of this type of organization would look something like this," continued the professor as he turned toward the board and chalked out Figure 1.

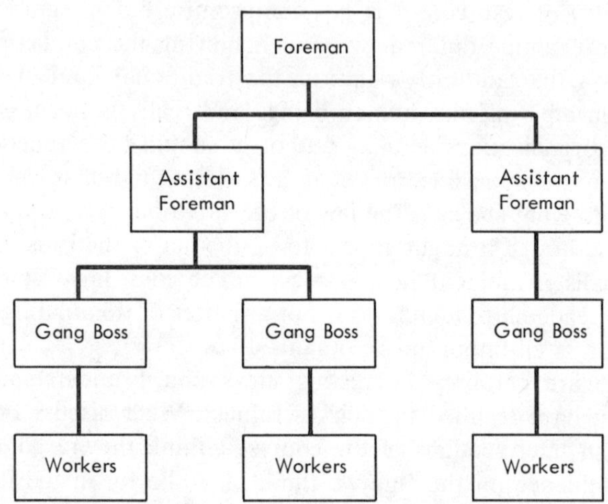

FIGURE 1
Military or Numerical-Type Organization

"You will notice that in this form," he continued, "all workers in Department 1 receive orders from the gang boss, who in turn is responsible to the assistant foreman, who is responsible to the foreman, and so on up the line.

"Within the military-type organization we also find specialization, under which similar duties are combined under a foreman and performed as a group activity. It is exemplified in manufacturing by such departments as the lathe, the screw machine, the milling department, and on the commercial side by such departments as correspondence, sales, accounting, and so forth. Also under specialization we can find distinct departmental types such as the tool design department, storage department, shipping department, cost department, and so forth.

"The next basic type is the functionalized type of organization, in which certain staff officers or departments have control over certain features that are common in all departments. This of course was the functional foreman type advocated by Dr. Taylor in his writings during the 1903 to 1911 period.

"At this point I should probably point out to you the difference between a specialist and a functionalist. We might define a specialist as being one who is expert in a certain trade or science essential to the manufacturing process of the given establishment, for example a tool design engineer or a time study expert. A functional staff officer or functional department on the other hand would investigate a single phase or aspect common to all handicrafts, trades, and sciences. For example, functional organization would be when one man is given the responsibility for performing the necessary routing of each and every order that goes to a plant. The advantage of the functional organization is that certain functions require an analytical mind perhaps beyond the capabilities of some of the first-line supervisors and foremen. When work is functionalized, we can find personnel with the skills necessary to make up the staffing of the particular functional department."

Definition of functional organization

At this point the professor saw a hand raised and stopped to answer the question. "Professor Mikeson, you mentioned Dr. Taylor's functional organization; did he combine functional with line or did he completely eliminate the line?"

"That's an interesting point," answered the professor. "Dr. Taylor insisted upon the complete abolition of the line organization of the shop, although in his works he dwelt at considerable length upon what he called the exception principle. Under this principle, executives were to receive only condensed, summarized, and comparative reports of what was going on in the plant; and further, before these were submitted, they were to have been gone over, and only the exceptions to regular routine or standards pointed out."

"Thank you, Professor Mikeson."

"I think it would illustrate the point better if I drew a functional organization, as Taylor envisioned it, on the board. Label this for your notes as Figure 2. You'll notice the difference between Figure 1 and Figure 2.

"Today, gentlemen, it is almost impossible to find any company that is organized strictly on a line-type or a functional-type basis. Our modern business enterprises are organized on a combination basis using staff, lines, and functions where needed. We might call this a column type of organization which utilizes line/staff or functional control whenever each is most appropriate. Again for ease of illustration let me draw an organization so made up. Designate this for your notes as Figure 3. You'll note that in this figure the industrial engineer and research engineer are staff advisers to the works manager. This relationship is indicated by horizontal lines connecting the squares containing their titles. The relationship is indicated by a vertical line connecting the square. The man in charge of production control is shown as being served in this example by two staff departments, the time and motion studies and the planning department, and these are indicated again by horizontal lines. The scheduling department, on the other hand, works directly for the production control department, and the various shop departments work for the scheduling departments.

Re-examining organizational charts

"Of course the advantage of this organization is that the works manager has a relatively small number of men reporting directly to him and thus has more time to handle some of the other activities of the plant. In a

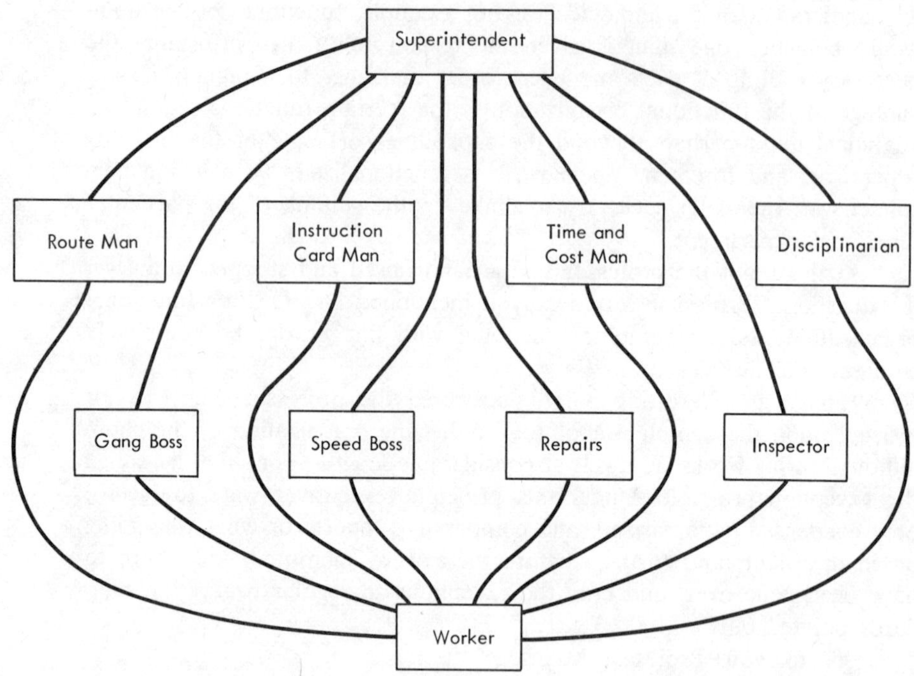

FIGURE 2
Taylor's Functional Organization

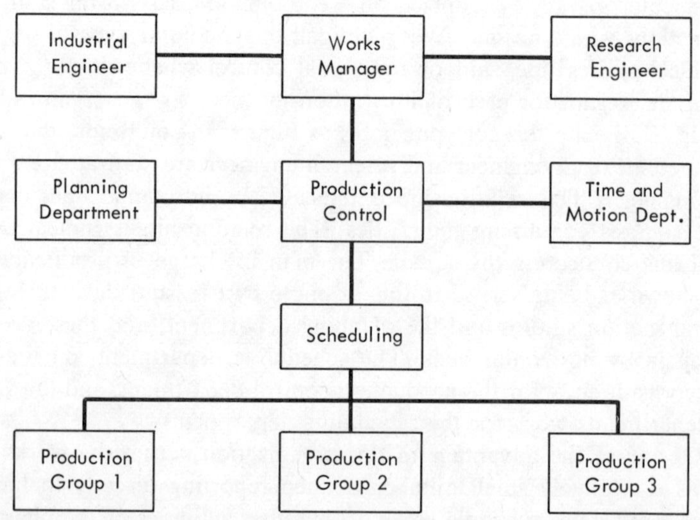

FIGURE 3
Modern Line/Staff Organization

larger plant, of course, you would have many such line/staff functional relationships, depending upon the activities required.

"One thing to bear in mind is that there is no single, correct form of organization, but every activity is organized. Various activities that are not industrial, such as churches, government, the Army, the Navy, educational and charitable organizations, all involve size, numbers, and complexity. And they're all organized. But good industrial organizations differ from these other organizations, and all organizations differ somewhat from each other, because the objectives, the results that are sought, and the way these results must be obtained are different; and, in addition, the material out of which the organization is made differs.

Organizations based on objectives

"It's true, of course, that there is much in common in all effective organizations. For example, the definite knowledge of what one wishes to accomplish, the principles of directing and controlling effectively large numbers of people, making the most of different kinds of skills, securing cooperation of each individual, the systematic and orderly way of doing things so that there are no neglected steps, no false movements, and no loss of time—these are all common in good organizations of any kind—but with differing purposes. The factors that make organizations have varying importances. In one situation, the principle of a division of labor for specialization or skill may be all-important; in another, this may be insignificant in comparison to proper control and direction of large numbers. In some circumstances the significant feature may be dispatch, where the question of economy may hinge much more on time required than on any other factor. As an example, the success or failure of a watch industry would certainly not depend upon instant obedience, definite evolutions of men, predetermined movement in emergency, and a definite line of succession and authority. No, gentlemen, it would depend upon such things as study, care, economy in the purchasing of materials, and the development of processes to make the most of each worker's special skill and ability and of delicate handling of the product.

Effective organizations depend on division of functions

"It sometimes becomes necessary to remind ourselves that organization as an end in itself is of no value. A business organization exists for the purpose of accomplishing definite pieces of work, of arriving at definite results with the least expenditure of labor and material, the smallest expenditure for plant, and shortest time of use at the plant. If organization does not prevent waste or enable us to get results obtainable in no other way, it has no value. And, finally, it is obvious that any organization depends upon the size and the degree to which it is specialized.

Organizations need a purpose

"In any discussion of organizations we must remember that organization is not management nor is the task of organizing a business the same task as managing a business. The organization of a factory might be considered as the design of the garden before management plants and nourishes the seeds which are to form the garden produce. Administration *makes* the design. Organization *is* the design. Management *uses* the design. Management, however, is not a simple function concerned with machines, layout accounts, and scientific methods. It is a human art, as I mentioned earlier. It is the art of directing and regulating the activities of human beings during great portions of their waking hours to the satisfaction of the material needs of their fellow human beings, and to the satisfaction and development of their own material requirements and moral and mental faculties. I can not overstress this point. Industrial management is primarily the management of men. Furthermore, the responsibility of management to direct men is further enhanced by the fact that industry exists for the satisfaction of human needs. Management, therefore, has a responsibility not only to the human element within the industry but also to the human element which industry serves. In other words, management has a definite social responsibility. Finally, in carrying out its work, management performs a group of related activities which we can categorize as functions and which we can recognize."

Social responsibility of management

At this point, Professor Mikeson stopped to answer another question. "Professor, would you clarify that social responsibility point? That's the first time I've heard that. And as a second question, are we going to cover it any more in our course?"

"Yes, we will cover it, to answer your second question first. And as to an example of social responsibility, it means that management is responsible for the health and well-being of the worker while on the job; because this relates to the worker's well-being at home. Management is responsible for a living wage, not just a wage that would be fairly sustaining of the absolute necessities of life. Management is also responsible to stimulate men to develop themselves while at work so that they can be better members of society as a whole, and management has a responsibility to ensure that a man has enough leisure time to carry on a rewarding life away from work. These are definite social obligations of management. We could sum up by saying that management is responsible for making the most out of each individual and not exploiting him for the sake of pure economic return. Does that answer your question?"

Are there more social responsibilities today?

"Yes, sir."

"I'd like to conclude this lecture with a discussion of what I would consider the fundamentals or the functions of management—first, from our own American businessmen and, second, from the standpoint of a noted French industrialist.

Compare these functions with those of today

"From our own viewpoint, I think that most of us in the business area would classify functions in management as (1) planning, (2) putting the right man in the right job, (3) direction, (4) supervision, (5) control, and (6) delegation and coordination of authority and responsibility. It is assumed, of course, that we first have definite and stable policies, an adequate organizational structure or functionalization definition, and incentives for men to do their work.

Policies

"Actually, policies, functionalization, and incentives are sometimes considered fundamentals of business organization. Briefly, because we are going to discuss them in much greater detail later on, policies include the definite statement of what must be done about the business. They are for the purpose of establishing aims, affording a basis for a plan of action, coordinating that action, creating and maintaining public confidence, reputation, and good will, and ensuring business permanency.

Functionalization

"Functionalization, of course, is the fundamental process of organization that requires that all the proper functions be recognized, granted existence, combined where similar or complementary, and placed under the direction, supervision, and control of properly qualified executives who have only one or at the most a few similar functions to perform. We really might call functionalization in organization a fundamental of management; because when we functionalize, we prepare the functional chart and an organization manual, and we consider the right man for the right job.

Personnel management

"Establishing definite and stable policies could be considered planning because planning is stating the objective of the organization and drawing up a detailed course of action for accomplishing that purpose. Getting the right man in the right place is a fundamental of organization. In essence, it is matching the man to the job. Under this function we have to consider that there are individual differences between people in addition to physical and mental capabilities. Only with education, training, and experience can people be developed. It is essential, therefore, to match their abilities with the requirements on the job. Where the abilities are lacking, it is necessary to train. Techniques of this management function include job analysis, job specifications, the interview, physical examination, and trade tests if necessary, including psychological testing.

Direction

"Direction would be the next fundamental of management. This is the factor that governs the conduct of the whole organization. In essence, it includes all factors that determine the type of action the organization is to take. Directive planning is the basis for the formulation of decisions which are made on the basis of concrete facts carefully segregated, evaluated, and correlated into a definite plan of action. As an aid to the directive function, we have policies, standard practices, values, standardization of works, methods, and techniques, written instructions, oral instructions, executive orders, standard practices, and a standard practices manual.

Supervision

"Supervision involves a carrying out of directions. Supervision, of course, occurs whenever there is a group of people whose collective energies must be utilized in the accomplishment of a definite purpose. Supervision can be personal or impersonal, but in any case someone must act. In many organizations it is difficult to secure adequate supervision, but we must remember that supervision is a positive yet intangible force that binds together all parts of the organization. Without its constant vigilance, inefficiencies creep in unnoticed; personnel lack the regulative force that make operations completely unified and harmonious; in the whole organization, men, methods, and equipment fall short of the organization's possible accomplishment.

Control

"The next fundamental, that of control, is a means of providing the manager and the executives of an organization with continuous, prompt, and accurate information concerning the efficiency of operations—what the business is doing, what it has done in the past, and what it can be expected to do in the future. Various controls include record control, standards of performance, standards of inventory, financial ratios, cost accounting, comparison of actual figures against scheduled ones in sales, finance, labor, production, and so forth. In essence, reports should be prepared in an easy-to-read manner so that management can tell at a glance what the situation is. They should be easy to read, prompt, and simple.

Authority and responsibility

"Finally, we have delegation and coordination of authority and responsibility as a managerial function. Authority, of course, is the right to command along with the power to enforce. Responsibility means being accountable for the performance—that is, being answerable for accomplishment. Responsibility without authority materially retards the efficient operation of the business, and, conversely, absence of definite responsibility to accompany authority is equally detrimental to the organization. Finally, when authority and responsibility have been delegated but not definitely fixed, it is a common occurrence to find that there are certan functions over which no one is in charge while others are subject to the overlapping control of two or more individuals. Authority and responsibility are often spelled out in the organization chart, the organizational manual, job descriptions, and functions. In summary, gentlemen, the above constitute the managerial fundamentals or functions from the American viewpoint.

"Finally, I would like to share with you my discovery of the ideas of a French Industrialist by the name of Henri Fayol. I learned of his works when I was in Geneva last summer at the International Management Institute. His work has just been translated into English by J. A. Coubrough of the British Xylonte Company. Fayol looked at the functions of administration, as he called them, from the top, because he was the managing director of COMAMBAULT, a large and successful mining operation. I would say from my examination of his works that his ideas and Taylor's theories were essentially complementary. They both realized that the problem of personnel and management at all levels is the key to industrial success; but where Taylor principally looked at the operating levels from the bottom of the organization looking upwards—Fayol concentrated on the managing director's spot and looked downward. Actually, Fayol's work, entitled or translated as 'General and Industrial Management,' first appeared in French in 1916 in the third issue of the *Bulletin of Société de L'Industrie Minérale.*

"The following are my notes from Fayol's works that I think are of particular interest to you. First of all he stated that all activities to which an industrial undertaking can give rise can be divided into six groups:

1. Technical activities (production, manufacture, adaptation)
2. Commercial activities (buying, selling, exchange)
3. Financial activities (search for an optimum use of capital)
4. Security activities (protection of property and person)
5. Accounting activities (stock-taking, balance sheet, cost statistics)
6. Administration activities (planning, organization, command, coordination, control).

"As he points out and as we all know, the first five activities are well-known and carried out by all organizations no matter what their size. But it is his sixth activity, administration, or as some might translate it, management, that he explains in much further detail.

"Before exposing you to Fayol's principles and elements of management, I'd like to point out that it's unfortunate that his work has not come to light in America. He sincerely believes that administrative ability can be acquired outside of the business area; specifically, he states that administrative ability can and should be acquired in the same way as technical ability—first at school, later in the workshop. He also feels that the real reason for the absence of management teaching in the vocational schools is absence of theory. Fayol's aim in publishing was to start the general discussion of administration with the hope that theory would evolve from the discussion.

"First of all he tells us that administrative functions operate only on personnel. He gives us fourteen principles of administration, pointing out that although he uses the term *principle,* he wishes to disassociate the word from any suggestion of rigidity, for there is nothing rigid or absolute in administration. He states that principles are flexible and capable of adaptation to every need and that it is the matter of knowing how to make use of them which is a difficult art requiring intelligence, experience, decision, and proportion. His principles are:

Do some of these look familiar?

1. Division of work
2. Authority
3. Discipline
4. Unity of command
5. Unity of direction
6. Subordination of individual interests to the general interests
7. Remuneration
8. Centralization
9. Scalar chain (line of authority)
10. Order
11. Equity
12. Stability of tenure of personnel
13. Initiative
14. Esprit de corps.

"You are all familiar with his division of work principle, because it is nothing more than what we have already discussed—breaking the job down into parts and assigning responsibility to individuals. His authority and responsibility principle again is not new because we have discussed this earlier in class. He makes the point that responsibility is a corollary of authority; it is its natural consequence and essential counterpart and wheresoever authority is exercised responsibility arises.

"Discipline, of course, is self-explanatory. Now the unity of command principle is perhaps one that you would not be aware of. In essence he is getting across that an employee should be receiving orders from only one superior. He makes a very strong point about direction from more than one superior, stating that if authority is undermined, discipline is in jeopardy, order disturbed, and stability threatened. In this respect it seems to me that he certainly does not agree with Taylor's functional foremanship, which really places each worker under the command of eight different foremen.

"His unity of direction principle is expressed as one plan for a group of activities having the same objective.

"His sixth principle is based upon the fact that in business the interest of one employee or a group of employees should not prevail over that of the concern. Principle seven is certainly self-explanatory. Principle eight, centralization, recognizes that orders radiate from a central spot and that information is directed toward that central location. Nine, the scalar chain, regards the chain of superiors ranging from the ultimate authority to the lowest ranks. The line of authority is the route followed as he says by every link of the chain, by all communications which start from or go to the ultimate authority. He gives an example of the scalar chain by use of the triangle, which I'll now draw on the board for you.

"The rigid scalar chain tells us that if the manager of Function *G* had to communicate with the manager of Function *Q,* his message would have to go up the left-hand side of the ladder to *A* and down the right hand side to *Q*. Fayol realizes that this might take much too long a time and develops the use of what he calls a gangplank—that is, allowing *G* to communicate directly with *Q* as long as *F* and *P* respectively are aware of and condone such actions.

"By order he meant a place for everyone and everyone in his place. His eleventh principle, equity, meant simply that employees should be treated with a combination of kindness and justice. Stability of tenure of

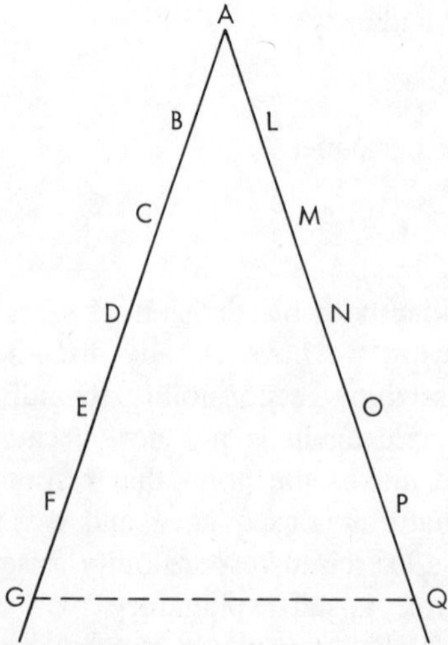

FIGURE 4
Fayol's Scalar Chain

personnel is self-explanatory, as I believe is initiative. Finally, esprit de corps represents the effort to establish harmony and union among personnel.

"After setting forth his principles, Fayol continued with the elements of management. First he listed *planning*—looking ahead and developing a plan of action; next he listed *organizing* or, in essence, seeing that the plan is judiciously prepared and strictly carried out. I think we have discussed organization enough. This introductory lecture certainly has gone into it in enough detail. Examination of Fayol's theories shows that his discussion of organizations does not differ too much from some of the things we have already discussed or will discuss later in this course.

"Fayol's next principle or element is *command*. As he states, the organization, having been formed, must be set in motion, and this embraces the mission of command. The manager who has command should, in Fayol's terms, have a thorough knowledge of his personnel, eliminate the incompetent, be well-versed in the agreements binding the business and its employees, set a good example, conduct periodic audits of the organization (and use summarized charts to further this), bring together his chief assistants by means of conferences at which unity of direction and focusing of effort are provided for, not become engrossed in detail, and aim at making unity, energy, initiative, and loyalty prevail among personnel.

"The principle of *coordination* refers to the harmonizing of all the activities of the concern so it can facilitate its working and its success.

"Finally, *control* consists in verifying whether everything occurs in conformity with the plan adopted, instructions issued, and the principles established. For it to be effective it must be done within reasonable time and be followed up by sanctions.

"That, gentlemen, is the essence of the principles of Fayol. You can see that they are similar to many of the principles established by industrial engineers and management specialists of American companies and universities. What is interesting is the addition of the few elements or principles that I have mentioned and the fact that these were first evolved in the very early 1900s but not published until the war years. Now, gentlemen, are there any questions?"

Professor Mikeson looked over the assembled body of students and recognized a young man in the third row, "Yes, Mr. Gregory."

"Professor Mikeson, was Fayol aware of Taylor's scientific management theories?"

"As a matter of fact he was, Mr. Gregory. Taylor's shop management, I found when I was in France, was translated in the *Metallurgy Review* in Paris in 1913. Fayol mentions Taylor's system in his book. However, Fayol thought that it was dangerous to allow the idea that unity of command is unimportant and can be violated with impunity to gain ground. In fact, he stated that, 'Until things change, let us treasure the old type of organization in which unity of command is honored.' For this reason he had reservations regarding Taylor's functional management. And now, if there are no more questions, class is dismissed."

EPILOGUE

What are they like?

They are the about-to-retire personnel who were in their teens during the twenties and received their business education—if they had a formal one—just before the "crash." They are also the professors who might well have taught today's forty to forty-five-year-old supervisor or co-worker. As such, the 1920s can have a profound influence on the teachers and students who are still active today.

During the period, the emphasis was still on factory management and industrial organization, again with the rigid hierarchy, the authoritarian structure, and with not too much thought to man as an individual. Training did, of course, include a glimmering of light as to man as an individual, but in general, overall policies hadn't changed too much. True, education would have mentioned the human factor. However, the emphasis on human relations would probably have been for the sake of getting the job done.

Exposed to a professor with a background like Mikeson's and having been raised during the Depression, we might expect our man to give lip service to getting along with other people. He probably would believe in human relations (it was stressed in the late thirties) but in the social man context. In fact he might have a Machiavellian attitude toward co-workers and, if a manager, toward employees. In the final analysis he probably is oriented toward organizational structure and Fayol's basic principles of planning, organizing, and controlling. He also is the "Establishment."

DISCUSSION QUESTIONS

1. To what extent are the organizational principles taught in 1929 similar to those in practice today?

2. Give examples and discuss firms that you think might have had good human relations in the 1920s.

3. Apply a 1929 managerial frame of reference in the discussion and solution of a chosen present management problem.

4. What social, political, and economic forces affected the thinking of the 1929-trained manager?

5. What influence would the 1920s have had on a professor of management who had received his training in the early 1900s?

6. List and discuss attitudes and values that might have changed in the 1900 to 1929 period.

7. How do you think the 1920 concept of the social responsibility of business affected the interrelationships between workers and management?

NOTES

(Books written in the 1920 to 1929 period included:

A. C. Anderson, *Industrial Engineering and Factory Management* (New York: The Ronald Press Co., 1928).

P. M. Atkins, *Factory Management* (Englewood Cliffs, N.J.: Prentice-Hall, Inc., 1926).

Alexander H. Church, *The Making of an Executive* (New York: D. Appleton and Co., 1923).

William B. Cornell, *Organization and Management in Industry and Business* (New York: The Ronald Press Co., 1928).

Hugo Diemer, *Factory Organization and Management* (New York: McGraw-Hill Book Co., 1925).

H. P. Dutton, *Business Organization and Management* (Chicago: A. W. Shaw Co., 1925).

Henri Fayol, *L'Incapacité administrative de l'état—les postes et télégraphes* (Paris: Dunod, 1925). (Originally published in Revue Politique et Parlementaire, March 1921).

G. L. Gardiner, *Management in the Factory* (New York: McGraw-Hill Book Co., 1925).

Edward E. Hunt, *Scientific Management Since Taylor* (New York: McGraw-Hill Book Co., 1924).

L. C. Marshall, *Business Administration* (Chicago: University of Chicago Press, 1921).

Henry C. Metcalf, *Scientific Foundations of Business Administration* (Baltimore: The Williams & Wilkins Co., 1926).

H. S. Person, ed., *Scientific Management in American Industry* (New York: Harper & Bros., 1929).

Webster Robinson, *Fundamentals of Business Organization* (New York: McGraw-Hill Book Co., 1925).

APPLES
NBC

8

The Lean Thirties 1930-1940

The objectives of this chapter are to enable you to

1. *understand* the managerial philosophy taught in 1940;
2. *identify* the changes in managerial philosophy that occurred in the 1930 to 1940 period;
3. *note* the shift in managerial thinking about man that occurred in the decade;
4. *comprehend* the reasons for the shift in managerial thinking;
5. *explore* the attitudes and philosophy that one would have acquired had he grown up or gone to school during that decade;
6. *appreciate* that many of today's supervisors and co-workers may have a 1940 frame of managerial reference;
7. *recognize* a 1940 frame of reference.

PROLOGUE

What was it like?

It began in gloom. There were bank failures and suicides. Financial disaster spread. Franklin Roosevelt was elected president, and the New Deal began. Drastic steps were taken to break the Depression. The National Recovery Act, the WPA, and the CCC created jobs for hundreds of unemployed citizens. Nevertheless, it was still a fiercely patriotic period. Parades, uniforms, chromed bayonets flashing in the sun, picnics in the park, flags waving, political rallies, barnstorming and radio were the rage. "God Bless America," "I'll Be Seeing You," "Begin the Beguine," "April in Paris," and "Betty Coed" were songs of the period. Best-sellers included *Gone with the Wind, North to the Orient, Good-bye, Mr. Chips, Anthony Adverse, The Good Earth,* and Dale Carnegie's *How to Win Friends and Influence People.* The Ford Motor Company turned out its 20-millionth car in 1931, and the Empire State Building was opened. Jigsaw puzzles became the fad while Adolph Hitler became "Der Führer" of the Third Reich in Germany. Heroes included Will Rogers and Wiley Post. The foreign situation was making an important impression on the older generation with the civil war in Spain, the abdication of Edward VIII, and the American involvement with European countries. Sit-down strikes were invented as a new CIO weapon. Bingo became the rage near the end of the period, and of course, World War II began—the war to end wars. Parents talked about the loss of Amelia Earhart and the sinking of the U.S. gunboat Panay by the Japanese. The country prospered because of war contracts which would soon provide a spurt to the economy under the lend-lease plan.

Against this background we renew our acquaintance with Professor Mikeson.

"Gentlemen, research has been conducted and articles and books published in the last ten years that have made a great change in our thinking about management. These discoveries will, I believe, have a profound effect on the way management is practiced in the future. Specifically, we have discovered that man is important as a human being working in a social setting—that we can accomplish more by considering the group and the social setting than we can be considering man by himself, as was the case with the advocators of scientific management. In essence, we can increase output more by concentrating on the social conditions on the job, the informal relationships which develop, and creating an atmosphere in which the worker feels important and feels that management really cares. We might say we are considering the human problem and its solution as more important to productivity than economic and technical problems." Thus Professor Mikeson began the introductory lecture to his course in Modern Industrial Management.

The social ethic

He always enjoyed this particular course because it was the last one the students took before graduation and it hopefully tied together the different management and administrative topics covered in the previous courses in the curriculum. As senior professor on the faculty, it was his duty to insure that the student had the overall broad picture and that no loose strings remained.

When he was preparing his notes for this particular lecture, he had thought to himself, "This is one course I certainly look forward to teaching because it gives me an opportunity to stop and, in retrospect, consider changes that have occurred over the years. I'm glad I only give the course every spring, because not only can I compare what's happened in the past year, but I can also compare changes that have occurred over the past several years. In fact, this year I can cover the whole decade.

Change in the 1930s

"Things certainly have changed. In my 1930 course the Depression had hit but certainly not as hard as it did in 1931 and 1932. We've seen a complete overhaul of the banking system, government relief programs such as the Civilian Conservation Corps and the Workman's Progress Administration, the development of government electric power plants in the form of the Tennessee Valley Authority, and the Homeowner's Loan Corporation. I know we needed these measures, but it seems that the government is taking over some of the duties that perhaps should be done locally. But it seems to be the way our country is going. I must say that

I was in agreement with the Wagner Act, which guaranteed our workmen the right to negotiate with employees through unions of their own choice. And it was gratifying to see the organization of the CIO. Competition, in my mind, is certainly healthy. It's unfortunate, though, that the government had to step in with the Fair Labor Standards Act rather than allow the workers and the corporations to work out their settlements. But we all know that if industry will not take the initiative, invariably government will take the side of the worker. And now here we are today on the brink of war—at least I don't see how we can avoid it. Our industry is gearing up for munitions manufacturing to help our allies, so it's probably more important than ever to get my message across this term. The message I want to stress is that we have to consider the *social environment of the worker,* the *informal organization,* and *true cooperation between management and workers.* So this will be my theme."

The 1940 frame of reference for management

With these thoughts in mind, Professor Mikeson outlined his opening lecture.

"To continue, gentlemen, the research I speak about was conducted from April 1927 to the middle of 1932 at the Hawthorne Works of the Western Electric Company in Chicago. The significance of the studies was published in 1933 in a book entitled *The Human Problems of an Industrial Civilization,* by Dr. Elton Mayo of the Harvard Graduate School of Business.

Fatigue studies

"To understand why the Hawthorne studies were undertaken and Dr. Mayo's interest, we have to go back in time to the period of the United States' involvement in the World War. The necessity of manufacturing large amounts of war materials made it essential to undertake scientific study of the maximum hours of work that labor could produce. It was essential to determine the effect of strenuous and sustained exertion imposed upon workers who provided the manual labor. As a result, the Health of Munition Workers Committee was established in 1915 by the British government. This particular English group found, or believed, that the factors affecting exertion that were uncovered in munitions plants might be of interest to or potentially applicable to industries in general. So, when the Munition Workers Committee was disbanded in 1917, the Medical Research Council and the Department of Scientific and Industrial Research, acting together, created the Industrial Fatigue Research Board with a mandate to embrace the whole of industry within its scope.

"The Board's initial work concerned studies in fatigue and monotony. Of particular interest to Dr. Mayo was Report Number 56 on the effects of monotony in work, by S. Wyatt and J. A. Fraser. Dr. Mayo was intrigued with Wyatt's conclusions which, in essence, reported (1) that boredom is fairly prevalent among operators employed in repetitive processes, (2) that boredom causes a reduced rate of working which is particularly noticeable about the middle of the spell, (3) that it causes a variable rate of work, (4) that it is responsible for an overestimation of time intervals, and (5) that it is dependent upon individual characteristics and tendencies. Furthermore, it is less likely to arise (a) when the form of activity is changed at suitable times within the spell of work,

(b) when the operatives are paid according to output produced instead of time work, (c) when the work is conceived as a series of self-contained tasks rather than as an indefinite and apparently indeterminable activity, (d) when the operatives are allowed to work in compact social groups rather than in isolated units, and (e) when suitable rests are introduced within the spell of work. The interesting conclusion was that boredom differs between individuals based upon intelligence and temperament and that social or personal aspects of the particular industrial group affects the situation in a profound way." [1]

Again we see an appreciation for man as a unique individual.

"With the foregoing information as background, the personnel research people at Western Electric wanted to study the effect of fatigue and monotony at Hawthorne on the output of workers. It was expected that exact knowledge could be obtained by setting up an experimental situation in which variables like temperature, hours of sleep, and humidity could be measured separately as a result of an experimentally imposed condition of work.[2]

Results of experiments

"Unfortunately, the results of the first series of experiments on illumination were nonproductive in that there was no direct relationship between the amount of illumination and the amount of work produced. Of course, we now know the reason for this, which I'll explain later. Even with this failure, Western Electric decided to conduct a second experiment to determine, if possible, the effect of various changes in activity, rest period, hours of work, and so forth, on the overall working conditions and output rather than attempt to test for the effect of a single variable, as was done in the illumination experiment. Because we will be studying Dr. Mayo's book in detail later in this particular course, I only want to give you the highlights of the results of the second experiment—the relay assembly room tests.

Output up no matter what

"During the course of the research, work periods were varied, rest periods were varied, and refreshments were either provided or not provided at different times. In fact, during one sustained period of twelve weeks the group returned to its original working conditions. The startling result of all the changes and combinations of changes was that no matter what happened or what change was made, output continued to increase. It became very clear that the different changes experimentally imposed, although they could perhaps be used to account for minor differences between output in one period and another, could not be used to explain the major change—that is, a continuing increase in production.

"As a result, the company concluded that among other things, (1) there had been a continual upward trend in output which was independent of the changes in rest pauses. This upward trend continued too long to be ascribed to an initial stimulus from the novelty of starting a special study. (2) The reduction of muscular fatigue was not the primary factor in increasing output; (3) there was an important increase in contentment among the girls working under test room conditions; (4) there was a decrease in absences of about 80 percent among the girls since entering the test room group; (5) output was more directly related to the type of working day than to the number of working days in the week; (6) observations of operators in the relay assembly test room indicated that their health was being maintained or improved; (7) the changed working conditions resulted in creating an eagerness on the part of operators to come to work in the morning; (8) important factors in the production of a better mental attitude and greater enjoyment of work were the greater freedom, less strict supervision, and the opportunity to vary from a fixed pace without reprimand from a gang boss; and (10) the operators had no clear idea as to why they were able to produce more in the test room; but as shown in replies to questionnaires, there was a feeling that better output is somehow related to the distinctly pleasanter, freer, and happier working conditions.[3]

Participation in change

"Actually, what was found out at the Hawthorne Works was that the increased production was probably based upon changes in the mental attitude of the workers. This can probably be attributable to the fact that before every change of program, the group was consulted. Their comments were listened to and discussed, and sometimes their objections carried weight in the decision as to whether or not to make a certain change. The group then must have developed a sense of participation in the critical determinations and became something of a social unit. This developing social unit was illustrated by the workers entertaining each other in their homes.

The group is important

"From the standpoint of the workers, they stated that they had no sensation of working faster than under previous conditions. They did feel that they had been relieved of the nervous tension under which they had previously worked. They ceased to regard the man in charge as a boss. They had a feeling that their increased production was in some way related to the distinctly freer, happier, and more pleasant working environment.

"Yet interestingly enough, the girls were getting closer supervision than they had ever received before, because it was essential to keep track of output and worker attitudes. However, the supervision was of a different quality. Thus, it would appear that quality or type of leadership or supervision might be important in productivity as well as the nature of the working environment from the workers' point of view.

"As a result of these conclusions, Western Electric instituted two additional studies, the mica room experiment, begun in August 1928, and an interviewing program which was instituted in September of 1928.

"The mica room experiments were in general the same as the relay test room experiment. Output increased regardless of the changes made—again based upon the absence of objectionable administration and supervisory practices and the attention paid to the group.

"The interview program was designed to discover how the workers felt about supervision and working conditions and how the workers liked or disliked their work.

"The main thing learned at Hawthorne that I want to emphasize is that it is not enough to have an enlightened company policy and a carefully devised plan of manufacturing. To stop at this point and, with a take-it-or-leave-it attitude, administer such a plan to workers, no matter how logical the plan, has much the same effect as administering medicine to a resisting patient. An individual must work with understanding of his work situation to be pleased with his work.

"Finally, human collaboration and work in primitive and developed societies has always depended for its perpetuation upon the evolution of a nonlogical social code which regulates the relationship between persons and their attitudes to one another. Insistence upon a merely economic logic of production, especially if the logic is frequently changed, interferes with the development of such a code and consequently gives rise in the group to a sense of human defeat. This human defeat results in the formation of a social code at a lower level and in opposition to the economic logic. In writing about the Hawthorne experiment, Mayo ends with an interesting point—that administrators face a human social problem and not an economic problem when they are dealing with workers."

> This is the importance of the group from another aspect. As we discussed the group in Chapter 3 it was from one's own standpoint as a member or potential member. Here we see the group as viewed by management.

"He further reminds us that as a consequence of the development of highly systemized industrial procedures upon a civilized culture, we see the relative annihilation of the cultural traditions of work and craftsmanship. This situation has seriously damaged the traditional routine of intimate and family life in the United States. The social disorganization has been so great that no form of political action can ever substitute for the loss. If then, the social unit is so important, there must be an effective and whole-hearted collaboration between the administrative and the working groups in industry. It is no longer possible for an administrator to concern himself narrowly with his special function and to assume that the controls established by a bigger social code will continue to operate in all areas of human life and action.

"Now, how is this awareness of man as a social being and the importance of the group being carried out in today's management? Well, to begin with, we're . . ."

A hand was waving vigorously in the third row. Consequently, Professor Mikeson stopped in the middle of his sentence and nodded to the young man. "Do you have a question?"

"Yes, Professor, I do. Would you explain your last statement just before you changed topics. I think you said something about social codes and other areas of human life."

"Yes, I did," said Professor Mikeson, referring to his notes. "I said that it is no longer possible for an administrator to concern himself narrowly with his special function and to assume that the controls established by a bigger social code will continue to operate in all areas of human life and action. What I'm getting at is that when the social organization disintegrates, people are often unable to formulate for themselves substitute attitudes and habits. In the past, when cities were small and people had room to maneuver, the social system established moral and ethical values by which people lived and were guided. Now, with the advent of the factory system and the large industrial areas, with people crowded into sometimes inadequate housing, often not their own, they do not develop the same value systems. Thus, their social order hinders rather than helps them to develop. Thus, if man doesn't find his social satisfaction away from the job, his work will represent his most important function in the society. Therefore, as administrators, we must be aware that the social environment of the work situation is most important. If the codes are not established in the social order outside the plant, codes of conduct must be established within the social order inside the plant. Does this answer your question?"

"Yes, sir, I believe I see the point you're making."

"Gentlemen, I certainly hope you all see the point, because I think we're coming to the time where we must pay more attention to what people do and the group within which they work rather than to keep on scientifically looking at man as an individual within the industrial setting."

This seems to smack a little of paternalism. The human relations movement has been criticized as being manipulative, insincere, and ignoring the reality of economic variables.

"Now, as I was saying, this new way of considering work and the worker is being carried over into the subject of leadership, the functions of the executive, and, in general, present organizational theory. As a starter, let's review the latest thinking on the principles of organization. Probably no better reference is available than the *Principles of Organization* by Mooney and Reiley. This 1939 edition is a revision of their book *Onward Industry,* written in 1931. My following comments will be, in general, along the lines of thinking in their book and my own comments from practical consulting experience over the past ten years.

Definition of the 1930s organization

"To begin with, whenever two people join together to achieve a common purpose, then organization begins. Thus, we can say that organization is the form of every human association for the attainment of a common purpose. Further, because two people work together, they coordinate their work. The first principle of organization is coordination or the orderly arrangement of group effort to provide unity of action and the pursuit of a common purpose.[4] Also, as it is the all-inclusive principle of organization, it must have its own principle and foundation in authority, or the supreme coordinating power.[5]

"At this point, gentlemen, be aware that there is a difference between authority and leadership. Also, there is a difference between authority and power. Authority comes from a position of right. It also can exist before organization. Leadership, of course, must have an organization to exist, and it comes from the person. Power also, as the ability to do things, is an individual possession.

"Mooney and Reiley next list the scalar principle, whereby they discuss the series of steps that allow the overall supreme coordinating authority to carry out this authority. And under this scalar principle they list the possession of leadership, delegation, and functional definition.

"Leadership, of course, should be self-evident to you.

"Delegation means the conferring of a special authority by a higher authority. In essence, Mooney and Reiley state that it involves a dual responsibility.

"Functional definition is that form which assigns all functions. It is the scalar form through which leadership delegates to each subordinate his own specific task.[6]

"The writers then discuss the staff phase of functionalization and go into various types of organizations. Actually, although their book is widely read today, it appears to be a rigorous approach to the study of organizations and does not stress the human element which we previously discussed in the Hawthorne study. Although what they say is correct, they say little as to how the principles would actually be carried out by the line executives. In fact, when we consider Henry Fayol, whom we discussed in one of your lectures last fall, we find that his administrative activities are probably far more encompassing than Mooney and Reiley's organizational principles.

"You remember that Fayol discussed planning, organizing, commanding, coordinating, and controlling. Also, one of his fourteen principles was a scalar chain, one was authority, and one was division of work. In comparing these two theories, I fail to see that Mooney and Reiley have actually added anything to the present field of management theory.

"If these and other writers have not really added anything to theory, if they have not emphasized the human element, then how have the results or the findings of the Hawthorne studies been integrated into management literature? In fact, has there been any revolution in the thinking about organizational theory?

"Luckily, there has been a complete new analysis of organizations and a new way of considering the functions of management and the work of the administrator. On this basis, let's take a different look at organizations. Rather than regarding them as the formal grouping of functions with line/staff relationships and efficiency of operations, let's consider for a moment how the organization builds up. Let's think of it as made up of individuals, of people. Let's really consider the human side.

The organization reconsidered

"First of all, let's ponder what an organization is. It would seem logical to suppose that an organization is a group of people—in fact, two people getting together forms an organization—but at least, it consists of a group of people who are able to communicate with each other and who are willing to cooperate or contribute their joint actions to accomplish a common objective. We have to start somewhere and this seems to be the basic starting point. One person, of course, is not, by this definition, an organization, because there is not the cooperation of someone else.

So essentially, then, we must have at least two people. They must be able to talk things over and agree to contribute their combined actions in order to get something done. By this definition the very basis and root of the organization is the individual or the person. Furthermore, individuals or human beings don't really operate by themselves. There must be an interaction with other people."

At this point a hand shot up. "Professor, would you explain that? I walk or ride my bike to school and I do quite a few things on my own. So why do you say that we can't operate without other people?"

"Good point, Mr. Bartholomue. It is Mr. Bartholomue, isn't it?"

"Yes, sir, it is."

"Well, again, good point. But consider this. Could you have survived after you were born without other people? Where would you have gotten your food and your clothing? You needed someone to take care of you. As you grew up, it would not have been possible to provide, on your own without any help whatsoever, all the physiological requirements necessary to sustain your life. And, as people grow older, they certainly do depend upon other people. They don't operate in a vacuum. Do you see what I mean?"

People still need people

"Yes, sir, I wasn't thinking of it in that connection."

"That's perfectly all right, Mr. Bartholomue. The point I was trying to make is that because we don't function in my context except in conjunction with other people, then the organization cannot function without the joint efforts of the human beings because they created the original organizational purpose. Now, getting back to our point, because human beings do operate in conjunction with others, when two people get together for a common purpose, we find that many times the actions of one or the other or both must be modified.

"Now let me explain that last point. Suppose I have a morning paper route that is expanding very rapidly. I normally get up quite early in the morning and I'm always on the corner when the paper is delivered. However, as my route expands, I find that I can't do the entire job myself and I team up with a couple of other individuals. Now we have an organization involved in delivering newspapers. If one of the other boys doesn't like to get up as early as I do—let's say there are two of us—in fact, he would like to get up as late as possible, yet all the papers have to be delivered on time, then perhaps a compromise has to be arrived at. I might get up a little later and start delivering the papers later if he will get up a little earlier than he would like to. Thus, we both have modified our behavior or our actions in order to achieve a common purpose."

An example of successful outward interaction and the fact that compromise is often necessary for the good of the whole.

"Now with the addition of two or three more people, we have a small organization with a definite purpose in which the participants have agreed to perform certain functions. Each one decides or agrees to what he will do so that the purpose can be achieved. This, of course, is the very smallest organization which would have few, if any, formal written practices and procedures as to how to do things. But the point is there. People have willingly cooperated and communicated their desire to work together to achieve a purpose. Unfortunately, very few of us have the chance to start an organization; but if we did, it would have to start in the way I've just described. The point to remember is that somewhere along the line people do have to agree, to cooperate, to get along together and to achieve a common purpose.

"Now larger organizations are composed of larger groups of people. However, there is a limitation to the number of people within any one particular group because of the number of relationships existing. Fayol, of course, pointed this out in his *General and Industrial Management,* and, of course, I know you're familiar with it. It is important now because of what I pointed out to you about the Hawthorne studies. The social aspects of the group are most important; and the social aspects can only be satisfied in a relatively small group. So there is a limit to the size of the basic organizational unit that has been created to form or accomplish a definite organizational purpose. If the size of the organizational basic group is limited, then we have to devise a way to integrate these units. Now this is the job of what we might call the basic supervisor or boss. Each group has a leader. Every leader in turn is part of another group which might be called the first-level executive group, and this first-level group also has a leader. Then as the organization gets bigger and bigger, the executive groups in turn have second- and third-level executive groups until we get to the group that is composed of the top manager or president of the company.[7]

The linking pin concept before Likert

"As for the functioning of these basic organizational units, the Hawthorne studies tell us that one of the most important aspects is the social function. In the past we've been organizing the basic groups around functions that had to be performed without regard to the people. In other words, we formed a warehousing function or a stockroom function or an earth-moving gang function or a toolroom function—whatever it might be—and we picked people we thought could do the job and put them into the group. Now, however, we must think of not only the ability to do the job but the social relationships that are going to be developing on the job. I'm certain that we can say that the social situation or outlook as seen from the worker's viewpoint is most important. If he does not believe that the social situation is correct, then I firmly believe that money alone is not going to be enough of an inducement to make him perform.

Attitudes, beliefs, and values revisited

"Now, what do I mean by 'acceptable social situation'? Well, I mean a situation based upon race, religion, nationality, education, customs, morals, social status, and the like. We have certainly seen the fruits of this in our history especially during the late 1800s, when the unions were being started. You may have read about, or remember from your course in unionism, the fights and discontents that developed in the industrial cities between the Polish, the Italians, the Germans, and the Hungarian immigrants; between the Catholics and those of Jewish origin as well as the Protestants; of the strifes developing between the negroes and the whites;

the dislike of the children of the richer, more educated families to associate in manual labor with the children from the poorer uneducated families. We know this happens, yet many times we fail to take it into consideration when assigning men to duties, or fail to realize that there are many subtle variations of prejudice, that affect the manner in which men and women are willing to perform on the job."

This is certainly an example of some of the problems associated with or influencing successful interaction.

"Another thing we've learned from the Hawthorne studies which we must consider now in dealing with organizations, in fact with administration, is that we must consider the opportunity for distinction and prestige. In other words, a good position or at least a position that other people will look up to and respect as being a 'good' position can be more important than monetary reward in the development of a good organization. Too much in the past we have assumed that all we had to do was pay high enough wages or high enough piece rates and production would increase and the workers would be satisfied. Unfortunately, this did not always prove to be the case, and we wondered why. I believe that we now know the answer. Recognition of workers as people, the establishment of the right social climate giving distinction and prestige and most important, participation, is or seems to be more important than wages. Remember how the girls in the Hawthorne study said that they felt better about their jobs, that they didn't think that they were being forced into doing what they didn't want to do? They thought their supervisor was really interested in them, and they had a complete change in thought about their work. This was the important thing in increasing productivity or output.

Maslow's need for recognition and esteem

"Another point that I believe we must consider again as a result of the Hawthorne studes is that there exists within every formal organization an informal organization—the relationships that develop between people that are not part of or controlled by the formal organization. These are the attitudes, habits, understandings, or customs of the group—how members get along with each other and how they communicate with each other outside the established formal network of communications in the organization. Actually, this is merely a recognition of the ladder effect that Fayol discussed. But, unfortunately, it's overlooked by many administrators. In considering the informal relationships that develop within the organization, as administrators we should be aware of the fact that sometimes these informal relationships can be helpful and sometimes they can be harmful. Remember from your readings that workers are sometimes very reluctant to make changes or are afraid of change. The informal relationships can cause them to band together to resist change. On the other hand, knowing that informal relationships exist, they can be used to help us in gaining the cooperation of workers if we learn to use this informal organizational communications network to our advantage.

The informal organization

"In analyzing what I've just presented, gentlemen, I'm not saying that we should throw away the traditional managerial functions of planning, organizing, and controlling. Nor should we throw out our scientific management principles of organizational structures, functionalization, specialization, line/staff relationships, and all the other things you've been taught. They all have their place. What I'm saying to you is that people are important in the organizational structure; that many times as they proceed into better jobs, people don't work for money alone but for the prestige of the job; that they enjoy participating in decisions that affect them; that definite social relationships exist on the job which can have a greater influence on the worker than the supervisor; that these factors must be considered when developing plans or considering leadership techniques.

The importance of the art of leadership

"You noted above, gentlemen, that I used the term 'leadership technique.' There is quite a bit of difference between a leader and a boss, as we are certainly finding out. The boss concept, a concept of ordering people and expecting compliance without question, has proven to be rather ineffective in the long run. As organizations grow larger and larger and tend to become less personal, the art of leadership becomes more important. Every group needs someone to make newcomers feel welcome and wanted, to show them the way, to be the example, to create a working experience that will be satisfying. This is the job of leadership. And another thing—leadership is different from command. Command might be considered as exercising a power over people. Leadership is creating a power *with* people, with the process by which results are obtained, rather than just the results themselves.

"The importance of the role of leadership is evidenced by the fact that entire books have been devoted to the subject. For example, a recent book by Ordway Tead entitled *The Art of Leadership* specifically draws our attention to the qualities necessary in leaders. These are:

These qualities are still applicable today

1. Physical and nervous energy
2. A sense of purpose and direction
3. Enthusiasm
4. Friendliness and affection
5. Integrity
6. Technical mastery
7. Decisiveness
8. Intelligence
9. Teaching skill
10. Faith.[8]

Tead further tells us that the techniques of leading include

1. Giving orders
2. Giving reproofs
3. Giving commendation
4. Maintaining a right personal bearing
5. Getting suggestions

6. Strengthening a sense of group identity
7. Care in introduction to the group
8. Creating group self-discipline
9. Allaying false rumors.[9]

"One other thing before leaving the area of leadership. I'd like to bring to your attention for further discussion a most interesting idea presented in a book I read last year entitled *The Functions of the Executive* by Chester I. Barnard, past president of the New Jersey Bell Telephone Company. His idea concerns the acceptance of authority in a leadership situation. He states that 'A person can and will accept a communication as authoritative only when four conditions are simultaneously obtained: (1) he can and does understand the communication; (2) at the time of his decision he believes that it is not inconsistent with the purpose of the organization; (3) at the time of his decision he believes it to be compatible with his personal interest as a whole; and (4) he is able mentally and physically to comply with it.' [10]

Acceptance theory of authority

"This is a most interesting thing to contemplate, gentlemen. There will be many times when communications that you issue will not be complied with because someone will not accept your authority or what you think is your authority. This is most interesting. We have been trained by scientific management as well as our experiences in wartime to accept commands and communications without question. Now, of course, you don't have to agree with Mr. Barnard. In fact, I presume that many of you won't. He's telling this based upon his experiences with industry; and AT&T is certainly not a small company. He believes this to be the rational action of people in many situations. He does go on to state that there is what he calls a zone of indifference wherein you accept an order or a command just because it doesn't matter that much. But the point is, if you do care at all, or if a person cares, then perhaps he does question authority and finds some way not to comply with the communication if he feels strongly enough about it.

"I can think of a way this might arise if the informal organization thinks that changes are being made which will endanger positions of certain members within a group. Malingering, goldbricking, and other things might be typical examples of purposeful delaying tactics in carrying out orders under this situation. But in any case, it's an interesting situation to contemplate. And we'll discuss it later on in the course.

"Now, as my last topic in this introductory lecture, I'd like to set forth the present concept of administration theory—that is, a view of the administrative process and the functions of management as applied today—that is, our latest organizational theory.

The systems viewpoint

"First of all, we must consider an organization as an overall system. Although we analyze parts and the various functions, we must consider how each part is related to every other part; because actually, the whole is greater than the sum of the parts. In any organization the activities performed or the results obtained are greater than those which could be obtained by each single individual or group acting on its own. Management applies to the directing of the overall organizational system and all its parts wherein administration, in its human relationships, can be described as the art of directing and inspiring the people who form the organization. My definition of manager would correspond to Fayol's word governor. Following this definition, a good manager might be a very bad administrator; but a bad administrator, on the other hand, might be a good manager.

"Now, by my early definition of organization as being two or more people willingly communicating and getting together toward a common purpose, the first principle of administration would have to be coordination. And by definition, coordination would have to be the orderly arrangement of the efforts of people in order to provide a unity of action in attempting to achieve a common, agreed-upon purpose.

"But under coordination as an overall title, we can discuss authority either in the classical sense or as Barnard discussed it. We can discuss service, doctrines, practices, procedures, discipline, and any other activity that creates the coordinative efforts.

"The next principle of administration would involve leadership and delegation. Leadership, as we have already discussed, is the exercising of authority and leading rather than bossing. In the leadership function we must learn to delegate, so delegation of authority would be another administrative principle. The delegation process, of course, sets up the scalar chain referred to by Fayol because authority can be delegated downward. The responsibility, unfortunately, goes upward.

"The next principle of good administration is functional definition of responsibility. Specifically, this involves who is going to do what and how, who reports to whom, and how the functions are carried out. This would lead us into the discussion of line/staff relationships and the various departmental functions. But this will be covered thoroughly in the rest of the class and in your assigned readings.

The importance of interaction again

"Finally, gentlemen, in your attempt to integrate the scientific philosophy, the functions of management which sometimes ignore people, and the human relations approach of Mayo as a result of the Hawthorne studies, consider one additional element. People do not act in a vacuum. They act based upon situations as they perceive them at the time they act. As a manager, you can plan the best organization possible, at least from your viewpoint, staff it with excellent individuals, and practice human relations and appreciate people as individuals in the social environment. But conflict and problems will still arise because of the day-to-day events that take place. People react to their environment, which is always changing. A reaction one day in a certain environment will not be the same reaction that will take place tomorrow in a different environment under different circumstances. Thus, your leadership style, whether it be democratic, authoritarian, or laissez-faire, is not the only consideration in your dealings with people. You must consider the situation or environment in which you and your workers find yourselves at the time the interaction takes place. Please remember that, gentlemen, in your dealings with people and in applying the general basic principles of Fayol as modified by Mayo. I thank you."

EPILOGUE

What are they like?

They are in their early fifties if they went to college in the late 1930s. They are also the professors who taught the supervisors and co-workers who are around the age of thirty-five today.

They have been taught that attitudes toward men have changed to the benevolent-authoritative structure with flexibility and concentration on group relationships, human relations, and the social man concept. They have been exposed to the human relations aspect of Mayo as seen in the Hawthorne studies, the comparison of management theorists during the period, and the writings of Chester Barnard concerning authority and responsibility. They have been taught that the human problem and its solution is as important to productivity as the economic and the technical problems. However the human problem emphasis would have been on the social group rather than on man himself.

Although exposed to these ideas, the Depression surroundings of the thirties would not have created an atmosphere in which it was considered essential for them to carry out the teachings of the period. In essence, when people are out of work and looking for jobs in great numbers, a manager doesn't have to be too particular about paying attention to the human element. There are always people to work no matter what the work situation. With this frame of reference, they would probably still be authoritarian, but the authority would be tempered with benevolence. That is, they would recognize the importance of groups and at least pretend to be interested in the opinions of other people. However, when the chips are down, their attitudes toward people might not be much different from those of managers with a frame of reference in the twenties.

DISCUSSION QUESTIONS

1. How prevalent do you think the social man concept is in interpersonal relationships today? Discuss.
2. Compare more recent studies in group behavior with the conclusions reached in the Hawthorne studies.
3. What impact do you think the 1929 Depression had on the training and education of teachers and managers in the 1930s?
4. What effect do you think the social conditions of the 1930s had on the development of managers and students trained during the period?

5. What effect do you think the social conditions had on the value systems of individuals who grew up during this period?

6. Take a stand on Barnard's acceptance principle of authority and cite examples from your own experience that either support or reject his premise.

7. Examine some of the writings of Mary Parker Follett and determine what she advocated as a managerial philosophy based upon individual motives.

8. Compare Ordway Tead's *Instincts in Industry* with his textbook written in the 1930s. Did his later book still consider instincts and the individual as being important in relation to the managerial team?

9. What was the effect, if any, of the war in Europe on the interpersonal relationships as practised in industry in 1939?

10. Give examples of how the informal organization can both help and hinder a manager.

11. Develop an interaction situation between two co-workers—one with a 1920 frame of reference, the other with a 1940 frame of reference.

NOTES

1. George E. Mayo, *The Human Problems of an Industrial Civilization* (Boston: Division of Research, Harvard Business School, 1933).
2. F. J. Roethlisberger and W. J. Dickson, *Management and the Worker* (Cambridge, Massachusetts: Harvard University Press, 1939).
3. Mayo, Human Problems, pp. 66–67.
4. James D. Mooney and Alan C. Reiley, *The Principles of Organization* (New York: Harper and Brothers Publishers, 1939), p. 5.
5. Ibid., p. 6.
6. Ibid., p. 23.
7. Chester I. Barnard, *The Functions of the Executive* (Cambridge: Harvard University Press, 1938).
8. Ordway Tead, *The Art of Leadership* (New York: McGraw-Hill Book Co., 1935), p. 83.
9. Ibid., p. 152.
10. Barnard, *Functions of the Executive,* p. 165.

In addition to works cited in the footnotes, the following books were available in the period:

H. S. Dennison, *Organization Engineering* (New York: McGraw-Hill Book Co., 1931).

H. P. Dutton, *Principles of Organization as Applied to Business* (New York: McGraw-Hill Book Co., 1931).

L. Gulick and L. Urwick, eds., *Papers on the Science of Administration* (New York: Institute of Public Administration, Columbia University, 1937).

Charles P. McCormick, *Multiple Management* (New York: Harper & Bros., 1938).

W. N. Mitchell, *Organization and Management of Production* (New York: McGraw-Hill Book Company, 1939).

F. J. Roethlisberger and W. J. Dickson, *Management and the Worker* (Cambridge: Harvard University Press, 1939).

CD

9

The Turbulent Forties 1940-1950

The objectives of this chapter are to enable you to

1. *understand* the managerial philosophy taught in 1950;
2. *identify* the changes in managerial philosophy that occurred during the 1940s.
3. *note* whether the changes in philosophy were basic changes or changes in the use of management tools;
4. *comprehend* the reasons for any changes in managerial philosophy;
5. *realize* that the forties would be the time frame of reference for the managerial philosophy of professors who are teaching many of today's students in their early twenties.
6. *appreciate* that co-workers and supervisors who are in their middle forties today would have received their management training in the late forties.

PROLOGUE

What was it like?

A turbulent period marked in the first half with the greatest war in the history of mankind—a war that ended with the first use of the atomic bomb (the most devastating destruction device ever conceived by man)—and in the second half by the biggest buying craze in the history of America, the communist threat, the Cold War, and television (during 1949 TV sets were being sold at the rate of 100,000 per week).

During the war there was gas rationing and food rationing with limited consumer goods being manufactured. Victory gardens, war bonds, Rosie the Riveter, blackouts, WACS, and WAVES were household words. In 1943 "pay-as-you-go" income tax was made law and the Pentagon was completed for $64,000,000. Money was being saved—mainly because there was nothing to buy. But after the war electric clothes dryers were marketed, garbage disposals sold at the rate of 50,000 per year with automatic dishwashers selling at a 225,000 annual rate. Supply could not keep up with demand and the same model Ford car that sold for $800 in 1941 sold for $1,400 in 1947.

Frank Sinatra was "the voice," slumber parties were the vogue, the juke-box industry blossomed, and the clubwoman became a powerful figure on the American scene. The radio and Saturday afternoon matinees, of course, occupied the younger generation, and cowboy stars became film heroes. RCA Victor pressed out its 1-billionth record—"Stars and Stripes Forever." War songs such as "Comin' In on a Wing and a Prayer" were popular during the war. Afterwards "Mona Lisa," "Tennessee Waltz," and songs from *Oklahoma* became hits. Book best-sellers became more serious, but *The Egg and I* still made it.

Parents became much more permissive and many a child was brought up with a strong mother-dominance. The adults of the era either saw wartime service or were part of the defense effort. They had grown up during the Depression and valued hard work—in addition, they were not used to having their values questioned.

Against this background we first meet Dr. Hugo Gregory in the spring of 1950.

"Good morning, ladies and gentlemen. My name is Dr. Gregory. I am professor of business administration and hold my doctorate from this university. In fact, during the final year of my undergraduate studies in 1929 I sat in this very lecture hall that you're sitting in now and participated in a course in organization and management, as you are today.

"I must say that a lot has happened in the last twenty-one years that has not only affected our country socially, politically, and economically, but has also affected the teaching of management and managerial philosophy.

"When I received my bachelor's degree, it was barely twelve years since World War I; the scientific management principles of Dr. Frederick Taylor were much in vogue in industry and very little thought in general was given to human relations.

"As you are aware, this situation has changed drastically. The discoveries at the Hawthorne Works of the Western Electric Company and the publishing of these experiments by Dr. Mayo of Harvard with the help of Dr. Roethlisberger have shown us the importance of social man as opposed to economic man.[1]

"The economic situation of the thirties also helped in many ways to intensify the social aspects of man's behavior. Although most of you were probably not born at the time, you must have heard your parents speak about the stock market crash of 1929 which, it is purported, cost investors approximately forty billion dollars. After that crash, the United States sank into the most acute depression in its history. Millions of people were financially wiped out. Factories shut down; stores closed; banks failed and almost all industry in the country slowed down to a bare walk. By the end of 1930 more than six million Americans were out of work, and one year later the figure had doubled. Men were forced to get together in groups because so many were in the same boat with the same problems: standing in soup lines, selling apples, and, in general, commiserating with each other. It's no wonder that the social aspect and group relationships that developed from the economic situation were recognized and carried over into the discussion of industrial problems.

"With the election of Franklin D. Roosevelt as president, we saw the initiation of the New Deal. With the establishment of the Civilian Conservation Corps, the Works Progress Administration, the Homeowners Loan Corporation, the Agriculture Rural Adjustment Administration, the Tennessee Valley Authority, the National Recovery Administration, and other agencies, we saw government acting in the broadest possible way for the betterment of human welfare. The Social Security Act was established during this period. The Wagner Act of 1935, the Fair Labor Standards Act of 1938, and the forming of the Congress of Industrial Organizations (CIO) were key labor advances during the period.

"In retrospect, however, complete recovery from the Great Depression did not occur until the oubreak of World War II in Europe, at which time the United States, through its lend-lease program, built up the war machines first of Great Britain and then of Russia. Finally, with our advent into the war, complete recovery occurred.

"Probably the biggest breakthrough or change in managerial philosophy during the last twenty years was the human relations movement uncovered at Hawthorne and promulgated by Harvard's Mayo in 1933. The printing of Henri Fayol's classic work in English in 1929 was, of course, another milestone. Unfortunately, even though the English translation did appear in Great Britain in 1929, it was not until last year (1949) when Pittman's of London published the translation by Constance Storrs with a foreword by L. Urwick that Fayol's work was given any wide American distribution.

"Another classic work that appeared in the thirties was Chester Barnard's *The Functions of the Executive*.[2] I recommend it heartily to all of you. In fact, I'm not only going to recommend it, I'm going to make it required reading for the members of this class.

Operations research comes of age

"Since the war, and particularly in the last few years, we have seen the publication of works in the operations research area applying the principles of mathematical analysis discovered during the war to the solving of managerial problems such as inventory, allocation warehousing problems, sophisticated breakeven analysis, maximum/minimum optimization procedures, and advanced statistical quality control. As you know, we have always used statistics in management; but the techniques now available were not developed until the advent of the war.

"Mathematics notwithstanding, gentlemen, the last twenty-year period has seen what I believe to be a shift in emphasis from the Protestant Ethic of Max Weber to a Social Ethic resulting from Mayo's writing."

"Professor, would you elaborate on that point? I'm not quite sure that I fully understand the terminology," asked one of the class.

These ethics have been covered in earlier "lectures." Even so, we are allowing the professor to repeat them for you here because they are so important. Many people today are still "hung up" on the Protestant Ethic.

"Yes, I'd be happy to," answered Professor Gregory. "In my opinion, I believe that the Protestant Ethic of Max Weber is what guided a majority of wage earners until the 1930s. Of course, there wasn't a complete switch; but, in general, until that period, the rugged individualist, the Horatio Alger hero, and the Protestant Ethic were all in vogue. Now the Protestant Ethic arises from the *Protestant Ethic and the Spirit of Capitalism* by Max Weber. Weber was a German professor who published this particular work in the early 1900s. In essence, Weber points out that according to the Calvanistic doctrine: (1) labor is an economic means to the spiritual end, (2) it is man's duty to work hard at his calling, and (3) labor should be considered in itself the life ordained as such by God. In essence, it was considered man's duty to work hard, to stay out of trouble, and not think of things alien to the teachings of God. This could be accomplished by hard work.[3] The teachings of the church, of course, intensified this feeling, and the Protestant Ethic would have obviously caused men to feel guilty if they didn't work hard. As a new input, however, because of the analysis made of the Hawthorne studies plus, as I just mentioned, the political and economic situation in the thirties, man grew to feel that perhaps the group was more important than the individual. Group effort, group solidarity, and the social aspects of the job as well as community relationships were considered more important than the individual striving for himself. This new thinking, labeled the Social Ethic, is perhaps even more important now than the Protestant Ethic. We are seeing, or have seen, the shift in emphasis from the individual man to the organization man. Also, the writers of the 1930s, such as Mooney[4] and Gulick[5] placed great emphasis on organizational studies and man's need for belonging. So you see, we apparently have switched from a Protestant Ethic to a Social Ethic. Does that fully explain the meaning of the terms?"

The Protestant Ethic

The Social Ethic emerges

"Now, I see what you mean, sir. I also see that my studies in history, looked at now from a different viewpoint, show how this could have happened too, because in the days before 1900 man could always move out West. And we still had stories of the rugged individualist. Now, we almost have to live together in groups in order to get by—that is, with the crowding in the cities and so many people coming from the farms and going into the cities."

"That's correct, young man. Your observation shows keen insight into the problem that's facing industry today, and it certainly does give another example of why the Social Ethic is in the forefront.

"With that background behind us, I'd now like to commence my first lecture in this, your final business course. I am going to make the assumption, and I believe rightly so, that you have completed all of your core courses in the curriculum. That is, you've had your course in organization management, behavioral science, statistical methods, economic analysis, and government and business relations. As a result, you should have been exposed to the authors mentioned during this introductory lecture. The purpose is to tie these various courses together, give you an integrated picture of management as a whole, and set the stage for the detailed discussions of authors and philosophies that will take place later in the course.

"To begin with, I would say that today we have at least three general schools of management thought or management philosophy. The first school would be the scientific management process school of Gulick, Urwick, Kimball, and probably Simon and Barnard. This might be called a modified classical school. The second is the human relations school of thought developed, as I mentioned earlier, as a result of the Hawthorne studies and the writing of Mayo, Lewin, Maslow, Likert, and other psychologists and behavioral scientists. Finally, I would say that we have a quantitative school. This latter school is just emerging, according to some of my colleagues in the consulting field. However, I feel that we will see many more advances in this area in the coming years.

The management process school of thought

"First of all let's review the scientific management or management process, as it is sometimes called, school of thought. You must remember that if we think of man in his economic sense and consider him motivated strictly by money and the authority of the supervisor, then the manager's job is to carry out the functions so ably spelled out by Fayol in France and by our own Davis, Gulick, and Newman. Basically, the functions of management include planning, organizing, coordinating, and controlling. At least the aforementioned individuals would agree on most of these. In addition, of course, Fayol included commanding where Gulick added directing, staffing, reporting, and budgeting. Newman adds assembling resources and directing while Davis limits his functions to planning, organizing, and controlling. Actually, if we define management as getting things done through the efforts of other people, management has at least three major responsibilities with which no one could argue. These three would be planning, directing, and controlling; because to get things done requires planning, to coordinate the efforts of other people requires directing, and to compare the results of the efforts to that which was planned requires controlling.

"We certainly saw the importance of planning during the war, when it was not uncommon for many companies, on short notice, to convert from peacetime to wartime production of products they had never before made on a scale never envisioned by the managers of the particular companies. To make this possible, it was necessary to plan intelligently and perform well.

"The directing function is the actual process of seeing that people get the job done—the leading or the supervising effort involved. We're seeing more emphasis on this function today from the top management viewpoint. It certainly is in this directing function of management that the human relations aspects should be incorporated. I firmly believe that good human relations are essential for good management.

"The management function of organizing is certainly as old as time itself, but it is a viable function, knowledge of which is essential to any manager. Basically, we still have our three types of organizational structures—the line, the line/staff, and the functional. You have studied all three, and we will study them again this term in conjunction with our latest thinking in behavioral science. Personally, I believe that organizing is an essential management function, because it logically follows planning.

"Because organization begins whenever any two people get together to achieve a common goal, organization must be the essential ingredient of any business operation. After any plan is established, we must organize to see how the plan can be carried out. The relationships between individuals certainly need to be spelled out—probably in the form of organization charts supplemented by written specifications defining the requirements of each level of management, each department, and each key job.

Delegation of authority

"In larger organizations, we sometimes organize on functional, regional, or product-lines bases. These regional and product-line organizations sometimes act as separate business entities on their own and are held accountable on a profit and loss basis. In this case delegation of authority must come from the central corporate offices which are probably responsible then for overall, long-range planning only. In this case corporate headquarters might consist mainly of staff units responsible for giving assistance to the autonomous, regional, or product-line subunits.

"We find many companies today also having a committee type of organization in which committees are established to coordinate viewpoints and pass collective judgment upon definite plans or proposals.

"Also, under the function of organization we must not forget the principles of organization. These include authority and unity of command, the scalar process, or the hierarchy and the division of labor. Of course, there are many more principles of management or elements of administration, and we shall study these later on in the term. I might list them for you at this time so that you may be thinking of them for later discussion.

1. Investigation
2. Forecasting
3. Planning
4. Appropriateness
5. Organization
6. Coordination
7. Order
8. Command
9. Control
10. The Coordination Principle
11. Authority
12. The Scalar Process
13. The Assignment and Correlation of Functions
14. Leadership
15. Delegation
16. Functional Definition
17. Determinative Functionalism
18. Applicative Functionalism
19. Interpretive Functionalism
20. General interest
21. Centralization
22. Appropriate staffing
23. Esprit de corps
24. Selection and placement
25. Rewards and sanctions
26. Initiative
27. Equity
28. Discipline
29. Stability

"These principles are contained in Urwick's recent book titled *The Elements of Administration,* which, as I said, we will take up in more detail later on in the term.[6]

"The latest thinking on control includes (1) an objective, establishing what it is desired to accomplish, (2) procedure, to satisfy how, when, and by whom the plan is to be executed, (3) criteria, as to what constitutes good performance, and (4) appraisal, as to how well it was done. This involves the plan of control. Most assuredly, we should have a control plan covering policies of the organization, key personnel, wages and salaries, costs, methods and manpower utilization, capital expenditures, service department efforts, product-line research and development, foreign operations, external relations, and general overall efficiency.

"Under the organization as a whole, certain principles apply as a result of the combined thinking of the writers in the area. They are expressed very well in the text that you used in your organization class—*Organization in Management in Industry and Business.* In this 1947 text Professor Cornell listed the following principles: [7]

1. *The Principle of Objective*—Prerequisite to the starting of any business enterprise, or to the carrying on of any activity by the concern as a whole or by any unit of it, a clear and complete statement should be made of the objectives in view.
2. *The Principle of Analysis*—A complete analysis of the entire problem should be made so as to make known and segregate all elements present and to assign to each element its relative weight.
3. *The Principle of Simplicity*—All activities which are not absolutely necessary should be eliminated and those activities which are retained should be handled in the simplest practical manner.
4. *The Principle of Functionalization*—The organization should be built around the main functions of the business and not around an individual or group of individuals.
5. *The Principle of Departmentalization*—The departments, divisions, and subdivisions of the enterprise and their functions should be clearly defined. The details of each department and its divisions should be logically and carefully coordinated so that each step of the work can be carried out to the best advantage in the shortest possible time.
6. *The Principle of Centralization of Authority and Responsibility*—There should be centralized executive control.
7. *The Principle of Limited Span of Executive Control*—The number of subordinates reporting directly to an executive should be definitely limited.
8. *The Principle of Personnel*—The personnel should be selected according to the individual's fitness for the particular position to be held."

Although many of these "principles" are similar to some discussed in earlier "lectures," we are allowing Dr. Gregory to quote them here so that you can compare them with those mentioned in earlier periods. Apparently Cornell had been influenced very little by "real" human relations. What do you think?

"Also according to your text, the basic principles of management are the following.[8]

1. *The Principle of Policy Making*—Definite, clear-cut policies are essential to effective management.
2. *The Principle of Improvement and Adjustment*—To be successful, a business must advance; it cannot remain dormant.
3. *The Principle of Balance*—To insure proper development of a business and efficiency in operation, a company must be well-balanced internally.
4. *The Principle of Relationship of Task and Accomplishment*—A person

works best and accomplishes most when he is given a definite job to be completed in a given time, the work being of a nature for which he is mentally and physically suited and of sufficient difficulty of performance to demand the best that is within him.

5. *The Principle of Individual Effectiveness*—Individual effectiveness is increased through training and improved working conditions.

6. *The Principle of Simplicity*—All elements which are not essential to successful operation should be eliminated and all those retained should be reduced to their simplest form.

7. *The Principle of Specialization*—Scientific distribution of work results in specialization of effort and specialization of task with the resultant advantages derived from concentration.

8. *The Principle of Standardization*—Whenever practicable, best practice should be determined, expressed in terms of definite units or standards and adopted as a pattern for use in operation or performance and in planning and control.

9. *The Principle of Financial Incentives*—Remuneration should be in direct proportion to the value of the accomplishment.

10. *The Principle of Human Relations*—Management succeeds or fails as human relations in business are intelligently or unintelligently handled.

11. *The Principle of Planning*—In order to accomplish satisfactorily everything of importance, there must be planning in advance of doing.

12. *The Principle of Control*—Planning is of little value unless there is subsequent control to make certain that the plans are carried out.

13. *The Principle of Cooperation*—The effort of two or more individuals working as a unit toward a common goal is greater than the sum of the effort of the individuals working as individuals.

14. *The Principle of Leadership*—Wise leadership is the most important single factor in successful operation.

15. *The Principle of Responsibility and Authority*—A person exercising authority should be held responsible for the carrying of all activities within the scope of his authority. Conversely: a person should be held responsible for the carrying on of an activity only in so far as he has authority over that activity.

16. *The Principle of Decision*—Decisions should be made at the lowest practicable organizational level.

17. *The Principle of Utilization of Executive Ability*—Executive ability can be utilized fully only when the executive is relieved of all matters that can be reduced to a routine, when standards of performance are set up and definite plans made, and the executive devotes his attention only to variations which are materially good or bad, to further planning, and to those matters which cannot be made a matter of routine.

"Comparing these principles and functions with those of Urwick, who also quotes Taylor, Fayol, Mary Parker Follett, and others, we see that there is duplication and overlapping in many areas. However, the point to be made is that these formal principles and functions have worked well in the past and undoubtedly will work well in the future if they are tempered with the human relations approach as developed over the past few years.

Economic man

"In discussing the principles and functions of management later on in the course, we will see that many are based upon the economic man assumption—the man who maximizes or selects the best alternative from among all those available to him in dealing with the real world and all its complexity. However, Dr. Herbert Simon tells us in his *Administrative Behavior* that we rarely find economic man. But we do find administrative man—the man who looks for a course of action that will get the job done. His decision is based on an elementary model of the actual situation. In other words, he makes his choice on the basis of the facts as he sees them, specifically the ones that he considers to be the most important, knowing full well that he will never know all the factors bearing upon the situation.[9]

Administrative man

"Now, let's consider the second—I'm sorry, gentleman, I should have asked; are there any questions at this point?"

"Yes sir, Dr. Gregory," came from a voice from the third row. "In mentioning Cornell's principles, you said something to the effect that they'll probably work well in the future if they are tempered with the human relations approach. And I believe I caught the words 'as developed over the past few years.' But I have in my notes from last term that his principle 10 was the principle of human relations. Was that principle different from the human relations you're talking about now?"

"Yes sir, Mr. Curtis, it was different. At least, it was different in my opinion. Expanding his principle of human relations, Cornell emphasizes fair treatment of labor by management, disciplinary action, the prompt attention to complaints, good labor policies strictly enforced, and a personnel department. This, in my opinion, is a somewhat different emphasis than Mayo and his followers were advocating."

"Thank you, Dr. Gregory, I see what you meant now by that inference."

"Now, ladies and gentlemen, let's consider the second school of managerial thought—that is, the human relations school. Let's particularly see how this might affect the economic man rationale that appears to be the key to the scientific or process field as some people teach it today.

"First of all, we need to trace some significant events during the past few years to see what their relationships might be or how they might affect traditional management philosophy. By traditional, of course, I'm referring to the scientific school or the process approach.

"First of all in importance, I believe, was an article in the *Psychological Review, Volume 50, 1943* by Dr. Maslow, in which he identified what he considered to be man's basic needs. Maslow stated that man's needs were arranged in a hierarchy whereby he would tend to satisfy his lower-order need first, then, when that was satisfied, his behavior would be oriented toward the next higher need. The order of needs were physiological, safety, belongingness or love, esteem, and self-actualization. Maslow's point was that needs motivated behavior and as one basic need was satisfied, behavior would be motivated toward satisfying the next higher need. Conversely, man's behavior would be motivated by a lower-order need if this need, having once been satisfied, should reappear as a need once more."

The professor would probably have covered Maslow in greater detail. However, you have already covered Maslow in Chapter 2.

"Now I'm sure that most of these needs require no explanation except perhaps that of self-actualization. Maslow doesn't explain this perhaps as well as he might, but my understanding of his self-actualization is that what a man can be he must be.

"The implication of the needs hierarchy is that perhaps recognition on the job may be as important to some people as is salary. In other words, we know that people have feelings—they like to feel important and have their work recognized as being important. This recognition can, perhaps, be as important to them as pay, which only satisfies the safety need and not the esteem need.

Maslow vs. Tead

"It's interesting to note that some of Maslow's needs are very similar to some of the instincts listed by Ordway Tead in 1918.[10] Tead's paternal instinct is similar to Maslow's physiological and safety needs. The instinct of workmanship, contrivance, or constructiveness is similar to Maslow's esteem need as is Tead's instinct of self-assertion/self display—in other words, the need to rise above the dead level of humanity and be an individual. Perhaps this is also close again to the self-actualization need. In any case, a thorough reading of Tead reveals that some of the instincts he names are very similar to Maslow's basic needs. However, the importance of Maslow's writing is that once a need is satisfied, it no longer motivates. This, apparently, was completely overlooked or not considered by Tead.

"Maslow's esteem need, of course, explains the importance of status in many organizations—status, referring to the prestige that a job has in the eyes of the work group or peers.

"Are there any questions to this point, gentlemen? I feel that it is necessary that you understand this particular line of reasoning, because I believe that it was not considered in developing organizational theory in the past."

The professor noticed a couple of hands raised and nodded at one. "Yes, ma'am?"

"Professor Gregory, what you have said is clear except for the self-actualization need. Could you explain that one in a little more detail?"

Self-actualization is the ultimate

"Well, all I can do is relate to you Maslow's interpretation. He's saying that once all the other needs have been satisfied, once a man has been recognized and has the esteem that he feels he must have, then he still must go on to something greater. At this point he is doing what he really feels he is actually capable of doing and can be himself because he is completely secure in his existence. He is motivated strictly to do what he wants to do. Painters, musicians, and writers fall into this category. They are really doing what they feel they can do the best. They know they are good and they want to continue. Esteem no longer is necessary as long as they are doing what they are capable of at the highest level. I don't know whether that clears it up or not, but that, in essence, is what Maslow means by the self-actualization need. In other words, man can never be satisfied; something has to motivate his behavior and if all other things are satisfied, then his motivation is to do what he must."

"Thank you, professor."

"Another discovery about the behavior of individuals which must be

Situational effect and field theory

taken into consideration when considering the direction function of classical organization theory is that people react to direction differently at different times, depending upon the external environment at the very moment behavior occurs. This is the essence of field theory, as published by Dr. Kurt Lewin. We'll be discussing this in more detail later on in the class, but the important thing to remember is that a man's reaction to supervision will differ from day to day depending upon the particular surroundings and interaction between the individual and the environment at the time. In fact, group dynamics has been applied to industrial situations by Dr. Lewin in the book *Resolving Social Conflicts,* published just two years ago.[11] We will review this work later in the term as we discuss the effects of democratic, authoritarian, and laissez-faire types of leadership upon individuals. In general, though, the results of studies have been that democratic leadership certainly gets better results in the long run than the traditional authoritarian type of leadership that would have been and still is in vogue in many organizations.

"An understanding of man's needs, face-to-face group relationships, and field theory is so important that during the past few years we have seen the establishment at the Massachusetts Institute of Technology of the Research Center for Group Dynamics now located at the University of Michigan, and the National Training Laboratory established by Dr. Leland Bradford at Bethel, Maine. Both of these institutes are carrying forward research on the interaction of people within groups and the importance of interpersonal behavior. Their results are having a profound effect on the thinking of many of our professors of business administration, and I predict that we will see many more articles and books published in this area in the next few years.

"The reason for making this statement is obvious. If management or administration is getting the job done through people, it appears that it is essential to have an understanding of people, how they get along with each other, and how they operate in groups. For an organization is simply made up of groups of individuals working together, supposedly, for a common purpose or goal."

This is the understanding of interaction from the downward point of view. Unfortunately it sometimes involves manipulative practices.

The development of group incentive plans

"As a result of the emphasis on the group rather than on the individual, we've seen the development of group incentive plans. One such plan was the Scanlon Plan introduced at LaPointe Steel Company in the late thirties. The basis of the plan was a suggestion and production committee that sought methods and means to reduce labor costs, because the steel plant was on the brink of bankruptcy. There were no individual awards for particular suggestions. Rewards, instead, were companywide on the basis of cost reductions evolved from the different suggestions. Of course, the uniqueness of this plan lay in the group reward system, the joint committee system, and finally, in the fact that the workers shared in reduced costs rather than increased profits. The other plan—that used at Lincoln Electric

—is, I understand, to be the subject of a book entitled *Incentive Management* now being written by Mr. James F. Lincoln. Lincoln's idea, as proved most effective in the operations of the company, is that recognition is the only real incentive. Bargaining power, security, seniority, safety, shorter hours, and money are not real incentives. He compares his incentives to those of the amateur athlete and comes up with the answer that 'recognition of our abilities by our contemporaries and ourselves' is the incentive that causes people to strive so mightily for success.[12] The plan is certainly effective, for Lincoln has stated that over the last sixteen years the average total bonus for each factory worker has exceeded $40,000.[13]

What a man does is important

"Another area of changing assumptions about the work and the worker based upon the human relations school of thought concerns the nature of work itself. Based upon the Social Ethic, Ordway Tead's instinct theory, and Maslow's writings, it would appear that work itself is important and that the nature of the task itself can be important. Certainly, the placing of workers in a production line goes against the social concept and the work group concept of man's life as well as the enjoyment of work. It also violates the principle of a rewarding job. This fact should be considered in the planning and organization functions of management. Of course, not too much has been considered in the area to date, because, unfortunately, the profit motive still seems to be paramount in the minds of many of the older managers. And why not? This was passed down to them through the company and has been the guiding light for many years. If not the profit motive, certainly the production motive has been paramount, as witnessed during the last war when it was essential that the division of labor be carried out to its utmost in order to mass-produce the means for defense in the war effort. However, now that we've gone back to a peacetime economy, we're hearing grumblings on the assembly line and perhaps the division of labor may not be as important in the future—especially when we consider that we have now entered a post-industrial society in which over 50 percent of the people are employed in government and the service industries.

Recognition of participation in management

"Another principle in the new human relations school of management is certainly that of participation in management by the workers themselves. This involves allowing them to participate in decisions affecting their jobs in the matter of how things are carried out. It certainly can assist in overcoming the resistance or fear of change found in many organizations. At a higher level, participation in management has been carried on by McCormick and Company, wherein junior boards have been set up to assist the senior boards in decision making. Thus, we can have participation from the top down in which the lower-level supervisors are consulted about changes in decisions affecting them, and we can have participation from the bottom up wherein workers at the lower level can contribute suggestions for change and discuss various aspects of their jobs with the freedom to interchange ideas at all levels. This, of course, is a carry-on of the group behavioral and interpersonal sensitivity training aspect.

The importance of the social system

"In speaking of change and resistance to change, we must never forget that technological changes certainly affect the work group situation. Work groups often develop a very strong social structure which, of necessity, must be changed by technological innovations. It is important that the manager realize the importance of the social systems that must be changed and let his workers participate as soon as possible in planning the change, so that there will be as little resistance as possible. Too many times in the past top management has developed a very logical technological change based upon economic conditions, passed the word to the workers, and found difficulty in carrying out the change because of the resistance at all levels of the organization.

"This, of course, leads directly into decision making, because the heart of change is the result of a prior decision. Decision making is covered very well in Simon's *Administrative Behavior*. I believe I mentioned to you earlier that Dr. Simon made the distinction between economic man and administrative man. But he also goes on to point out all the problems involved in the decision-making process. I would certainly recommend his book for reading, because we will be discussing it in detail later on in the course.

New quantitative techniques

"Finally, let's move to the quantitative school to see what new developments are available in the statistical and mathematical areas to assist in making decisions. We know from our readings that mathematical approaches to the solving of management problems are certainly not new. An economic lot size model was first published in 1915. Dodge and Romig at Bell Telephone Laboratories in conjunction with Shewhart developed statistical sampling procedures in inspection in the Shewhart X-Bar R Charts. T. C. Fry, another Bell engineer, developed the statistical basis for queuing theory in 1928, and the breakeven chart was developed in the 1930s. These methods and other methods that developed during the war were discussed in your course in nonmilitary applications of operations research. Accordingly, I am not going to go into these mathematical techniques in this class. However, you certainly should be aware of them.

"In conclusion, gentlemen, I would like to leave you with the following thoughts. Perhaps you've sometimes wondered why it is necessary to review the development of management thinking. At least you wonder why I do so in this particular course. I realize that in many of your other courses you only studied the latest trend or current vogue in management thinking. However, you must remember that when you go out into industry or government, as the case may be, and approach your first job, you are going to be working for supervisors and working with co-workers who have very often not been exposed to the latest in management principles. Therefore, I believe it is essential for you to know what management principles were being taught at different periods of time so that you will have an understanding of what I call the frame of reference of the people with whom and for whom you work.

Managerial frame of reference for interaction

"As an example, many of you who are 21 or 22 years old today have no recollection whatsoever of the Depression of the early thirties. Yet, certainly, if you are working for a supervisor who is 50 years old today, he most certainly is going to remember the 1930s, because he would have been in his thirties at the time. Moreover, his management training would very likely have occurred in the late twenties and he would not have been exposed to our present managerial philosophy. Thus you might expect that he would be an authoritarian type manager who believed in the Protestant Ethic and couldn't possibly see the reason for participation in management or considering the group and people's feelings about their jobs. To him the job might mean "Do it or else because, what the hell, you're getting paid for it."

"I have seen the changes taking place because I am in the academic field. I know what training I had in the late 1920s and I know how that training has changed today. I know it from practice, from reading, and from experience as a consultant for business. You, of course, must learn it from books because you don't have the actual background. Your supervisors, on the other hand, will have had the practical background, but it will be based upon conditions existing in the various plants in which they serve as managers. Thus, don't try to change the world overnight. Have an appreciation for the other person's point of view and try to get along if possible.

"Now, let's sum up the interaction influence of the three schools of management thought. First of all, we still have the classical school based upon the managerial functions of planning, organizing, staffing, directing, and controlling. These functions are essential, and probably we always will have them. However, the manner in which they are carried out must be tempered with our understanding of human behavior as a result of current theories. We must remember in the planning stage that we are planning for people, that people have associations and social relationships, that they want esteem and recognition, and that they will work better if they participate in the planning.

"Under the organization function we again must realize that people work together in groups and that sometimes the attitude of the group is much more important than the attitude of the individual—remember the Gestalt Theory that you were exposed to in your psychology courses. It might not always be possible any more to put the right man in the right job, but compromise and pick the man who could probably do the job best based upon his relationship with the group.

"In directing, we most certainly need to realize that men must be consulted if they desire to participate, at least in general, and they prefer to think for themselves. The autocratic, dictatorial-type leadership style is not going to work as effectively as a democratic style, in which people are allowed to participate. In fact, the *Art of Leadership* by Tead, if you'll remember, even suggests that the best leader is one who suggests the courses of action rather than orders work to be done.[14] And, finally, in the control aspect we are now able to use mathematical techniques which were not available before. In fact, these are not only available for control, but are also available in the planning stage.

The developing importance of the individual

"Thus, gentlemen, we find that although the principles of the classicists are still with us, they must be tempered with a human relations approach. The individual is important, particularly now that we are in a post-industrial society in which more people work in government and service industries than in actual manufacturing and agriculture. Unfortunately, too much emphasis seems to be placed on the industrial setting by the writers in management. Not enough is given to the nonindustrial setting where people relationships are paramount."

EPILOGUE

What are they like?

They are the teachers of some of today's college students. They are the co-workers and supervisors who are in their middle to late forties today.

We would expect them to be well-grounded in the human relations side of management. They are probably the benevolent/authoritative type of leader/teacher. They understand the importance of the group but they also know the importance of planning, organizing, directing, and controlling (PODC). They consider the importance of the individual but still might be apt to manipulate.

Participation may be condoned but when the chips are down, they know that the boss is judged on results and the buck stops at the top.

Change is difficult based on their personal philosophy.

EXERCISE QUESTIONS

1. Compare Cornell and Fayol's theories in relationship to the human element. Was there much change?
2. Contrast the human relations teaching of 1950 to 1940. What changes occurred, if any?
3. What significant attitudes and values might have changed from 1940 to 1950? What might the reasons have been?
4. List the major contributions to the human relations thinking of the 1940 to 1950 period.
5. Identify and give examples of the needs according to Maslow.

DISCUSSION TOPICS

1. What effect do you think World War II had on the development of managerial philosophy—especially the human relations movement?
2. What social, political, and economic factors would have affected the 1950-trained manager?
3. What effect would TV have had on the personal philosophy of the person who grew up in the 1950s?
4. Would you expect the value system of the young child in the 1941 to 1945 period to have developed differently from one in the 1945 to 1950 period? Explain your thinking in detail.

PROJECTS

1. Role-play the following interaction situations:
   a. The discussion of a form change, affecting a number of people, between a 1929 frame of reference man and a 1950 frame of reference woman.
   b. a 1950 frame of reference male suggesting a new idea to a woman supervisor with a 1940 frame of reference.

NOTES

1. George E. Mayo, *The Human Problems of an Industrial Civilization* (Boston: Division of Research, Harvard Business School, 1933); and F. J. Roethlisberger and W. J. Dickson, *Management and the Worker* (Cambridge, Massachusetts: Harvard University Press, 1939).
2. Chester I. Barnard, *The Functions of the Executive* (Cambridge: Harvard University Press, 1938).
3. Max Weber, *The Protestant Ethic and the Spirit of Capitalism,* translated by Talcott Parsons (New York: Charles Scribner's Sons, 1958).
4. James D. Mooney and Alan C. Reiley, *The Principles of Organization* (New York: Harper and Brothers Publishers, 1939).
5. Luther Gulick and Lyndall Urwick, eds., *Papers on the Science of Administration* (New York: Institute of Public Administration, Columbia University, 1937).
6. L. Urwick, *The Elements of Administration* (New York: Harper & Brothers Publishers, 1943), pp. 118–129.
7. William B. Cornell, *Organization and Management in Industry and Business,* 3rd ed. (New York: The Ronald Press Co., 1947), pp. 39–44, with permission.
8. Ibid., pp. 50–61, with permission.
9. Herbert A. Simon, *Administrative Behavior* (New York: The Free Press, 1947).
10. Ordway Tead, *Instincts in Industry* (New York: Houghton Mifflin Co., 1918).
11. Kurt Lewin, *Resolving Social Conflicts* (New York: Harper & Row Publishers, 1948); also selected papers on group dynamics edited by Gertrud Lewin and Gordon Allport.
12. James F. Lincoln, *Incentive Management* (Cleveland: The Lincoln Electric Co., 1951), p. 101.
13. Ibid., p 111.
14. Ordway Tead, *The Art of Leadership* (New York: McGraw-Hill Book Co., 1935).

In addition to works cited in the footnotes, the following books were available in the period:

Chester I. Barnard, *Organization and Management* (Cambridge: Harvard University Press, 1948).

George Filipetti, *Industrial Management in Transition* (Homewood, Ill.: Richard D. Irwin, Inc., 1946).

Mary Parker Follett, *Freedom and Coordination* (London: Management Publications Trust, 1949).

B. B. Gardner, *Human Relations in Industry* (Homewood, Ill.: Richard D. Irwin, Inc., 1945).

P. E. Holden, L. S. Fish, and H. L. Smith *Top Management Organ-*

ization and Control (Stanford, Calif.: Stanford University Press, 1941).

James D. Mooney, *Principles of Organization,* rev. ed. (New York: Harper & Brothers, 1947).

I LIKE
IKE

10

The Fabulous Fifties Decade of Suburbia 1950-1960

The objectives of this chapter are to enable you to

1. *understand* the managerial philosophy taught in 1960;
2. *identify* the changes in human relations thinking in the 1950 to 1960 period;
3. *trace* the origins of the behavioral scientist movement in the 1950s;
4. *note* the basic change in man's thinking about man that occurred in the late 1950s;
5. *comprehend* the reasons for changing attitudes;
6. *realize* that supervisors and co-workers in their thirties today received their managerial training in the late fifties;
7. *appreciate* the fact that members of the present generation were in their formative years (age 1 to 7) in the 1950s. This was their time frame of reference for personal philosophy.

PROLOGUE

What was it like?

It was the decade of suburbia—the great move to the suburbs, resulting in transportation problems, promotion of sales for power lawnmowers, floor polishers, automatic washing machines, and new homes. Little League, Girl Scouts flourished. Bicycles and encyclopedia salesmen abounded, and musical instruments and juvenile booksales boomed. Because help was hard to find, the campaign for the do-it-yourself man emerged. Suburbia became known for its consumption of liquor, the new way to live, more active sports, "simple" fun, swimming pools, and other recreational activities. Hula hoops became the rage and then went.

It was the beat generation with songs of protest, Negro blues, and depressing ballads. Liberace made a million dollars a year, and Mitch Miller sold 1.75 million records in 15 months. Harry Belafonte became the first to sell 1 million LP records. It was really the first TV generation, with TV taking over the role of baby sitter, mother, father, and teacher.

The Korean War came and went during this period, and the launching of Sputnik in 1956 had a profound influence on the American educational system. Commercial art in the period underwent a major revolt against tradition, and wound up with more sophisticated, more cosmopolitan design. Paint-by-number kits were popular. And the price of a first-class letter was increased from 3c to 4c.

The experience during this particular decade was under the shadow of the Bomb. There was a growing awareness of poverty and racism, economic affluence, and computerized technology. It was certainly a time of questioning and awakening.

Against this background we renew our acquaintance with Dr. Gregory. This time it is February of 1960.

Professor Hugo Gregory was not happy as he tooled his little VW through the afternoon traffic on his way home from the university to the suburbs. He just couldn't understand this modern generation.

"You'd think they'd realize," he thought, "that we have to get serious if we're ever going to keep up with the Russians. Sputnik I was a great triumph for the Russians; and if we're going to catch up and surpass them, these students have got to be serious. Yet all they seem interested in is seeing how many of them can fit into a phone booth or into a VW. And these sack dresses and shorter shorts and hula hoops—my God, when are they going to realize that they have to get down to business? Well, maybe its the fact that they haven't gone through a depression. I remember how it was back in the thirties, but the present college classes certainly don't. Most of them were born just before World War II and were probably brought up without the influence of a father, at least during their formative years. So I guess I can't blame them too much, but it certainly is frustrating when you want them to get serious about future plans. As far as they're concerned, the Protestant Ethic might be just another rock group!

"Come to think of it, that probably is the reason—they didn't live through a depression. They were given everything they wanted. Our country certainly provides welfare programs for families who don't have enough, so that there is very little starvation any more. And they really don't have to work as hard as the young people in my day. This might very well explain some of the differences in attitudes. Not only is the cultural environment different but the social and political environment is certainly also different. Perhaps if I can keep that in mind more when I see some of the shenanigans going on on the campus, I won't get quite so upset."

Maybe Dr. Gregory is beginning to see that successful interaction requires much thought and a little hard work.

"But at least in my business course the students are more dedicated. I think that most of them realize that business training will be essential for securing an adequate job in business and government today. Not only do the students seem to be smarter and realize the need for education, but the whole country is increasing its median school years completed. If I remember correctly, the number of years completed was 8.6 in 1940, 9.3 in 1950, and up to 10.6 today.

"Well, all this is interesting but really doesn't have any bearing on my present administrative management course. It's a wonder that I don't get tired of this particular course, but I must say it's one of the most interesting ones that I've taught; and I certainly would never give it up. It's the one place where students can tie together all the different schools, if you want to call it that, of management thought and get the big picture. At least, that's what I started out to do twenty years ago when I began my teaching career, and luckily, I've been able to keep it up. Of course it is a little difficult for me now, because the amount of literature written in the field of management is doubling almost every year. But I've been able to keep my eye on the general trend. And I think they get a lot out of my course."

The incessant tooting of a horn behind him snapped the professor out of his daydreaming, and he realized that the light had turned green. "Well," he thought, "I'd better concentrate on my driving the rest of the way home and not give any more thought to this lecture until I get to the office in the morning and start preparing my notes."

At 9:16 A.M., Professor Gregory turned the handle of the glass-paneled door with the words "BUSINESS ADMINISTRATION, DR. GREGORY" stenciled in large black letters. As he closed the door, he thought to himself that it certainly was nice having an office to himself now that he was a full professor. But at times he did miss the bantering with Jack and Harry, with whom he had shared an office when he was an associate professor. But now he had time to complete uninterrupted research on the book that he was preparing, so he really did like the privacy. And besides, with the new stereo on, it was rather soothing. He pulled the chair up to his desk, pulled out his note pad, and began making some notes. Under the heading "Modern Managerial Philosophy," he wrote a few observations concerning formal organization, wrote the words "human relations," "behavioral science" and "Herzberg," then reached for a book on his shelf. He finally finished his detailed outline around noon.

Dr. Gregory walked into classroom 210 at about five minutes of two. He always tried to be a little early the first day because he had to call the roll, usually sign a couple of add/drops for students who were in the wrong class, and, in general, hand out the assignments for the term and get things rolling. As usual, he was correct; the process took about 20 minutes; and he wasn't able to begin his lecture until approximately a quarter after two.

"Ladies and gentlemen—it's nice to see that so many of you have been able to successfully maneuver your way through what I am sure must be a frustrating curriculum until you're sitting in the final course of the last term of your program leading to the business degree. As you know, in this course we're going to try to pull together the various aspects of administration and management that you have been exposed to in other courses so that you can develop your own managerial philosophy and decide what's right for you when you go out into the field of business. I feel particularly honored in conducting this course because it is probably the last time I will do so. I have been with the university for approximately twenty years now, and next year I will be going on a sabbatical to complete my book; probably after that, I'll only teach on a part-time basis. But be that as it may, I am pleased to be here because I feel we are witnessing a change in management thinking today—a change that I believe will have profound effect on all future practitioners of management and particularly you when you graduate. Specifically, I am speaking of the change that I see occurring in the way we look at the individual in the organization—in fact, perhaps the way that we look at all mankind. I believe we're seeing a switch from the Protestant Ethic which, of course, led to the Social Ethic, to a new ethic today which, for lack of a better name, I'll call the Self-Actualization Ethic. I believe we are seeing a shift to the realization that what a man does—the type of work that he performs —is more important in motivation and management than a realization of the group effect of the Social Ethic or on the innerdirection of man as a result of the Protestant Ethic.

The advent of the Self-Actualization Ethic

"Now, I'm not saying that we're going to see a change in the formal organizational structure or in the general functions of management—that is, planning, organizing, directing, and controlling, which, incidentally, have changed very little over the years. But I think we will be seeing a new emphasis on the structure of work.

"This course will include a review of current management thinking as far as organizational structure, staff/line relationships, functions of management, participative management, newer human relation approaches, and behavioral aspects are concerned. In addition, we will thoroughly explore the writers in the field over the last years as well as the classical theories of management. In today's class, however, I only want to give you some background which I hope will stimulate you as we study writers and current philosophies through the remainder of the course.

"Now, before considering the newer management philosophies, let's review the formal or classical theory as practiced today."

"Dr. Gregory," a voice called from the back of the classroom, "would you mind reviewing just for a minute the Protestant Ethic and Social Ethic. Perhaps I should know what they are, but I just transferred here last year, and I haven't had all my work here. I don't believe I'm clear about the Protestant Ethic."

This has been covered in earlier lectures; but, as we pointed out at that time, its importance cannot be overstressed. Note the different slant this time.

The Protestant Ethic again (see Chapter 9 for a more thorough explanation)

"Certainly, I'd be glad to. The Protestant Ethic was a terminology coined by the German political economist and sociologist Max Weber in 1904 and 1905 in his essay entitled *Protestant Ethic and Spirit of Capitalism.* Weber's theory was that the rise of capitalism was due to a change of moral standards as a result of Calvinistic theology. The Calvinistic theology, according to Weber, placed great emphasis on what is named 'a calling'—which is a strenuous and active way of life to which the person must devote himself with a sense of religious responsibility. In other words, labor is an end unto itself, the way of man's salvation. Man must be diligent, thrifty, sober, and prudent if he is to have complete happiness and obtain his reward in heaven. In other words, his conscience must be his guide. He does not have access to confession as the Catholic does—he must make his peace directly with God. Therefore, work is the spiritual end unto itself. In fact, it is a sin not to work. This, in essence, is the Protestant Ethic. It also, according to Weber, gives us some of our hang-ups, particularly concerning sex, because he tells us that the Calvinistic doctrine states that sex is permitted solely for the purpose of reproduction and for no other purpose. In other words, it was considered morally wrong to engage in sex for pleasure. Does that explain it?"

Parent values

"Yes, sir, it does; and based upon that, I can now see why my father said some of the things he told me about the value of work and idle hands and some of his general clichés."

"Now, gentlemen, as I mentioned before, I think we are seeing a shift today. But, before looking at that let's consider for a minute this Protestant Ethic. If we consider the growth of our country, we find that the Pilgrims settled in New England for religious freedom. They were certainly indoctrinated in the Protestant Ethic, and if they had any doubts in their minds about it, the hard times, cold winters, and the Indians certainly would have left no doubt in their minds that work was necessary for the salvation of man. In fact, it was a must for survival itself. So out of necessity they worked hard and were successul.

Early managers instilled with the Protestant Ethic

"As the country grew and industry developed, these settlers and their descendants, instilled with the Protestant Ethic, became the managers and leaders of the new industries. At first there was enough labor available within the United States. But rapidly it was necessary to import laborers from abroad. In 1780, for example, more than three out of every four Americans were descendants of the original English and Irish settlers. Between 1840 and 1860, however, over 4,300,000 immigrants came from Ireland, Germany, Great Britain, and France—you see these people became the workers in the industrialization of the United States while the original descendants, those instilled with the Protestant Ethic according to

Weber, became the supervisors and managers. The general philosophy toward immigration was wide open during those days and was expressed very well in the poem by Emma Lazarus inscribed on the tablet on the pedestal of the Statue of Liberty. I'm sure you remember the famous lines:

Give me your tired, your poor,
Your huddled masses yearning to breathe free,
The wretched refuse of your teeming shore,
Send these, the homeless, tempest-tost to me,
I lift my lamp beside the golden door!

"Now the rise of big business in the form of the steel mills, copper mills, railroads, and oil industry with the names of men such as Vanderbilt, Carnegie, Rockefeller, coupled with the Protestant Ethic as an excuse to amass wealth, led, of course, to the development of the rigid hierarchy of business organization in which we find man as the common laborer being, in general, looked down on and ignored.

"And, as I am sure you remember from your studies of the labor movement, the lot of the laborer was not very good until the formation of labor unions. Now, we realize that the bureaucratic organizational structure led to the development of the functions of management; that is, planning, organizing, and controlling, which are common to most writers in the field of management. There are, of course, other functions mentioned by different authors which I will discuss with you later. But what I want to emphasize now is that the Protestant Ethic gave rise to the very formal organization with its specialization of labor, emphasis on span of control, the scalar principle, departmentalization, and a strong authoritarian type of management, the unity of command and acceptance principles, and the very rigid hierarchy. This thinking on organizational structure, in general, carried on at least through the early 1930s until the publishing of Mayo's book on the human problems of the industrial civilization, which was a direct result of the Hawthorne studies. We thus arrive at the point of time at which the Protestant Ethic begins to be replaced by the Social Ethic.

Were there any other reasons for the formal bureaucracy?

"You all studied the Hawthorne experiments in your managerial psychology class; but just in case you've forgotten, I'll refresh your memories. The Hawthorne studies were the experiments conducted at the Hawthorne Works of the Western Electric Company to determine what effects lighting might have on the output of workers. Of course, the results of the relay test room experiments showed that no matter what varied, either the lights up or down or rest periods increased or decreased, output per man hour still increased. Accordingly, the general consensus was that the group itself was more important than other factors in increasing productivity. The social side of work, then, was emphasized and managers began to have an appreciation of the group and its effect on and within the organization. Although it was not played up as much as it should have been at the time, I believe, the participation in this particular Hawthorne group was important. It originally started with six girls, but two were replaced because they didn't get along; so there was a compatible group of six girls

Hawthorne reviewed (see Chapter 8)

working together who were consulted before every change occurred—in other words, true participative management. Not only that, but when the girls were asked why they thought their production had gone up, they indicated that the working conditions were nice, and they liked to be consulted, and besides they didn't have any supervisor looking over their shoulders all the time. The interesting part is that they had closer supervision than the girls in the rest of the plant because the men with the stop-watches who were conducting the experiment were right there all the time. The important point was that it was a different type of supervision. It was a supervision in which the leader really cared about how the workers were producing and wished to help them in all ways possible—certainly different from the normal authoritarian type of supervision that the girls had been used to before they became part of the experiment. Thus we find that, or we should have found, that the group is important, yes, but the manner of supervision is important and the fact that workers can participate in changes before they occur is of great importance."

An example of the interaction process being condoned by management.

"Now, of course, as you know from your studies of the fundamentals of management, the Social Man Ethic has carried over into managerial practice; and we see such things as participation in management, the Scanlon Plan, the McCormick Plan, the Lincoln Electric Plan, the National Training Laboratories, Group Dynamics, and human relations movements in general occurring in management literature as well as management practice. We're seeing more emphasis being placed upon the group and its position in the organizational structure, and I hope we're seeing a breaking down of the traditional bureaucratic patterns. Certainly in leadership training, we're seeing some changes taking place. But, again, we have not seen the great changes that I feel will evolve in the next few years as a result of some interesting philosophies and writings that have been published over the last three or four years. This, as I mentioned earlier to you, is the change into the self-actualizing man concept of Maslow. As you will remember, in his hierarchy of needs the self-actualization need was at the highest level. This is when man is realizing his full potential, as it were, getting the most he can out of his work.

"Now, before proceeding any further into this ethic or way of looking at man in his work situation, I'd like to briefly review what's current in the literature still along the classical theory line.

"One of our recent texts is the third edition of *Industrial Organization and Management* by Ralph C. Davis, Professor of Business Organization at Ohio State University. In Chapter 3, entitled 'Management Responsibility and Authority,' Dr. Davis discusses scientific management, creative planning, organizing, controlling, factors in operative performance, standards and standaridization, responsibility, authority and accountability, organizational structure and the division of responsibility, units of supervision and the span of control, authority and the democratic process, delegation, de-

The same emphasis as in the forties

centralization, and functional analysis.[1] His book is widely read, is along the classical line, and gives a lot of insight into production management. It discusses the human side, but I'm afraid it misses the behavioral science side.

"Another recent text, *Management and Organization,* by Louis A. Allen, president of Louis A. Allen and Associates, was published in 1958. Allen's concept of management includes planning, organizing, coordinating, motivating and controlling. In his unified concept of management in Chapter 2, under motivating he lists selection, communication, participation, appraisal, counseling, coaching, training, compensation, direction, and dismissal.[2] Perhaps this is good human relations, but it certainly isn't motivation from the standpoint of the behavioral scientist."

As Dr. Gregory paused at this point for a sip of water, he noticed a hand raised on the right side of the lecture hall. "Yes, ma'am, you have a question?"

"Yes I have, Dr. Gregory. I believe you used the term 'behavioral scientist.' In fact, I believe you used it once before when you said something about missing the behavioral science side. Is behavioral science different from human relations?"

Human relations is NOT behavioral science

"As a matter of fact, Miss Steinman, there is a difference, at least as far as I'm concerned. In my opinion, the human relations approach was the be-nice-to-workers approach in order to try to improve morale and output. It put them together in social groups so that they would be happier, and concentrated on fringe benefits, company-sponsored recreational activities, and the friendly attitude by the boss to the workers. I think it tried to make the workers feel like they were a part of one big, happy family; but the intent was again, in my opinion, to get more work from the worker. In essence, I think it was a phony approach."

Some of the earlier management writers—Dutton and Diemer, for example—shared the professor's views. In fact they warned against a patronizing attitude.

Do you agree?

"Now, on the other hand, what I'm calling the behavioral scientist approach is that taken by psychologists and sociologists who actually conduct experiments, as did Dr. Herzberg and others, to actually determine how people really feel. It's an applied science, humanistic and optimistic, oriented toward economic objectives, but concerned with the total climate of the organization. It's concerned with development of interpersonal competence, and it concentrates on a scientific basis for determining company organization and the administrative practices of management.

"Now do you see the difference in the two, or why I'm referring to one as human relations and to the other as behavioral science?"

"Yes, sir, I see the difference. I don't know as I had thought about it that way, but I guess I do see that human relations as you call it is kind of phony."

"All right, now; let's see where I was in my notes. Ah, yes—I was discussing some of the books written in the last few years in the general area of management. All right, to continue, Dr. John G. Glover of New York University states that, 'With the basic principles of industrial economics as the keystone, research has made it possible to define clearly the responsibilities of management and to develop principles for the administration of an enterprise. These management principles are:

1. Principle of research application
2. Principle of policy creation and application
3. Principle of planning
4. Principle of action or performance
5. Principle of measurement and appraisement
6. Principle of control.[3]

In my opinion, Glover's discussion of management's influence on human behavior has a Machiavellian approach.[4] Glover seems to believe that specific job descriptions, practices, and procedures will insure obtaining the right type of worker who will react in the correct manner.

"Koontz and O'Donnell list planning, organizing, staffing, directing, and controlling.[5] In addition, they go into considerable detail concerning the human relations side of the organizational structure. I think they do the best job of presenting the management process school of thought.

The element of leadership is common to most authors who believe in the management process

"Implicit in the writing of most authors who espouse the management process or functions of management doctrine is the element of leadership, which in some cases comes under direction or command. This facet of management, of course, has been covered in separate books; a recent one, in particular, is a study describing the leader as he sees himself, then the reaction of his followers, and finally lessons to be learned by the study.[6] The conclusions of this study by Argyris were that leaders do not see themselves the same as do the followers. It's generally found that the followers depend upon the leader for most of their reward, praise, authority, communication, and so forth, and thus become leader-centered. Consequently, they vie for his attentions, filter information so that each one will look good in the leader's eyes, let him know only what he wants to hear or at least what they think he wants to hear; they depend on him to tell them what he would like to have done; they tend to resent him and their attitude creates pent-up feelings. The answer to the problem, of course, would be true participation, where all members of the group feel that they're on a team and that no one in particular is in charge. In other words, they all have to realize that they are human beings subject to error, and get along accordingly. As Argyris says, 'Such a leadership philosophy minimizes such leadership roles as pusher, aggressor, director or mover and emphasizes roles such as helper, supporter, clarifier, encourager.'[7]

Classical management principles against human nature

"At this point let's turn to some of the findings uncovered in the last few years concerning classical organizational theory or managerial func-

Rigid chain of command unhealthy

tions and principles as pointed out earlier. First of all, let's review the findings of Dr. Chris Argyris, who recently completed a book integrating the existing research literature relevant to understanding human behavior in the organization.[8] His first observation is that task or work specialization goes against the grain of the average man, who, in effect, would like to use all of his abilities rather than just a few. Remember that the idea of work specialization is to break work down into the smallest fragment that can be studied. The study leads to the best method of doing that particular fragment. Then the man is trained to repeat it over and over again. Obviously, this is a most monotonous operation, yet it is what we find in most of the industrial production lines today. What one can do becomes more important than who one is, and man thus loses his identity in the work situation. This, of course, goes completely against the philosophy of Maslow's need hierarchy, which shows man needing esteem, self-respect and, finally, self-actualization."

It goes against the grain of Tead's teaching also.

"The next observation regards the chain of command. Under this management principle, we have a hierarchy of authority with each person higher in the ladder having the power to reward or penalize those below. This naturally leads to individuals being 'depended upon, passive toward, and subordinate to the leader.' [9] As Argyris points out, this situation is not normal for the healthy adult. It would only be normal to the adolescent. Argyris points out that there are three solutions to this sorry state of affairs. One is rewards in the form of higher pay, position, title, rank, or some other reward. This solution, of course, rewards a person for putting up with the dissatisfaction of the job and assumes that he can find satisfaction outside the work situation. Another solution to this problem would be one in which the leader is so dynamic and technically competent, objective, and rational that the workers look up to him. This, of course, would imply keeping one's personality out of the job, which is virtually impossible. The third solution is to have the subordinates compete with each other and thus be motivated to have more initiative and drive. The fault with this solution is that people aren't necessarily better learners or better workers just because they're in competition with each other.

What are your thoughts on unity of direction?

"Next, he discusses unity of direction. This principle states that each unit in the organization must have a single activity aimed toward a specific goal planned by the leader. This violates the basic psychological analysis of people that a person must define his own goals. Therefore, one would be completely frustrated if he had to forego his needs for those of the unit or organization at all times.

"Finally, under the concept of span of control is the much-discussed principle that one man can only effectively supervise a minimum number of subordinates. Analysis of research on the subject leads Argyris to conclude that 'Span of control to keep the number of subordinates at a minimum will tend to increase the subordinates' feelings of dependence, submissiveness, passivity and the like. Again, these are typical of a work situation which requires immature rather than mature participants.' " [10]

Argyris' point seems well-taken. The February 24, 1973, issue of *Business Week* (page 81) told of organizational change at Kaiser Aluminum: "Indeed, Kaiser had almost a classic form of pyramid management. Since he landed the top spot last July, Maier (the new president) has changed all that and the changes seem to be paying off. One of Maier's first moves was to sweep away the old multilayered management structure and replace it with a 'flat' organization in its purest form. Now, ten operating managers and an equal number of staff specialists report directly to him."

"In concluding the particular section on the formal organization, Argyris points out that its aims and objectives are certainly not in context with the aims and objectives of a normal psychologically healthy individual.

"Another thing basically wrong with classical organizational theory is that apparently it considers the employee as an inert instrument performing the tasks assigned to him in a logical, predictable way at all times rather than considering him as a variable, subject to different ideas and feelings on a day-to-day basis. In other words, classicists ignore individual behavior and, particularly, psychological theories of motivation.

Attitudes about people

"Undoubtedly, many of the problems that occur in organizations and in managing people are the result of the way many managers think of people. These managerial attitudes or assumptions about people have been categorized by Dr. Douglas McGregor. He feels that they are implicit in most management literature and in current management philosophy. He entitles this view of human behavior as Theory X, the traditional view of direction and control. Dr. McGregor states that the assumptions are that

1. The average human being has an inherent dislike of work and will avoid it if he can.
2. Because of this human characteristic of dislike of work, most people must be coerced, controlled, directed, threatened with punishment to get them to put forth adequate effort toward the achievement of organizational objectives.
3. The average human being prefers to be directed, wishes to avoid responsibility, has relatively little ambition, wants security above all." [11]

Based on past lectures it would seem that Theory X assumptions strongly prevailed until at least 1930. In fact, probably many people still hold these convictions today.

"McGregor feels that based upon the accumulation of knowledge about human behavior, it is now possible to formulate another set of generalizations about how management should think of the worker. This he calls Theory Y, which states that

1. The expenditure of physical and mental effort in work is as natural as play or rest.

2. External control and the threat of punishment are not the only means for bringing about effort toward organizational objectives. Man will exercise self-direction and self-control in the service of objectives to which he is committed.

3. Commitment to objectives is a function of the rewards associated with their achievement.

4. The average human being learns, under proper conditions, not only to accept but to seek responsibility.

5. The capacity to exercise a relatively high degree of imagination, ingenuity, and creativity in the solution of organizational problems is widely, not narrowly, distributed in the population.

6. Under the conditions of modern industrial life the intellectual potentialities of the average human being are only partially utilized." [12]

Theory Y assumptions probably did not influence very many managers until after 1960. Between 1930 and 1960, the group–human relations attitude probably held sway.

Which theory do you believe in?

"The implications of Theory Y are fascinating. If managers really believe in Theory Y and the workers adhere to it, then there can be true participation in management because the workers will want to see the organization succeed. They will want to work. They will want to integrate their goals with the goals of the organization. They will wish to be consulted upon changes affecting their operation. They will want to have more meaningful jobs, and they will be motivated from within if the right occupational setting is achieved.

"Luckily, we don't have to guess whether or not McGregor is correct. Dr. Frederick Herzberg has already confirmed this as a result of his study of accountants and engineers in and around Pittsburgh. By a directive questionnaire asking the surveyed individuals to relate an experience or tell about a situation in which they felt exceptionally good about their jobs and also a story about a particular situation in which they did not like or felt badly about their jobs, Herzberg arrived at some interesting conclusions. He found that in the satisfaction stories, achievement, recognition, work itself, responsibility, and advancement were the most often-mentioned characteristics of the situation. On the other hand, in the dissatisfied story situations he found that company policy and administration, supervision and technical aspects, salary, impersonal relationships with the superviser, and working conditions had the highest percentage of mention.[13]

How do you feel about salary?

"The interesting point about the "satisfiers and dissatisfiers," as he called them, is that salary is not nearly as important in the satisfier side as it is in the dissatisfier side. I would presume, of course, that this is after one gets beyond a salary high enough to live on. Obviously, salary is going to be a most important satisfier at the lower economic levels. But beyond that level, what seems to be more important, at least based upon

Herzberg's findings, is the nature of the work itself—the job one does. Apparently this has very little to do with the group, but it certainly has much to do with the self-actualizing need set forth by Dr. Maslow.

"The significance of Herzberg's findings are most important because they back up Argyris' contention that work itself is important and that meaning has to be placed in the job. Argyris reports that job enlargement, wherein the individual is given a greater opportunity to use more of his abilities, increases feelings of satisfaction on the part of employees. In addition to reporting the research findings, Argyris points out himself that 'this type of job enlargement cannot be restricted to the tasks found along the flow of work. The employee must be provided more "power" over his own work environment and therefore he must be given responsibility, authority and increased control over the decision-making that affects his immediate work environment. He must become self-responsible.' "[14]

Job enlargement

Realize here that Argyris is speaking of the manual worker in an industrial setting. However, the same contentions are true for the knowledge worker as substantiated by the December 1972 report of HEW entitled *Work in America*.

"Herzberg also refers to restructuring of jobs, stating, 'First, jobs must be restructured to increase to the maximum the ability of workers to achieve goals meaningfully related to the doing of the job.'[15] He is realistic about the situation, though, when he points out that many jobs probably cannot be made more meaningful. Specifically, I believe he is referring to the assembly-line jobs at the lower level. This would seem to be what he has in mind when he states that 'It may be that for them the good life will have to come from fruitful hobbies and from improved lives outside the job.' "[16]

It is amazing how close this comes to Tead's philosophy.

"But, ladies and gentlemen, consider that over 60 percent of the work force is employed in government and service industries. These people are in a position where work can be made more meaningful. They are not on the assembly line. We can certainly practice participative management and mean it. We can consider the job itself; we can include people and treat them as human beings. And we certainly can, if possible, develop our own philosophies hopefully along the lines of thinking that McGregor calls Theory Y.

"In doing so, we will of necessity concentrate more on the individual man, the work he does, and the work he is capable of doing. We are not, then, looking at man in light of the Protestant Ethic or the Social Ethic, but in terms of what he is capable of doing; the self-actualizing man of Maslow gives rise to what I call the Self-Actualization Ethic.

"Remember, ladies and gentlemen, that we still must consider the functions of management in order to run any business whether it be industry, government, or service. It is necessary to plan, to organize, to direct, and to control. In carrying out these functions, we also have management tools such as mathematics and the computer. However, the way we use the tools and the way we carry out the functions must be tempered with the way we think of people. The way we think, I hope, will be in terms of the Self-Actualization Ethic.

"Thus we have seen a change from the Protestant Ethic to the Social Ethic to the Self-Actualizion Ethic. I certainly think that this latter ethic is most important. I hope that it is the answer to solving some of the work-oriented problems that are taking place today and certainly some that will take place in the future. I am sure that you will look forward to later sessions in this particular course in which we will thoroughly go into the works of Argyris, Herzberg, Simon and March, White, Drucker, McGregor, Roethlisberger and Dickson, and Leavitt, to name but a few. When we've completed our program, I hope you will be able to integrate all the theories to date and devise your own managerial philosophy based upon the organization to which you will eventually become attached."

EPILOGUE

What are they like?

They are the co-workers and supervisors who are in their middle thirties today.

They are well-grounded in classical management theory, the Protestant Ethic, and the Social Man Ethic. They grew up in a permissive society after World War II, and they have really known no poverty. They have been exposed to operations/research techniques and the complex man proposition.

Many have been exposed to the behavioral scientists and Theory Y assumptions—whether they believe them or not we will probably never know. They are willing to change but probably only if they can achieve self-esteem.

EXERCISE QUESTIONS

1. List the behavioral scientists who made the greatest impression during the 1956 to 1960 period. How did they make their contribution?

2. Has the work of Maslow been integrated into the thinking of behavioral scientists of the period? If so, how?

3. How was the work of Simon and March influenced by Maslow, if at all?

4. List Herzberg's satisfiers and dissatisfiers. Explain the significance of each.

5. List the Theory X and Y assumptions of McGregor.

6. What political influences were strong in the 1950s that may have caused a shift in managerial philosophy?

DISCUSSION TOPICS

1. The "self-fulfilling prophecy" is explicit or implied in behavioral science literature. What is it and how is it applied?

2. Compare Argyris and Herzberg as to job enrichment and/or enlargement. Do the terms mean the same thing?

3. What are the basic differences between human relations and behavioral science? How do you feel about them both?

4. Do you agree with the professor's summation of managerial philosophy for 1960?

PROJECTS

1. Solve an employee lack of interest in work problem from:

   a. a 1960 managerial frame of reference.
   b. a 1950 managerial frame of reference.
   c. a 1930 managerial frame of reference.

2. Role-play an interaction situation involving a change in procedures between co-workers (one with a 1960 frame of reference, the other with a 1950 frame of reference).

3. Find an example of a local firm that operates on Theory X assumptions. Compare and contrast it to one in your area that operates on Theory Y assumptions.

4. See if you can find anything in the literature that goes beyond Theory Y. If so, explain.

5. Read McGregor's 1960 book. What else did he have to say about management?

NOTES

1. Ralph C. Davis, *Industrial Organization and Management,* 3rd ed. (New York: Harper and Brothers, 1957).
2. Louis A. Allen, *Management and Organization* (New York: McGraw-Hill Book Co., Inc., 1958).
3. John G. Glover, *Fundamentals of Professional Management* (New York: Simmons Boardman Publishing Corp., 1958), pp. 9–10.
4. See Anthony Jay, *Management and Machiavelli* (New York: Holt, Rinehart & Winston, Inc., 1967). Machiavelli's work, *The Prince,* was published in 1592.
5. Harold Koontz and Cyril O'Donnell, *Principles of Management: An Analysis of Managerial Functions* (New York: McGraw-Hill Book Co., 1955).

6. Chris Argyris, *Executive Leadership* (New York: Harper and Row Publishers, Inc., 1953).
7. Ibid., p. 112.
8. Chris Argyris, *Personality and Organization* (New York: Harper and Row Publishers, Inc., 1957).
9. Ibid., p. 60.
10. Ibid., p. 66.
11. Douglas McGregor, *The Human Side of Enterprise* (New York: McGraw-Hill Book Co., 1960), pp. 33–34.
12. Ibid., pp. 47–48.
13. Frederick Herzberg, Bernard Mausner, Barbara B. Snyderman, *The Motivation to Work* (New York: John Wiley & Sons, Inc., 1959), pp. 81.
14. Argyris, *Personality and Organization,* p. 181.
15. Herzberg et al., *Motivation to Work,* p. 132.
16. Ibid., p. 138.

In addition to the works cited in the footnotes, the following books were available in the period:

Russell L. Ackoff, "The Development of Operations Research as a Science," *Operations Research,* IV (June 1956), 265.

Stafford Beer, *Cybernetics and Management* (New York: John Wiley & Sons, Inc., 1956).

C. West Churchman, Russell L. Ackoff, and E. Leonard Arnoff, *Introduction to Operations Research* (New York: John Wiley & Sons, Inc., 1957).

Peter F. Drucker, *The Practice of Management* (New York: Harper & Brothers, 1954).

Manley H. Jones, *Executive Decision Making* (Homewood, Ill: Richard D. Irwin, Inc., 1957).

Harold J. Leavitt, *Managerial Psychology* (Chicago: University of Chicago Press, 1958).

J. G. March and H. A. Simon, *Organization* (New York: John Wiley & Sons, Inc., 1958).

Paul Pigors and Charles A. Myers, *Personnel Administration* (New York: McGraw-Hill Book Co., 1956).

F. J. Roethlisberger and W. Dickson, *Management and the Worker* (Cambridge: Harvard University Press, 1956).

Herbert A. Simon, *Administrative Behavior: A Study of Decision-*

Making Processes in Administrative Organization, 2nd ed. (New York: The Macmillan Company, 1957).

Ordway Tead, *The Art of Administration* (New York: McGraw-Hill Book Co., 1951).

George R. Terry, *Principles of Management* (Homewood, Ill: Richard D. Irwin, Inc., 1953).

JFK
Betsi

11

The Sixties to the Present

The objectives of this chapter are to enable you to

1. *understand* current managerial philosophy;
2. *identify* the changes in behavioral science thinking since 1960;
3. *appreciate* the situational theory of management action;
4. *develop* your own managerial philosophy.

EPILOGUE

What was it like?

You tell us what it was like. It was the period during which you developed your beliefs, attitudes, and values—the period when your philosophy jelled.

The decade saw the outbreak of the most unpopular war in the history of the country, the Vietnam conflict. The transistorized, miniaturized radio put the spoken word in the earphones of the city streets and the automobiles. Value systems changed, with a cry for social reforms and identity crises with the young. Because of radio and television, it was probably the best-educated generation in the history of any civilization. The Cuban crisis arose and passed. It was a time of turmoil, with the assassinations of President Kennedy, Bobby Kennedy, and Martin Luther King. Campus unrest, strikes and riots added to the turmoil. Questioning government intentions and involvement in Vietnam was accepted. The space program was in full sway and the cold war was beginning to thaw. The youth revolution flourished and the question was always "Why?" Mass production made it possible for the standard of living of the majority of Americans to be the highest in the world and government welfare programs made it almost impossible to starve. It was, indeed, a decade of the affluent society.

Against this background the current lecture is delivered.

"Ladies and gentlemen, if there's one thing certain today, it's that there is no one contemporary managerial philosophy. I know this must

No one managerial philosophy

seem rather disconcerting to you, inasmuch as the title of this course is Contemporary Managerial Philosophy. But before we're finished, I'm sure that you'll see the reason for my statement." Thus began the first lecture in the seminar course in Contemporary Managerial Philosophy by Dr. Curtis—the last course in the business administration curriculum at Tidewater University.

Develop your own

"Because there is no one contemporary managerial philosophy, what I hope you will obtain from this final seminar is enough information from readings and discussions to develop your own managerial philosophy—a philosophy that will guide your actions in carrying out the managerial duties you will be assigned in your first working situation.

"You've all had courses in accounting, marketing, finance, production, business mathematics and statistics, business management and human relations—in fact, some of you have even had senior-level courses in operations research, advertising, and organizational theory. However, you have not had one course that attempts to pull all these different areas of management together into one neat package. To do that very thing is the purpose of this particular course.

"Now, to begin with, let's distinguish between the tools of management and the practice of management. But even before we get into that, let's define the word "management," because you may have found it defined differently in different courses. For the purpose of this course, we'll define it as getting the job done through and with people. Some authorities might well consider this definition as the definition of *administration.* I can't say that I would disagree with them; because if you go back to the original French version of Henri Fayol's *Administration industrielle et générale,* the literal translation is: 'to administrate is to plan, organize, command, coordinate and control.' Of course, you recognize that these are what we call today the functions of management. But, unfortunately, the most common English version of Fayol's work has his word *administration* translated as *management,* and this has pretty well carried forward to today.[1] So, again, for the purposes of this course, we will define management as getting things done through or with people.

Definition of management

Do you agree?

Tools vs. practice

"Now, to distinguish between the tools of and the practice of management, planning things would be a tool of management; statistics, operations research, and other mathematical techniques would be tools of management; accounting, finance, marketing, and advertising all would appear to be tools of management because they assist us in getting the job done through people.

"The practice of management would seem to me to be staffing and directing. By staffing, I mean placing people in the job, with directing being another name for leading.

"At this point you'll probably realize that I haven't mentioned organizing or controlling. If we split the organizational function into the mechanical part of charts, job descriptions, job titles, and so forth, then these are only tools of management. However, the minute we plunk people into the organization we are getting into the practice of management. Thus organization can be a tool of management or one of the practices of management, depending upon your outlook. As far as controlling goes, if using the tools of management is controlling, then it in itself is a tool; if it's controlling by the manipulation of people, then it's part of the practice of management. Although this might seem confusing, I think it is essential to recognize that by our definition of management many of the techniques, methods, and practices you have been exposed to today are only tools of management.

Schools of management thought

"The reason I'm making this distinction is that in much of the literature today we find references to schools of management thought. The word *schools* was probably coined by Harold Koontz in an article entitled, 'The Management Theory Jungle' appearing in the *Journal of the Academy of Management* in December 1961. I'm sure you've read articles that refer to the management theory jungle, so it's interesting to know the source. Basically, Koontz identified six main groups or schools:

How different are they?

the management process school
the empirical school
the human behavioral school
the social systems school
the decision theory school
the mathematical school.

"The management process school of course referred to Koontz' own thinking in his textbook, *Principles of Management: An Analysis of Managerial Functions,* written in conjunction with Cyril O'Donnell.[2] This has been the basic textbook in many courses in management, and presently is in its fifth edition. Basically, the management process school develops the definition of management as I have—that is, the idea of getting things done through and with people operating in organized groups. The process school identifies the management processes or functions as planning, organizing, staffing, directing, and controlling, and carries on Henri Fayol's work as modified by present interpretation. We might also call this the universalist approach because it's contended that the functions of management are universal to all organizations—government, military, service, or industrial. It is only the way in which the functions are carried out that differs from organization to organization."

This was also Fayol's viewpoint.

"The second school—the empirical one—makes use of case studies for analysis and interpretation. Cases are so devised that students recognize management problems and arrive at logical solutions. By analyzing enough varied cases, the student gains an appreciation of what is required by successful managers under as many situations as possible.

"The human behavioral school was interpreted by Koontz as human relations or behavioral science. It makes use of psychology and sociology to understand the people side of management. Now to my mind, there's a difference between human relations and behavioral science; but we'll discuss that a little later on.

"The social system school was considered that which concentrated on the interaction of groups and the cooperation between groups. Sociological theory was considered to be the backbone of this school.

"The decision theory school was considered to be a school of management thought, probably fathered by Herbert A. Simon in his work on the decision-making process in administrative organizations.[3]

"Finally, the mathematical school was viewed as including all the mathematical, statistical, and operations research techniques available to solve management problems.

"The reason I bring these up is because in reading some of your management books, you will find reference to the quantitative school, the human relations school, the behavioral science school, and the management process school—these are among the most common—and also perhaps the social systems school. Accordingly, I want you to be familiar with the terms.

General systems theory

Is it really a theory or just good common sense?

"Another school which Koontz had not considered when he wrote his article in 1961 is the general systems theory school. This school, began by Bertalanffy, tells us that we must study the organization as a whole, that the organization has an equilibrium state and is affected by its environment and, in turn, affects its environment.[4] In essence, we have to consider the whole organization, its internal and external environment—the relationship of all the parts—with a realization that often an action involving one part affects other parts in some way. Consider, for example, a purchasing department which would like to buy steel by the carload in order to reduce the unit price. From the purchasing department's point of view, this would be a logical approach. However, from an overall management standpoint, it must be determined whether the company has facilities to store that amount of steel, whether the controller's department has the funds to pay for the steel when received, and whether the engineering department wants to commit itself to that quantity of steel. This is an example of the internal system interaction. As an example of external system interaction, consider a company contemplating a switch to a four-day, forty-hour week. From the internal standpoint, it looks fine, but how about the company's customers? Can they accept orders over a four-day period that they are used to receiving over a five-day period? Also, how about the company's suppliers? Are they geared to supply in four days what they are normally used to supplying in five days? Again, in this situation, how about the transportation company? Does it have enough busses available during the revised four-day week to take care of the traffic problem? From this example, it's obvious that, in taking the systems approach, this particular company would have to consider the external system as well as the internal system.

Management thought, management functions, management principles—a semantic jungle

"Now when we consider that these are just the different schools of management thought and that in addition to management functions we have the management principles such as unity of command, span of control, the scalar chain, specialization of labor, and others, we begin to see the semantic jungle that confuses everyone. Thus, to get back to my original point, there is no one contemporary managerial philosophy. In view of this, what I would like to review with you is some of the changes that have taken place over the last few years to show you their impact on the various functions of management and, in particular, on our thinking about the practice of management—getting the job done through people.

"First of all, I'd like to give you *my* thinking on the subject. I don't believe there is any one school of management thought. Now this may bother you in view of your readings in the management area, especially in such textbooks as Koontz and O'Donnell, Terry, Dale, Haynes and Massie and others; but look at it this way. The minute anyone decides to do something, he must plan. He has to decide what he wants to do, how he's going to do it, if it will take anyone to help him other than himself, how much money it will take, if money is a factor. In other words, he has to consider all the things that must be done to accomplish his objective. In the most elementary undertaking, once the planning is done, a person by himself can carry out his plan. However, he usually finds that this isn't possible. He finds that he will need someone to help him. Thus, an organization is formed—two or more people working together to achieve a common objective. The minute an organization is formed, it must be decided who is going to do what (again, let's just consider the two people), who is going to make decisions in what areas, how the work will progress, and how the two will work together. They must also decide which one, when the chips are down, is going to have the final say.

Interaction of the plan and the organization

"With the advent of the organization we may have to go back and alter the plan, because now the plan must include two people where before it perhaps only included one. Of course, you realize that in a large operation the plan includes many people, as does the organization. But there always must be an *interaction* back and forth.

"Next, of course, we must have direction. Someone has to have the final say, and someone has to give the orders; hopefully, the two people in our first organization have agreed as to who will give the orders. Actually, the giving of orders or the directing stage must occur in any group effort.

"Finally, some type of control must be exercised so that we know if the objective is being achieved and if not, what can be done to achieve it.

"Therefore, it seems obvious to me that no matter who is doing what, there must be planning, organizing, directing, and controlling. However, the thing that differs is how these particular functions are carried out depending upon the organization and the situation."

PLANNING

Planning need not involve people

"Now let's go back and look at planning. I think I made it rather clear in my little example that planning either can or can not involve people. You can plan an operation without people, but you certainly can't organize people without a plan. In planning, we can make use of statistics, charts, graphs, quantitative analyses, PERT, and all sorts of sophisticated

Changing concepts of planning

mathematical and electronic methods. How, then, can there be a quantitative school when mathematical techniques at this stage are only used to assist us in planning?

"Another aspect of planning is that it must involve more factors today than it did say fourteen or twenty years ago. Traditionally, planning involved only economic and technological consideration. Today, however, planning must also involve social and political considerations. Planning for nuclear reactors is a perfect example of a situation in which all four factors must be taken into consideration. Ecology groups have made loud noises about thermal pollution, thus delaying construction of many reactors. Government, also, has changed regulations which, in turn, have caused delays in the nuclear power industry. The supersonic transport project is another example of political and social aspects far outweighing the technological and economic factors involved in future planning.

Is the concept that people *must* be considered in planning new?

"The behavioral scientists also give us an input into planning by telling us that it is essential that we now consider people. As an example, we're finding more and more unrest within industry with the production line and with the monotonous jobs in many plants. The problems have been written up in *Fortune, Newsweek,* and many other publications. In fact, the term 'Lordstown Syndrome' was coined to describe the condition existing at the GM Vega plant, where the workers were so concerned with the monotonous repetitive work that it became one of the negotiation points in the next contract. 'Blue Collar Blues on the Assembly Line,' an article in the July 1970 *Fortune,* also discusses the same thing—workers' unhappiness with the job that they have to do."

Does this sound familiar? It should! Refer back to the discussion of Tead's instincts in Chapter 7.

"Another example of this particular factor and its influence on planning was cited in a newspaper article concerning the new Volvo assembly plant under construction at Kalmar, Sweden.[5] The plant is constructed in the form of a five-pointed star with each section isolating a part of the assembly process (such as electrical or transmission work). There are no standard conveyor belts. Work teams of ten to twenty-five men, operating under the group principles already in use at this particular plant, have car bodies coming to them on self-propelled carriages. The groups control their work pace with a stockpiling system that will let a series of car bodies accumulate at their work station if they choose. About 600 men are expected to turn out about 30,000 cars a year for the same cost as a standard assembly line. Of course, one of the company spokesmen has been quoted as saying that this is a risk investment that is costing about $2.5 million more than building a standard factory. He went on to say that the company expects problems. 'Not everyone will be able to learn everything. Our psychologists tell us that groups will be unequal and there will be human difficulties, but we are convinced we'll have people who like, or at least don't hate, their jobs. And that is something.'

"This same plant had already experimented with having teams of two or more members completely assemble car engines rather than using the assembly-line practice in effect until that time. Of course, the experiment was only conducted with a small number of workers, but officials report that productivity is the same while absenteeism and turnover is reduced. It would appear that perhaps overall productivity has not decreased but perhaps productivity per unit worker might have. This is possible in considering the fact that absenteeism and turnover improvement allows a longer period of time per worker while still maintaining overall productivity rates.

"It's obvious, then, that planning can no longer be done without considering people. One plans for an objective, and that objective can only be achieved by a person—in the majority of the cases more than one person. Therefore, people must be considered. Of course, the minute we consider people in the planning side, then we are also considering organization; because to carry out the plan involves, as I mentioned, more than one person. When this occurs, we have to organize in order to carry out the plan. Organization in this case involves setting up some type of a structure so that the people can work together to carry out the planned objective."

ORGANIZING

"Traditionally, the first organizations were probably the military type with the straight-line organization in which *A* reports to *B* reports to *C* reports to *D* reports to *E* right up to the top leader. The next historical change was probably the line/staff organization, in which the staff of experts helped the managers at different levels of the organization. Of course we still find this today in the accounting, controllership, legal, advertising, and marketing departments, considered staff functions of most organizations. Another innovation is what is called the functional type of organization in which one segment has functional responsibility over other segments. An example of this would be the accounting department that has functional authority over all other departments as to how they will prepare their budgets and their cost sheets. Of course all of the above-named organizational types eventually led to the strict bureaucratic type of organization with its rigid chain of command and very formal lines of authority. Bennis lists the functions of the formal bureaucracy as

Bureaucracy was the rule

1. A division of labor based upon functional specialization
2. A well-defined hierarchy of authority
3. A system of rules covering the rights and duties of employees
4. A system of procedures for dealing with work situations
5. Impersonality of interpersonal relations
6. Promotion and selection based upon technical competence.[6]

Bennis also goes on to list the criticisms of bureaucracy, to wit:

1. Bureaucracy does not adequately allow for personal growth and the development of mature personalities.

The demise of Weberian bureaucracy

2. It develops conformity and group-think.

3. It does not take into account the informal organization and the emergent and unanticipated problems.

4. Its systems of control and authority are hopelessly outdated.

5. It has no adequate judicial process.

6. It does not possess adequate means for resolving differences and conflicts among ranks and, most particularly, among functional groups.

7. Communication (and innovative ideas) are thwarted or distorted because of hierarchical divisions.

8. The full human resources of bureaucracy are not being utilized because of mistrust, fear of reprisal, etc.

9. It cannot assimilate the influx of new technology or scientists entering the organization.

10. It will modify the personality structure such that man will become and reflect the dull, gray, conditioned 'organization man.' [7]

Do you agree?

As a result of the criticisms of the bureaucracy, Bennis can see the demise of the bureaucracy and a new form of organizational structure taking its place.

What will replace bureaucracy?

"I certainly would agree with Dr. Bennis that we are seeing the end of the bureaucracy with all the characteristics listed by him. However, I believe that some kind of formal structure is going to be required whenever men work together. Of course, we're seeing different organizational groupings take place. One is matrix management as practiced by TRW Inc.

Matrix Management

"The matrix involves both permanent and temporary lines of authority. When the two lines of authority meet, of course, there are inherent conflicts. Ideally, organizational development applications of behavioral science techniques can keep the communication channels open, minimizing the difficulties that result. Actually, the system looks something like this." Here the professor turned to the board and chalked up Figure 1. "The manager of laboratory B1 may agree, for example, at the start of project Y that the project manager is the 'boss' of departments III, IV, and V as far as work on his project (Y) is concerned. The laboratory manager also lends people from his lab to be managers who report to project Y's manager and recruit expertise from a number of departments including departments I or VI in other divisions. Under the matrix management, an engineer in department III may work on several project teams at once and have any number of bosses. For instance, he may work for subproject manager Y1 and project manager Y as well as for the head of project X in another division.[8]

Other organizational types

"The matrix management technique is just one of many in which we see the decline of the rigid bureaucracy. We are reading about the beehive, the donut, the bell, the supergriddle, and the ladder as organizational structures that are being used to overcome the inadequacies of the pyramid—the most faithful of all hierarchical designs.[9] CIT Financial Corporation has adopted a circular organizational structure which has been called a donut. The president and the vice-president sit in the middle, and the outside ring consists of the heads of all the staff departments, none of which is shown as being subordinate to any particular vice-president in

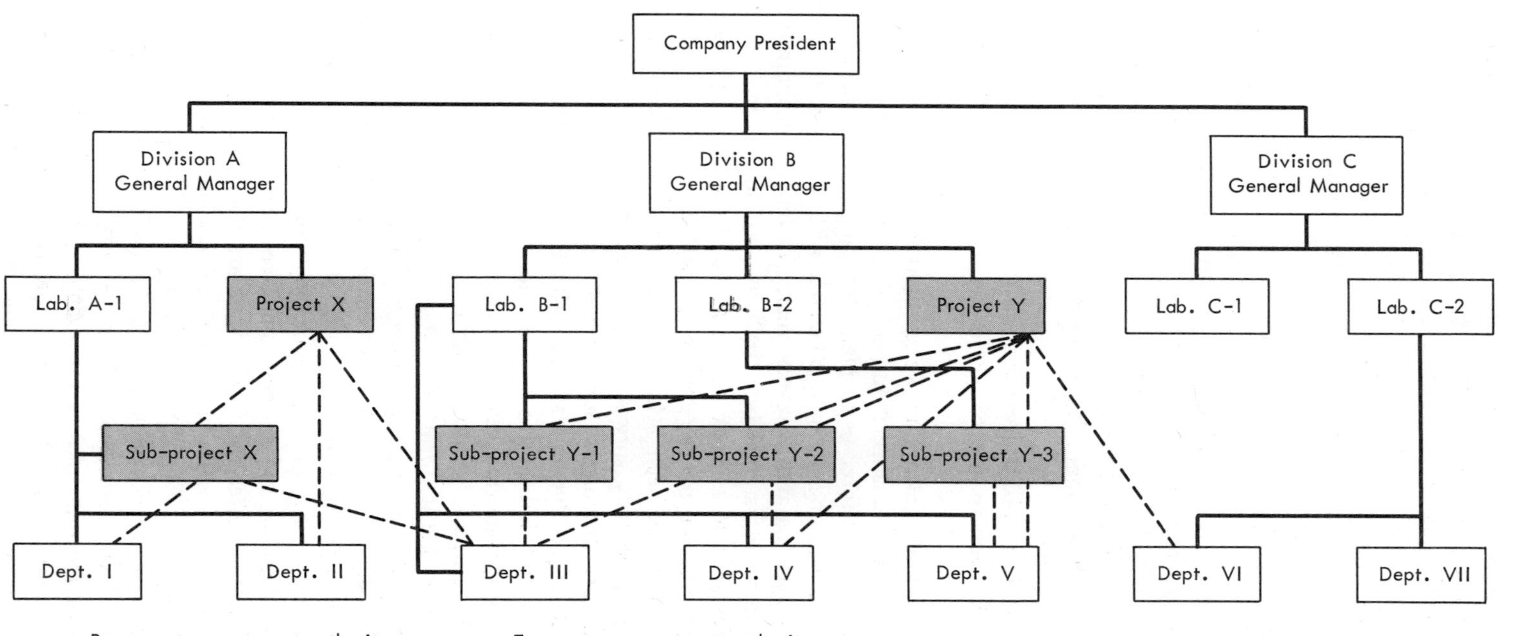

FIGURE 1
Matrix Operation

© *Business Week*, **March 20, 1971. With permission.**

the center circle. Outside the ring the various divisions and subsidiary companies are located, again, not connected to any particular operating department. Actually, what the chart is intended to show is that there is a high degree of interchange between managers of every level and freedom to talk and exchange communication throughout the organization. The other names are again simply ways to try to depict the dynamic aspects of how an organization works and the personal interrelationships among the people in the organization.

The circular concept

"In considering organizational types, it's interesting to note that Chester Barnard, himself, gave an opinion that organizations are best regarded as circular or spherical with the chief executive position in the center. He further states, 'I have, however, followed the conventional figures here because they are well established, and because there appears to be no practicable way to diagram the system of authoritative communication that does not result in a "pyramid." Probably all spatial figures for organization are seriously misleading; but if they are used to cover the functioning of organizations as distinguished from their structural aspects, either the center of a circle or of a sphere better suggests the relationships.' [10] I would certainly agree.

The temporary organization

"In any case, no matter how we envision the organizational structure, it certainly is going to change if for no other reason than that the rapid pace of life is going to force us to plan for change. As Toffler points out, knowledge is accelerating at an exponential rate. One out of every five Americans changes his address every year. We have a temporary society wherein allegiance to fraternal organizations and clubs is more important now than allegiance to a work organization. As a result, we will have temporary organizations put together for a specific purpose then disbanded when the purpose has been achieved.[11] Under these conditions a rigid hierarchy cannot possibly survive. In place of permanence, we have to think of temporary structures. Our organizations cannot be rigid and fixed but must be fluid and dynamic to cope with today's modern society.

Flexibility is a must

"Another point that must not be overlooked in considering organization structure is the informal organization which can be a help or a hindrance depending upon the use we make of it as managers. At least we have to remember that its formation is based upon companionship, understanding from friends, a desire to belong and to be helped in solving work problems. Actually, the informal organization consists of all the interrelationships among people that are not officially established by the organizational chart or by job descriptions. Although we can't design our formal organization around the informal, because the informal doesn't come into being until after the formal slots are filled with people, we can make the formal loose or flexible enough so that the informal—we know it will develop—can be used for the betterment of the organization as a whole. In other words, it can be used to facilitate formal work, to fill in the gaps in the formal structure, add to the span of control, compensate for violations of the principles of management, provide an informal communications channel, make the organization as a whole a better place or a more enjoyable place to work, and allow managers to be more sensitive

The importance of the informal organization

to the feelings of the individuals.[12] This, in essence, is what we want when we organize; and by realizing that the informal organization can accomplish this, we may achieve our purpose.

"Now you certainly see that this is an entirely different attitude toward organization than that which existed as little as fifteen to twenty years ago. However, I'm afraid that the old attitude still exists, particularly in the Civil Service—at least, in my opinion it does. Here we find job titles and job descriptions and whole departments that are engaged in writing out detailed practices and procedures. It would seem that in many cases this stifles individuality and growth rather than fostering a viable organizational system. However, as I said before, this is a personal opinion, and perhaps those who have had long attachments with the Civil Service system would not agree with me.

No one best way to organize

"At any rate, what I want you all to realize is that there is no one best type of organization, just as there is no one best managerial philosophy. If you are placed in a position where you must build up an organization, then do so by allowing the most flexibility possible and the most opportunity for employees to actually participate in the management process. This is assuming, of course, that you have asked them whether they want to participate; some people would rather be told what to do so they do not have to think.

"The changes in organizational philosophy and thinking that I have mentioned are a result of behavioral scientists' thinking. Significantly the findings have proved McGregor's Theory Y assumptions about people:

1. The expenditure of physical and mental effort in work is as natural as play and rest.
2. External control and threat of punishment are not the only means for bringing about effort toward organizational objectives. Man will exercise self-direction and self-control in the service of objectives to which he is committed.
3. Commitment to objectives is a function of the rewards associated with their achievement.
4. The average human being learns, under proper conditions, not only to accept but to seek responsibility.
5. The capacity to exercise a relatively high degree of imagination, ingenuity, and creativity in the solution of organizational problems is widely, not narrowly, distributed in the population.
6. Under the conditions of modern industrial life, the intellectual potentialities of the average human being are only partially utilized." [13]

McGregor's theories were covered in Chapter 10. Theory Y is repeated here for emphasis and comparison. Its importance cannot be overstressed.

"We need to allow people to develop as much as possible, to determine their own best way of carrying out their general responsibilities, and to participate in decisions affecting them. These things certainly must be kept in mind when implementing an organizational structure and certainly must be kept in mind in the planning stage. Thus it is most difficult to distinguish between planning and organization.

Is behavioral science a school of management?

"Now at this point, do you see that it is almost impossible to say that there is a behaviorial science school and not discuss any other aspects of management? No, behavioral science is a tool in carrying out the planning and the organization side of management itself. It has had its greatest contribution, however, in the next area of management, that of directing.

"Before considering directing, however, one last word on planning and organizing. We must never forget 'that the actual physical task of carrying out an organization's objectives falls to the persons at the lowest level of the administrative hierarchy. The automobile, as a physical object, is built not by the engineer or the executive but by the mechanic on the assembly line. The fire is extinguished not by the fire chief or the captain but by the team of firemen who play a hose in the blaze.' "[14]

DIRECTING

"Now let's go on to directing as the third and perhaps most important aspect of getting the job done through people. Directing is the function of management that initiates action. Up till now we planned what we wanted to do considering the people side. We've drawn up a structure that we feel will get the job done, including the people side from the behavioral science point of view. Now we actually have to direct the people in their efforts to achieve the common objective.

Direction and leadership styles

"Traditionally, direction has involved leadership and leadership styles. Today we're also finding that direction involves providing the climate for the individual to be motivated. Nevertheless, many people still feel that directing involves leadership styles alone and that leadership characteristics or skills are attitudes that can be acquired. Moreover, some individuals think that leadership is a character trait. Fortunately or unfortunately, as the case may be, leadership has been found not to be a property of the individual but a complex relationship among the characteristics of the leader, the attitudes, needs, and personal characteristics of the followers, the characteristics of the organization, and the social, economic, and political situation at the time.[15]

The three basic leadership styles

"You have certainly completed enough readings in management, though, to realize that there are basically three types of leaders—the autocratic, participative, and the laissez-faire. Other terms, of course, have been used such as authoritarian or leader-centered for autocratic, democratic for participative, and free reign for laissez-faire. But in any case, three types are commonly recognized. Any of you who took my principles course last year will remember that I recognized four types of leaders—the exploitive-authoritative (type 1), the benevolent-authoritative (type 2), the consultative (type 3), and the participative (type 4). These four types are identical to Likert's systems of organizations and are based upon management's assumption about people, as we will discuss later on in this lecture.[16]

"In connection with leadership styles, research results tell us that people react differently to different styles—that in the majority of cases the authoritative type of leadership does not work as well as the consultative or participative group. With these results in mind, several techniques of leadership development have been devised during the past few years. The first is the managerial grid technique. The second is sensitivity or T-group training, which actually began in 1947 when the National Education Association joined the Research Center for Group Dynamics in a pioneering effort in re-education through the workings of face-to-face groups.

The development of the managerial grid

"The grid development grew out of the belief of Dr. Robert R. Blake, formerly a professor of psychology at the University of Texas and a trainer for National Training Laboratories, that there existed in the minds of many managers a conflict between concern for production and concern for people.[17] If a manager really had to produce, then he couldn't be that involved with people problems. On the other hand, if he were involved in solving people problems, then production or output most assuredly would fall off. Blake's idea was that concern for people and concern for production were complementary, that you could have both and that the solution lay in pointing out to managers how this could be possible. As a result, the grid developed. You will find this as Figure 2.

Does it really help?

"The idea behind the grid is that a manager can locate himself; then, based upon the detailed descriptions of the five principle positions—that is, the four corners and the middle—he can move toward a position that will integrate concern for people and concern for production. Most managers in government and service industries today probably fall in the 5, 5 bracket. The ultimate, of course, is 9, 9; if possible, managers should take steps to achieve this objective.

Sensitivity training

"Sensitivity training, or T-group training, as it is sometimes called, is an attempt to have people examine themselves and see each other as they really are—in other words, how they function as actual human beings. Typical T-groups are of two kinds—one wherein group members, usually ten to twelve, are members of different organizations and do not know each other; the second where members are from the same organization—usually of the higher-echelon management group. In either case there is no agenda or list of topics for discussion. There is no established goal or objective other than interpersonal and group learning. There is no common chairman or discussion leader. In the T-group sessions in which people come from different companies, participants are without hierarchical status."

This appears to be an attempt to teach interaction. However, we are still of the opinion expressed in the preface. Interaction cannot be taught—but it can be learned.

"Chris Argyris, in one of the BNA Communications, Inc., training films, describes a typical T-group session with top executives from the same company. They were to meet all day Friday to explore sensitivity training. Argyris was the trainer—the professional paid group leader. Normally, when this particular group met, there would be an agenda prepared by one of the staff men and the president would go down the agenda and

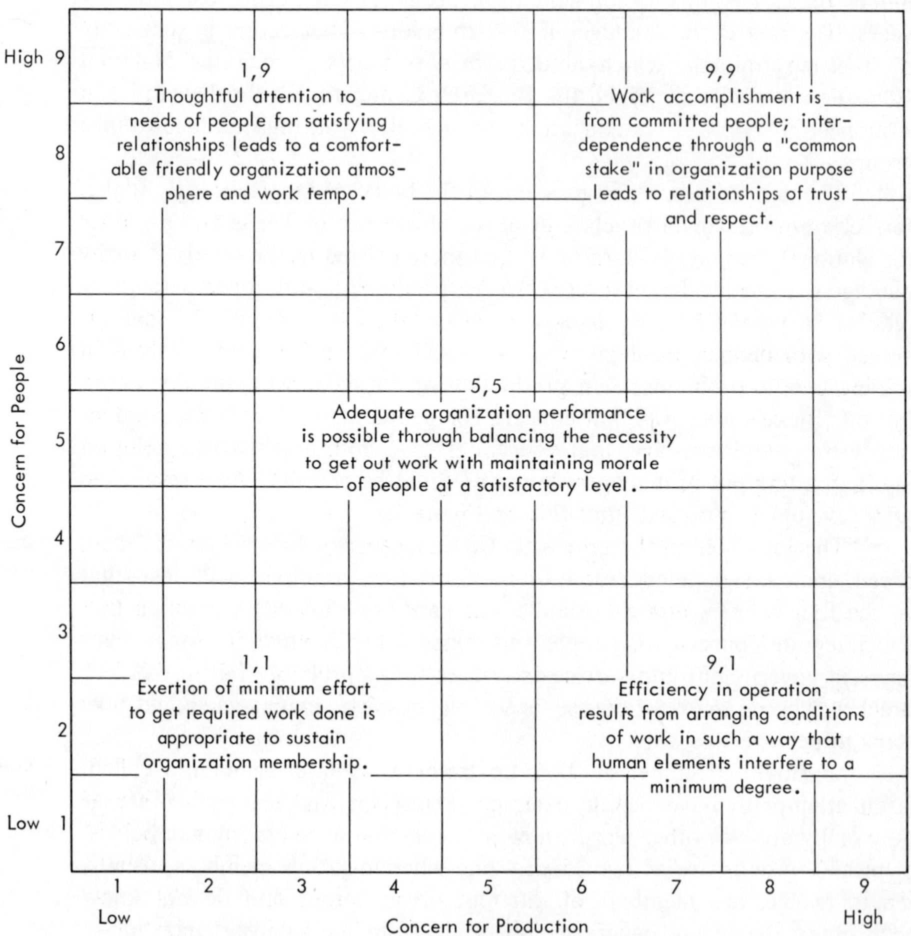

FIGURE 2

The Managerial Grid ®

Copyright, R. R. Blake & J. S. Mouton, and Gulf Publishing Co., Houston, Texas. Reproduced by special permission.

things would be discussed in order. At this particular meeting all were assembled when Dr. Argyris walked in. However, he didn't say anything. There was dead silence. After a few minutes, one of the members of the group asked for the agenda. Again, more silence. After another few minutes, one of the individuals pushed back his chair with a remark, 'Well, if nothing is going to get done, I'm going to go back to my office because I certainly have a lot of work to do.' At this point, the controller stated that a considerable amount of money had been spent for this particular day; and as far as he was concerned, everybody was going to stay there until five o'clock. After another period of silence, one of the members stated that he felt a little funny with nothing happening. At this point, another one said, 'I feel a little fearful.' This brought forth a remark by the vice-president to the effect that it was interesting that this comment had been made, because he felt that the company was run on a basis of making people a little fearful. The president interjected with, 'I don't think we run this company that way, and I don't think you should have said that.' Argyris says that at this point he was about to interject the thought that the president was not being open and accepting remarks from the employees, but the president cut him off with the remark that he saw what he was doing. The president then turned to the vice-president, saying that he had been waiting quite a few years to hear one of the staff discuss how he really felt about the running of the company; and now when someone did make such a remark, he, the president, cut him off completely. After this, the group relaxed and was able to explore feelings about the company and each other.

"Now, of course, this is the ideal condition. Many times people are not honest—in fact, it is the exception rather than the rule. The specific pattern people develop which certainly affects their leadership style and their ability to communicate is brought out in Argyris' new book on organizational development.[18] He defines organizational development as vitalizing, energizing, actualizing, activating, and renewing of organizations through technical and human resources. Technical development is achieved through areas of marketing, finance, engineering, and manufacturing. Human resource development concerns people, interpersonal relationships, small groups, intergroups, and organizational norms and values.[19] He then goes on to make a study of three companies, one that was deciding to incorporate organizational development (OD), one that had incorporated OD and had a few years experience, and one that had incorporated OD for quite a few years and had considerable experience. Unfortunately, in all three companies, he noticed the same behavioral pattern. Rarely, and in most cases never, were individuals and groups observed expressing feelings, being open to feelings, or experimenting with ideas or feelings. Rarely observed were feelings of concern and trust. Also rarely observed were individuals helping each other be open and experimenting with ideas or feelings. In other words, most individuals do not say what they really feel about important issues if they think that these ideas might be threatening to any other member. They prefer to be diplomatic and careful and not make waves. Their concern is with conforming and taking the 'I' position. This, of course, was the behavioral pattern that was evidenced at the beginning of the T-group sensitivity training session. If we are honest with ourselves, it is probably the same behavioral pattern that most of us exhibit in dealing with other people in an organization. However, if we really want to develop the proper atmosphere in which employees will be motivated to do their best work, we'll have to make a conscientious, honest effort to change."

Most people hide their true feelings, making honest interaction difficult

Again, successful interaction is difficult to achieve and requires real effort.

"This logically leads into the question of 'why change?' If we're the boss, why not just tell people exactly what to do in detail, hold them to it, and if they don't do it, use the threat of punishment, firing, no raise, or another threat in order to gain compliance. Well, obviously, many studies have shown that this type of leadership doesn't work in any organization. It's based upon the assumptions about people that McGregor calls Theory X rather than assumptions based upon the Theory Y outlook—more truly representing the majority of people today. This isn't to say that everybody should be treated with an X philosophy or everybody should be treated with a Y philosophy. However, generally speaking, in the past most philosophies have been X-oriented where they probably should have been Y-oriented. Edgar H. Schein brings out this point very well in his book entitled *Organizational Psychology*. He recognized four types of people based upon the assumptions of management. First would be the rational economic man based upon McGregor's Theory X assumptions. These assumptions lead to the philosophy that 'the organization is buying the services and the obedience of the employee for economic rewards, and the organization assumes the obligation of protecting itself and the employee from the irrational side of his nature by a system of authority and control. Authority rests essentially in designated offices or positions and the employee is expected to obey whoever occupies a position of authority regardless of his expertise or personality.' [20]

Many people have an X philosophy—do you?

Rational economic man

Social man

"The next assumption would be that of social man as evidenced by the Hawthorne Studies, Mayo, and subsequent interviews with workers in industry. The assumptions of man that Mayo developed are different from those assumptions leading to the rational economic man theory and are:

Do you have this philosophy?

1. Man is basically motivated by social needs and obtains his basic sense of identity through relationships with others.
2. As a result of the Industrial Revolution and the rationalization of work, meaning has gone out of work itself and must therefore be sought in the social relationships in the job.
3. Man is more responsive to the social forces of the peer group than to the incentives and controls of management.
4. Man is responsive to management to the extent that a supervisor can meet a subordinate's social needs and needs for acceptance.[21]

Is man really this important?

"Based upon these assumptions, Schein tells us that the manager needs to pay more attention to the needs of the people rather than the specific task that must be performed; that he needs to be more concerned about people's feelings regarding acceptance, belonging, and identity rather than to be concerned with controlling the subordinates; that managers need to think about group incentives rather than individual incentives; and finally, that the manager's role shifts from the functions of management—that is, planning, organizing, directing, and controlling—to acting as an intermediary between men and higher management. Now remember, this is only one view of man based upon the social man aspect of Mayo and is only the opinion of one man, Dr. Schein, in stating what managerial strategies would be implied from Mayo's assumptions.

Self-actualizing man

"Schein's third way of looking at man is to classify him as the self-actualizing man. He states that the assumptions that are implied about the nature of man under the self-actualizing concept are that (1) man's motives fall into classes which are arranged in a hierarchy, (2) man seeks to be mature on the job and is capable of being so, (3) man is primarily self-motivated and self-controlled, and (4) there is no inherent conflict between self-actualization and more effective organizational performance.[22] The implied managerial strategy in this case is not whether the employee can fulfill his social needs, but whether he can find in his work meaning that gives him a sense of pride and self-esteem. Authority in this case would shift from the office or the man to the task itself.

Is this a realistic assumption?

Complex man

"Finally, he ends with a concept of complex man which, in my opinion, is the best way of looking at man. The assumption in this case is that man is not only complex but highly variable. He has many motives arranged in shifting hierarchies. He is capable of learning new things and thus developing new patterns of behavior. His motives vary in different organizations and at different periods of time. Finally, man can respond to many different kinds of managerial strategies.[23]

But man is unique and does not always conform to a specific theory

"This, to me, means that there is no one particular assumption that will work with all individuals, nor is there any one particular management strategy, tactic, or device that will. In other words, if we think of man as an individual, then we have to assume that some people do fall into a Theory X category, some people do fall into a Theory Y category, and many people fall somewhere in between. Some people do not want to participate or be consulted in the matter of decision making, while other people would like to have full participation and be consulted in all cases. In other words, how you lead, how you get along, and how you react must be based upon the individual and the circumstances. Because these are changing at all times, we would expect that managerial strategies and styles must also change to fit the circumstances.

"Now before discussing this particular aspect of changing managerial styles in more depth, let's consider the specific motivating principles brought out in the studies by Herzberg and Argyris.

"In 1959 Dr. Herzberg published with other authors the results of studies concerning accountants and engineers in the Pittsburgh area in a book entitled *The Motivation to Work*.[24] The results of this study were based upon the analysis of stories told by the 200 participants in the survey. They were asked to think of a situation that made them feel exceptionally good or bad about their job—in other words, a situation in which they felt satisfied or happy and a situation that made them feel dissatisfied or unhappy. As a result of these stories, the authors were able to identify the factors that appeared most often in the satisfying story episodes and the factors that appeared most often in the dissatisfying story

Refer to Chapter 10

instances. The results are shown in your handout at Figure 3 and show a most interesting trend. Achievement, recognition, work itself, responsibility, and advancement showed the highest percentage in the satisfying stories. Company policy and administration, supervision, salary, interpersonal relationships, and working conditions appeared the highest percentage of

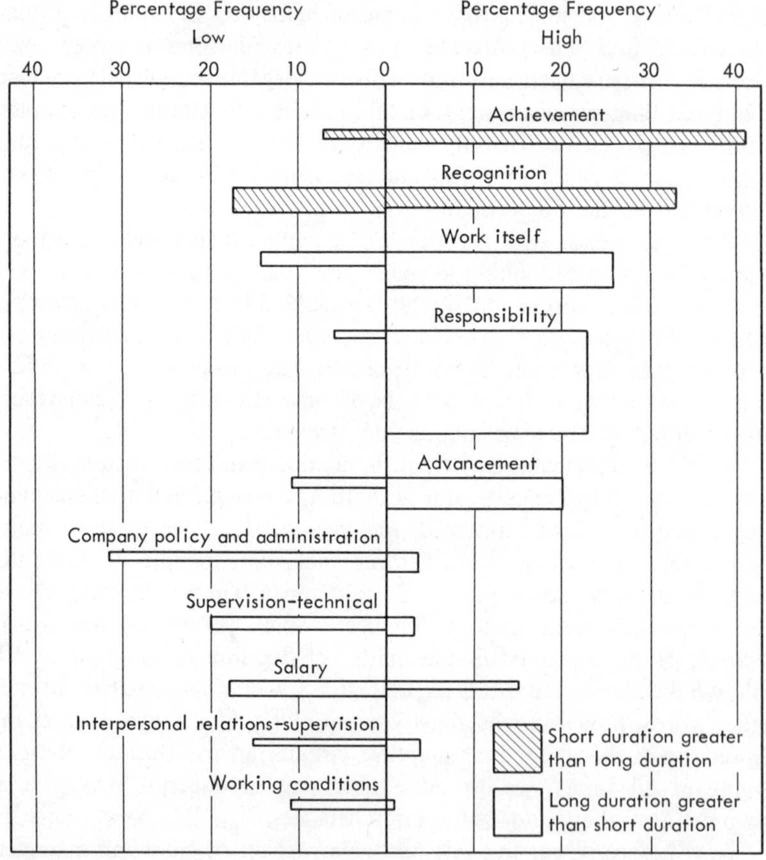

FIGURE 3
Comparison of Satisfiers and Dissatisfiers

From: Frederic Herzberg, Bernard Mausner, and Barbara Snyderman, *The Motivation to Work* (New York: John Wiley & Sons, Inc., 1967), p. 81. Reprinted with permission.

times in the dissatisfying stories. The conclusions drawn from the studies were obvious. A person is more interested in what he does—the content of the job itself—the responsibility, recognition, and achievement he gets from the job rather than company policy and administration, salary, working conditions, and other side effects. In other words, the work itself is most important. A *man cannot* then *be motivated* to do a better job.

Motivation

Motivation must come from within. This is, of course, in keeping with the dictionary definition, which states that motivate 'is to provide with a motive' and that motive is 'something that prompts a person to act in a certain way.' The dictionary goes on to point out that 'motive is applied mainly to an inner urge that moves or prompts a person to action.'[25] Thus, motivation comes from within and the job of the manager is to create an atmosphere or a climate in which a man can be motivated to do his best work. This leads to job enlargement and job enrichment.

Job enrichment

"On the assembly line in particular, ways are being sought in which the worker can be more involved in the job. In addition to the Swedish example cited earlier, *Fortune* reported that the Corning Glass Works Plant in Medfield, Massachusetts, is incorporating job enrichment by having employees put meters together entirely on their own from beginning to end, including inspecting and packaging. This has done away with the old assembly-line basis and enlarged the job so that the workers can take pride in what they do. Another example—Precision Cast Parts has reduced its reject rates on castings from 24 percent to 7 percent by allowing workers to decide how the castings will be made.[26]

Management by objectives

"The whole behavioral science field is leading us toward different styles of management as well as different techniques to get the job done through people. Management by objectives is one approach that has been given considerable publicity of late.[27] In MBO, objectives are mutually arrived at and agreed to between the supervisor and the subordinate. The system usually starts at the top of an organization with the board of directors or the president deciding upon the objective for a particular unit for the year. The president then gets together with his operating executives, vice-presidents, or department heads and goes over the one objective. Each one sees what his part must be and decides whether he can meet his subobjective. In other words, the subobjectives are arrived at mutually between the top executive and his staff. Then each staff member, in this case a department head, meets with his lower-echelon supervisors to determine what further objectives each lower unit must meet in order to contribute successfully to meeting the overall objective. In this manner each supervisor and subordinate works out objectives that can be reached and can be met by the working unit. The purpose behind MBO is that if the group is committed to the objective, the chances of reaching it are greater than if it is simply established on a one-way basis from top down. (It is important to note that the objectives have to be measurable.) If it appears somewhere during the work cycle that they are not going to be met, the subordinate should immediately bring this to the attention of the supervisor so that they can sit down and decide what action must be taken. It is a system that must be based upon mutual trust and openness among individuals or it will not achieve its purpose. If MBO is based on a reward-punishment basis or as a basis of management appraisal, then the system will fail. The reward-punishment psychology serves to intensify the pressure on the individual while really giving him a very limited choice of

Should MBO be used for performance appraisal?

objectives. He is continuously on the defensive and does not feel that the organization has a genuine interest in having him meet his goals but is using the objective to 'rap him on the knuckle' if he doesn't succeed.[28]

Participative management vs. participation in management

"Participative management is another technique advocated by the behavioral scientists. It's the system 4 style of Likert and is geared toward involving the personnel of the organization in the decisions that must be made. However, I believe that we should distinguish between participative management and participation in management. Participation in management could be construed to be the situation in which the group gets together, and the leader asks for opinions concerning decisions that have to be made, manner of conducting work, and so forth. Members of the group give their opinions, and the leader then makes his decision, weighing comments by the group. This, to me, is participation in management.

"True participative management would be the situation in which the employees actually decide among themselves what the decision will be and how they will carry out certain projects. The decision is the consensus of the group or the majority opinion and all are committed because it represents the combined thinking of the group. This is true participative management and should certainly commit the group to supporting the action taken by the supervisor who, in the long run, has to be the one to carry out the actions of the group. I am probably making the distinction here between the consultative and participative group form of Likert. However, in much of my reading in managerial journals, I find that often participative management and participation in management become confused.

The organization climate

"If we use the systems approach in directing, we also must consider the organizational climate as discussed by Lippitt, et al.[29] We must consider that our directing style not only affects the particular group with which we are involved but other groups within the organization, as well as groups external to the organization both on the input and the output side. This organizational climate point of view is obvious when you realize, as was pointed out earlier, that most people belong to more than one group. Specifically, they belong to the small group with which they work, a larger informal, social group within the organization, and exterior groups such as PTA, bowling clubs, bridge clubs, and lodges. They influence these groups and are in turn influenced by them. They carry their thoughts and views from the external to the internal organization. An awareness of this interaction is essential for the manager."

CONTROLLING

"Finally, we have the controlling function of management which, in essence, is the regulating of activities in accordance with the requirements of plans. We have many tools available to assist the manager in carrying out the control process. In industry we have statistical quality control in the form of control charts and statistics. We have PERT, which was discussed under planning, but is also a control device. We have accounting reports and analyses. We have various ratios such as employee turnover, spoilage of parts, and other quantifying techniques that let us know how

Tools for control

well we are doing the job. This is fine as far as industry goes, but what kind of control do we have in services or government industries where the output cannot be quantified?

Budgets are objectives

"Perhaps the budget is a control device. If we accomplish the objectives, say the report that is supposed to be prepared within a certain time and within the allocated funds, then the system is in control. If we're not getting the job done, if the report isn't completed on time, if taxes have to be raised to provide additional services, then perhaps the objective is not being met and steps need to be taken to insure that objectives are being met. In fact, this is the case in any method of control. If the objective, by whatever method arrived at, is not being achieved, then changes have to be made. Decisions have to be altered, and this involves change and the whole philosophy of resistance to change. And not only do we have the problem of resistance to change, but we have the problem of recognition of the right problem. As Joseph L. Massie said, 'A good decision is dependent upon the recognition of the right problem. Too often a decision maker is so intent in jumping to the right answer that he fails to look first for the right question.' [30] Also, in trying to make decisions in our own organization because we feel that the objectives are not being met, we must consider that 'in this day and age, the day-to-day decisions of management are greatly influenced by factors outside its control—such as policy, integration, fiscal and monetary affairs, social welfare legislation, regulations affecting government contracts, and many other public matters.' [31]

The importance of understanding the resistance to change

"Considering resistance to change, we know from human experience that people are creatures of habit. It is much easier not to make a decision if we don't have to. As an example, look around you in this particular classroom. How many of you are sitting in the same seat that you sat in yesterday and the day before yesterday and the day before that? You tend, after you have picked out a seat on the first day, to gravitate back to that seat; because if you don't sit in that seat, you really have to make a decision. Also, admit to yourself that if someone else sits in that seat, you're rather annoyed. Here a change has taken place. You have to sit somewhere else, and you don't like the idea. This feeling is not unique to anyone. It's a natural feeling in all individuals. Once we have things planned out and in a routine, we don't like to change. First of all, it takes some extra thought; second, it can break up relationships that have been established; third, it causes us to establish new relationships, thus involving additional effort on our part. Certainly, it's a situation that has been recognized for quite some period of time. Ordway Tead, as far back as 1918, referred to the "possession instinct" when he described a situation in which shop girls who used different sewing machines cried because their original machines had been taken away for repair when the new machine that they were using was identical.[32] He cited this as an example of resistance to changed conditions and attributed it to the possession complex or instinct.

Expect and plan for resistance to change

"But whatever it is, it's essential to realize that resistance to change should be expected. Accordingly, in any control situation in which people must change (and most assuredly in management, just about everything does involve people), we have to, as Bennis points out, plan for change and take steps accordingly.[33] We should involve everyone in the change as soon as possible, explaining it to them, why it is necessary, in fact, getting complete participation in carrying out the various steps. This participation in the change and the planning by employees should commit them to the particular process, because they have been involved and feel that they have planned it; and in realty, they are now responsible for it.

"Now, in conclusion, ladies and gentlemen, I hope you see why I made the statement in the first part of this lecture that if there is one thing certain today, it's that there is no one contemporary managerial philosophy. Of course, a manager, in order to get the job done through people, must plan, organize, direct, and control. But how he does this is particular to the situation in which he is involved. He must use all the tools available to him in the terms of quantitative methods, accounting techniques, behavioral science techniques, economic planning, technical information, and the latest word on government regulations in carrying out his job. The manager must be aware that people are unique and that all cannot be categorized and treated the same way. Each person is an individual and must be handled as such. Some want to participate; some do not. Some want to be told what to do; others want to be left as free as possible to carry out their assigned tasks as they see fit as long as the results are forthcoming. Thus, we have to look at management from a new aspect. Let's call it the *situational aspect;* that is, act according to the situation and realize that it changes from time to time."

This sounds very similar to Mary P. Follett's law of the situation. Is anything in management really new?

Situational theory

"This way of looking at management was covered in a recent *Harvard Business Review* article entitled 'Situational Theory of Management.' The author states that the situational approach starts with a manager, working in a specific situation, who recognizes that he must adapt any theory to meet his specific needs. Any conflicts of theory arise from the job situation. For example, if the work situation involves reconciling behavioral and business needs, the manager looks at both kinds of factors, human and business, determines the impact of each on the situation, and balances any conflicting requirements in his selection of and administration of a course of action.[34] Actually, what we take is an eclectic approach—that is, we select the best of all possible methods of carrying out the management function. We must consider that all things are relative and pick the best course of action depending upon the circumstances. In other words, 'guide our actions in the light of multiple values and goals, subjective as well as objective. Employ a wide variety of ways of making and carrying out decisions, avoid following rules of thumb about administration and realize that the validity of a decision is dependent upon other decisions and actions and events about which we generally have imperfect knowledge.'[35]

"Finally, I leave you with this thought. This course is designed to help you develop your own managerial philosophy, which will probably be unique to you because you are a unique individual. Develop a philosophy that you feel most comfortable with, consider all aspects of the situation, bring to bear as much knowledge as possible, and then carry out your management philosophy as you see fit based upon the situation prevailing at the time. And remember, you are not set in concrete when you make a decision. You can probably change if you see that circumstances have changed."

As he finished the statement, the professor looked at his watch and remarked, "Perhaps it's a little early, but I have nothing else to cover this morning; so I'll see you next Wednesday, same time, same place." With that he strode out of the lecture hall.

The minute the door closed, the usual buzz of conversation began. "Yeah, that dude's kinda cool, man, but you know he's not with it," came from one of the students.

"What do you mean?"

"Yeah, how can you say that? We've only had him for one day."

What would YOUR reaction have been?

"Well, what I mean is," said the first voice, "it's the same old stuff. You get it in all the management courses, and you get it in most of the textbooks. It's the preaching style, telling us how we're supposed to act as managers. Hell, we're not going to be managers in our first job. We're gonna be workers. All this stuff is fine if you're in the driver's seat. But how do you get along at our level?"

The second voice piped in with, "Well, that isn't exactly what the business administration curriculum is for. It's to try to teach us how to be managers."

A female voice said, "I can see the point of what he's getting at, though. We're going to have to work with people. But another thing, have you ever noticed that all the lectures don't say anything about age? At least the Prof didn't say anything about age. The stuff he's sounding off about seems to me more applicable to an older manager. I just don't think he's figured out what's going on in our age group."

Number four added, "I agree with the chick. I don't think he realizes that our value system isn't the same as his. His generation was brought up to have respect for the system and authority. Motherhood and the flag were "in." And all of us know that that garbage is pretty stale to many of us now."

"Yeah, you're right. Just because a guy's in a boss position doesn't say that you can't question his competence. I know. I got a letter from my brother in the army the other day, and he said the same thing. Damned, if he wants to get himself killed because some stupid lieutenant thinks he knows what to do."

"I agree," came from another student. "We certainly do have a right to question why. I don't know that I agree with you about the military situation, but it seems to me that in a work situation we certainly have a reason to question why. Why should we take everything as gospel and not question anything? We, as individuals, are important, and the organization isn't everything."

"Man, how true that is. In this day and age everything's changing so fast, you gotta figure out nothing's going to be the same anymore. You know, my old man was so afraid to change anything; he kept telling me all the time about the importance of consistency. Heck, he'd blow his top if he were alive today."

Do you agree with this point?

A new voice offered, "It sure seems to me that his lecture was stressing the Work Ethic too much, and that principles are maybe more important than people. Geez, the way things are today with welfare and government programs, who has to work if he doesn't want to? And another thing, people are more important than anything. Boy, it's the quality of life that counts! Do your own thing; be an individual. And another thing, the moral code that the older generation digs just isn't "in" any more. Me, I believe in situational ethics."

"Ah, come on, you don't know what the hell situational ethics are."

"The hell I don't. What it means to me . . . all right, I know I read it in the paper, but what it means to me is: OK if you want to live with someone, if you don't want to get married, if you want to experiment, if you want to try it out, what the heck's wrong with that? This is the age of the new morality."

"OK, I've been listening to all of you for awhile. What are we all trying to get at? What's this leading to?"

"Well," according to the first voice, "I think what we're all trying to get at is that we don't think that the professor realizes some of the shifting values. He doesn't realize some of the beliefs and ideas of our generation, and his lecture looks like it's geared to just any old age group rather than specially to ours. I don't know—what he says makes a lot of sense. I guess if I can be in a boss situation someday, I'll develop a managerial philosophy; but right now, especially on my first job, I gotta get along with the group. I'm going to be working for some dude who probably doesn't feel the same that I do, and I'm probably going to have problems. I sure hope he brings that out somewhere in this course."

"I think he will," someone else said. "I was in the mimeograph room this morning and saw the master copy of the course outline that he's going to pass out to us next week. Near the end of the course we do go into what he calls interaction outward and upward, which is supposed to give us an appreciation of how to get along with the people we work for and with. Also, I asked around; some of the guys who had him last year said he did a pretty good job—when he finally gets around to it in the end of the course—of cluing us in on some of the problems we're going to encounter on that first job."

"I sure hope so. See you all tomorrow."

EPILOGUE

What are they like?

You can answer that better than we can because "they" are you. They are also the co-workers of your age group—the ones who have just received their managerial training or who are being trained today.

What are they like? You have to decide for yourself. In any case, you will have to *interact* with them. Part IV should help you—good luck!

EXERCISE QUESTIONS

1. What are the characteristics of the bureaucracy as listed by Bennis? What would a behavioral scientist have to say about each one?
2. List Likert's four systems of organization and give some comparative characteristics of each.
3. List Schein's concepts of man. Which one do you agree with?
4. Where are you on the managerial grid?
5. Bring in some examples of organizations in the local area which do not have rigid hierarchies. Explain with examples.

DISCUSSION TOPICS

1. Explain Likert's linking-pin concept.
2. Give some examples of the situational theory of management.
3. What do you think about the student conversations at the end of the lecture?
4. What were the major influences in the application of behavioral science to management since 1960?
5. What do you think Peter Drucker's place will be in the history of management?
6. Are leaders made or born?

PROJECTS

The following situations are for role-playing. In each case the decision to be reached is first whether to expand a service organization and second how to proceed. Assume a discussion between co-workers, then between worker and supervisor:

Co-workers

a. Current frame of reference versus 1960 frame of reference.

b. Current frame of reference versus 1950 frame of reference.

c. Current frame of reference versus 1933 frame of reference.

Worker–supervisor

d. Change all situations to current frame of reference versus supervisor with the frames of reference indicated above.

NOTES

1. Henri Fayol, *General and Industrial Management,* Storrs translation (London: Sir Isaac Pitman and Sons Ltd., 1949).
2. Harold Koontz and Cyril O'Donnell, *Principles of Management: An Analysis of Managerial Functions* (New York: McGraw-Hill Book Co., 1972).
3. Herbert A. Simon, *Administrative Behavior* (New York: The Free Press, 1945).

4. Ludwig von Bertalanffy, "General Systems Theory: A New Approach to the Unity of Science," *Human Biology,* Vol. 23 (December 1951).
5. John Vinocur, "Sweden Attempts to Humanize Assembly Line," *Daily Press,* Newport News, Virginia, November 16, 1972.
6. Warren G. Bennis, *Changing Organizations* (New York: McGraw-Hill Book Co., 1966), p. 5.
7. Ibid., p. 6.
8. "Teamwork through Conflict." *Business Week,* March 20, 1971, p. 44.
9. David Oates, "Is the Pyramid Crumbling?" *International Management* (New York: McGraw-Hill Book Co., July 1971).
10. Chester I. Barnard, *The Functions of the Executive* (Cambridge, Mass.: Harvard University Press, 1938, 1968), p. 112.
11. Alvin Toffler, *Future Shock* (New York: Random House, 1970).
12. Edwin B. Flippo, *Management: A Behavioral Approach* (Boston: Allyn and Bacon, Inc., 1966).
13. Douglas McGregor, *The Human Side of Enterprise* (New York: McGraw-Hill Book Co., 1960), pp. 47–48.
14. Herbert Simon, "Decision-Making and Administrative Organization," *Public Administration Review,* Vol. IV (Winter 1944).
15. McGregor, *Human Side of Enterprise,* p. 182.
16. Rensis Likert, *New Patterns of Management* (McGraw-Hill Book Co., Inc., 1961). See also Chapter 3 of this book for a discussion of leadership styles.
17. Robert R. Blake and Jane S. Mouton, *The Managerial Grid* (Houston, Texas: Gulf Publishing Co., 1968).
18. Chris Argyris, *Management and Organizational Development* (McGraw-Hill Book Co., 1971).
19. Ibid., p. ix.
20. Edgar H. Schein, *Organizational Psychology* (Englewood Cliffs, N.J.: Prentice-Hall, Inc., 1965), p. 49.
21. Ibid., p. 51.
22. Ibid., p. 57.
23. Ibid., pp. 60–61.
24. Frederick Herzberg, Bernard Mausner, Barbara Bloch Snyderman, *The Motivation To Work* (New York: John Wiley & Sons, Inc., 1959).
25. *The Random House Dictionary of the English Language,* unabridged ed. (New York: Random House, 1966).
26. Judson Gooding, "It Pays to Wake Up the Blue-Collar Worker," *Fortune,* September 1970, p. 135.
27. George S. Odiorne, *Management Decision by Objectives* (Englewood Cliffs, N.J.: Prentice-Hall, Inc., 1969). See also W. J. Reddin, *Effective Management By Objectives* (New York: McGraw-Hill Co., Inc., 1971).

28. Harry Levinson, "Management by Whose Objectives?" *Harvard Business Review,* Vol. 48, No. 4 (July–August 1970), pp. 125–134.
29. Gordon L. Lippitt, Leslie E. This, Robert G. Bidwell, Jr. editors, *Optimizing Human Resources* (Reading, Mass., Addison-Wesley Pub. Co., 1971).
30. Joseph L. Massie, *Essentials of Management* (Englewood Cliffs, N.J.: Prentice-Hall, Inc., 1964), p. 35.
31. Marion B. Folsom, *Executive Decision-Making: Observations and Experience in Business and Government* (New York: McGraw-Hill Book Co., 1962). p. 4.
32. Ordway Tead, *Instincts in Industry* (New York: Houghton Mifflin Co., 1918).
33. Bennis, op. cit.
34. Robert J. Mackler, "Situational Theory of Management," *Harvard Business Review,* Vol. 49, No. 3 (May–June 1971).
35. George F. F. Lombard, "Relativism in Organizations," *Harvard Business Review,* Vol. 49, No. 2 (March–April 1971), p. 58.

part IV

MODUS OPERANDI

Having acquired an understanding of the individual, the group, and managerial philosophies—the three essential elements needed to develop a plan for successful interpersonal relationships in organizations—it but remains to develop the plan—the modus operandi—for *interaction* (interpersonal relationships) both *outward* (with co-workers) and *upward* (with supervisors)—IOU in organizations.

The objectives of Part IV are to enable you to

1. *understand* the attitude of everyday life and the propositions thereunder;
2. *recognize* the scientific attitude and its underlying principles;
3. *identify* the steps necessary for successful IOU when approaching a job;
4. *identify* the steps necessary for successful IOU on the job;
5. *appreciate* the significance of sex roles in IOU;
6. *realize* the effect of managerial philosophy and frame of reference in the IOU situation;
7. *understand* the factors that make successful interaction difficult;
8. *learn* the eight general guidelines available in developing a plan for successful IOU.

OUR WAY
OUR WAY
ROUTING
Betsi

12

Interaction— Outward and Upward

Basis for behavior

At this point we have a pretty good idea of why we, as individuals, behave the way we do. We have seen that our behavior is the result of our philosophy as modified by our needs and that this complete relationship is affected by our frame of reference, past experiences, the current situation, and our future expectations. We have further seen that the philosophy portion of the above relationship is the result of beliefs and attitudes as modified by values.

Develop a plan of action

In addition to realizing why we are what we are, we also at this point have an understanding of groups—how they function and operate—considering the characteristics of norms, role relationships, power and influence, and cohesion. Finally, we have an appreciation of managerial philosophies—that often they vary among individuals and that they have developed during a particular time period which gives each one a managerial frame of reference. With this understanding we can now develop our own plan of action to interact favorably with people on our own level as well as with those on a higher level.

ATTITUDE OF EVERYDAY LIFE

Before we can really develop our own plan for successful IOU (Interaction—Outward and Upward), we need to know one more thing about people in general. That is that most of us adopt a perspective in our day-to-day activities that we can call the *attitude of everyday life*. This attitude of everyday life is made up of three propositions: first, that a person views the world about from his personal perspective, not from a general perspective; second, that a person is constrained to routinize the world about him; third, that a person is engaged in a process of typification, a process of forming generalized judgments about the world about him.[1]

Personal Perspective

We only see our own point of view

The personal perspective tends to cause us to look at things from our own point of view—from our own beliefs, values, and frames of reference. If we are interested in the local ecology movement, we assume that everybody else is. If we are concerned about speeding on a certain section of highway, we assume that everybody else is. It seems illogical to us that other people are not interested in ecology and are not interested in speeding problems. We often fail to see that what is work to us, such as mowing a lawn, might be pleasure and recreation to someone else who needs exercise and likes the outdoors. Again, if we were brought up according to a strict Protestant Ethic, it is difficult for us to see why other people do not go to church and feel that work is not important. In general, most of us develop an attitude that everyone is interested in us, in what we think, what we feel, and how we act. We tend to look at the world through "rose-colored glasses" and assume that everyone sees things as we do—the "I" position.

Routinization

Events are as unique as people

Routinization is the process of developing patterns of action on the assumption that because something occurred a certain way one time, it will occur that same way a second time. This results from a failure to realize that every event, even human experience, is unique. It occurs at a certain place, at a certain moment, to persons of a specific age and under conditions and in an arrangement of all of these which will never be repeated. Never again will the event happen at that place, at that time, to those people under those conditions.[2] In spite of this uniqueness of events, what most of us try to do is classify events into categories and then attach names and labels to such categories. We look for predictability and repetition of pattern. Once having found the pattern, or at least what we think is the pattern, we try to develop a routine so that we don't have to make the same decisions again and again; therefore, life is more bearable, because we can identify supposedly predictable patterns. We assume, for example, that if the bus comes along two or three mornings at eight o'clock, it will continue to come along at eight o'clock. If we sit in the same seat in the same classroom for three classes in a row, we assume that no one else will take our seat and that it will be available or empty for us at the fourth class session. We assume that because in the past, when everything is going all right, the boss wears a big grin, that whenever he wears a big grin, things are going all right. Have you ever driven a car over a familiar road, say from the house to school or from the house to the office, and all of a sudden realized at a certain stop light that you have no recollection of starting out or of driving to that light? Such an event can really give you a scare. But it certainly serves to point out that we tend to routinize, fall into a pattern, and sometimes give little thought to what we do.

Along the lines of routinization and uniqueness we also have to consider that, even if circumstances were identical at the time of an occurrence, patterns may not be repeated because of external influences occurring before the unique act. This is the essence of field theory. Consider, for example, the supervisor who comes in two days in a row with a cheery smile and a "hello" for everybody and at the same time on the third day comes in grumpy and out of sorts. His problem is that everything was going nicely at home for those first two days, but on the third day he woke up a little late, had to rush through a cold breakfast, the kids gave him a rough time, and his wife borrowed all of his money to go on a shopping trip. The external situation affected his general attitude for the day with the resultant behavior at the office.

External influences alter patterns

Typification

Typification, or forming generalized judgments about events and the world about us, is based upon our perceptual processes, which often lead to first impressions and stereotyping. The perceptual process refers to becoming aware of things, knowing or identifying by means of the senses. Unfortunately, we often get wrong information from our senses or we may process information on insufficient information. Perception may be influenced by many factors. First, it may be influenced by hues or inferences we get from things unsaid or unseen; a certain look passing between two people to whom we are talking can give us a sense of uneasiness or inferiority. The forehead wrinkled in concentration can be misread as a sign of disapproval or anger. An unanswered question can lead us to believe that an individual is indifferent when perhaps he didn't hear the question. We perceive these minor nuances and react accordingly. Second, perception may be influenced by irrelevant clues; for example, in trying to assess honesty we can be wrongly influenced by a person's winning smile. Third, perception is often influenced by emotional factors. We tend to think that what we like is right. If we become emotionally involved, we can often overlook factors that might lead to a different interpretation. Consider the trusted controller who is embezzling funds from the company. The supervisor notices an error and accepts the answer that it was strictly a mistake in copying down a figure by the inversion of a number. His friendship—an emotional factor—makes him overlook the fact or not perceive that perhaps more could be involved. Fourth, we tend to weigh perceptual evidence coming from respected sources more heavily than those coming from other sources. For example, we might rely on what a friend says about someone based upon the friend's value system rather than what we observe and know based upon our own value system. We will probably never be aware of all the factors on which we base our judgment.[3]

Typification often based on perception

Perception influenced by nonverbalized clues

Perception influenced by irrelevant clues

Perception influenced by emotions

Many times our perceptual process leads to the making of first impressions based upon material and information which may not be significant. Unfortunately, these first impressions tend to stick with us and influence the way we classify all sorts of different data about a person or a group. Generally, they are likely to be inaccurate.

First impressions are lasting

Stereotyping

Finally, in our generalized judgments, based upon the perceptual processes, we tend to stereotype people—that is, we tend to assign qualities to people based principally upon group membership, occupation, status in life, financial position, and other relationships. This stereotyping tends to give us a generalized idea of what people ought to be like and how they might behave. Consider what comes to your mind when you hear the terms banker, supervisor, union member, poor people, rich people, the country club set. They bring a picture into your mind as to what people might be like.

Stereotyping can be prejudicial

Stereotypes have developed about many types of groups and relationships that prejudice our perception of their members. Germans are industrious; Jews are businessmen; Protestants work hard; bankers are rich; union members are out to get management; bosses exploit the workers—these phrases are examples of stereotyping. These stereotypes come from our own background, reading, associations in general, beliefs, and attitudes that we have developed about people over the years whether based upon fact or fiction (remember the uniqueness of individuals discussed in Chapter 2).

Do you have an attitude of everyday life?

The preceding enumerated characteristics of attitudes of everyday life serve most individuals who are confronted with an ongoing round of life and who must give it meaning consistent with expectations. It is much easier to take everything at face value and not question the motives of others, much less those of ourselves. Unfortunately, to do this, we sometimes act like the ostrich who puts his head in the sand to hide from his enemy.

SCIENTIFIC ATTITUDE

Because an attitude of life based on personal perspective, routinization, and typification cannot very well lead to the development of realistic and meaningful interaction, we need to adopt a scientific attitude. Certainly, the scientific attitude isn't new. It has been advocated by the earliest practitioners of management—Frederick Taylor, Gantt, and Emerson—as well as modern behavioral scientists with their logically planned experiments.

The scientific attitude must be based upon a general perspective, a posture of doubt, and realistic typifications.[4]

General Perspective

Consider all sides

A general perspective would cause us to look at any situation from as many points of view as possible; certainly, to try to see a particular situation from the other person's point of view as well as from our own. In taking the general perspective we know that everyone is a unique individual and that differing points of view are the rule rather than the exception. In fact, we should generally make the assumption that it would be a rare occurrence if other people saw things the same way we do. In a group relationship, the general perspective gives us the viewpoint that everyone in the group might have different attitudes and beliefs and that to interact and get along, there is going to have to be a compromise.

The Posture of Doubt

Question assumptions

A posture of doubt makes us question the assumption that just because something happened one way once, it will happen that same way again. It causes us to question broad generalities not backed up by empirical data, logical references, and facts. No longer can we always accept at face value; we have to look beneath the surface to see whether things are really as presented. We must question certain situations or actions, not just shrug things off with a "that's life" attitude.

This doesn't mean that we always have to be suspicious and look for ulterior motives in all actions. It just means that we should be cautious about taking things for granted and realize that some things are culturally determined—vary from one culture to another. We should be suspicious of proverbs, sayings, and folk knowledge. We should be careful of broad, sweeping generalities. We should always get the facts before acting.

Realistic Typification

Making realistic typifications involves being suspicious of perceptions based only upon senses, stereotyping, and first impressions. We need to get as many facts as possible before forming an impression. We must realize that in the majority of cases stereotyping is apt to be wrong and that we really can't tell what a person is thinking and what he's really like from facial expressions, unspoken words, and unsubstantiated information.

Discover the facts

Realistic typification about people with whom we will be working and, in particular, persons we will be working for, involves finding out as much as possible about their managerial philosophy frame of reference, attitudes, beliefs, and value systems. This way we may be able to determine what their behavior might be compared to ours and the degree of interaction that may be possible.

Successful interaction is not easy

Based upon the scientific attitude, we must assume that we really have to work at getting along—that it isn't going to come easily—and that in view of the uniqueness of individuals we might have to compromise in order to successfully interact. We have to realize that the first letters of interaction outward and upward are IOU. In any interaction I owe you something. Also, you owe me something. We owe each other the consideration to see each other's point of view, to realize that each one of us is different and to try to work out a compromise.

People need people

At this point you might very well ask, "Why do I really care about successful interaction with other people if it's so much work? Why not go on my merry old way and to hell with other people?" Well, it sounds great, but unfortunately it won't work out. Why? Because no one operates in a vacuum. No one can get along without contact with other people, and, by definition, the minute one has contact with other people interaction occurs. Agreed, in our dealings with other people we don't *have* to worry about their feelings. We can run over the top and around them, causing hurt feelings and general unhappiness. Maybe it won't matter. But in the work situation such actions will matter. Such actions will not gain acceptance from the work group or a supervisor and will, in the end, probably lead to much unhappiness and perhaps discharge. So, back to the answer to the original question: successful interaction is necessary for sane survival.

Take a systems approach in interaction

Assuming at this point that we have decided to develop a satisfactory IOU relationship, the next step is to get as many facts as possible—make use of the scientific attitude—analyze the situation and act accordingly. This can be accomplished by taking the systems analysis approach. Individuals operate within groups, which operate within companies, which operate within communities, which are located within states. We look at each element of the system in turn, finding out as much as possible about each element and how it interacts with other elements. If we're looking toward successful IOU in approaching a job, we start our analysis from the outside in—that is, looking at first the community, then the company, then the group, then the individuals. If we are already working, then we use the inside-out approach—that is, we study the individuals, then the group and then the company. In either case, however, we must consider the synergistic effect—the system is often more complicated than the sum of the parts.

APPROACHING THE JOB

Community Philosophy

Communities also have philosophies

The first step in approaching a job is to understand as much as possible about the community in which the organization for which we will be working is located. What is the predominant religion, the predominant political party? What is the range and variability of the cultural values held by the majority of the people? What is the average educational level? Is the community urban or rural? Does it have a cosmopolitan atmosphere? How many different civic organizations and groups are there? What we are trying to get is a feel for the philosophy of the community; in other words, what are its beliefs, attitudes, and value systems? In reality a community is made up of a group of people. Admittedly, in large cities the community consists of a very, very large group of people; and within the overall community there are subgroups and sub-subgroups, each with a unique philosophy. Even so, there is a general overall philosophy in one particular area, which can and often does affect organizations located within the community. As individuals, we should attempt to determine how this general philosophy might affect us. Let's take for an example a government office in a small southern town. Suppose that the community is mainly rural-agricultural. The pace of life is easy. Church influences are strong, and the government is very conservative. Knowing this, we might wonder how a person from a large northern

Community philosophies affect organizations

industrial city raised in a radical neighborhood would get along as a junior clerk in the city government. We purposely used an extreme example in this case. But the point is there nevertheless. The more divergence between the general philosophy of the community and the general philosophy of the individual, the greater will be the problems that arise and the work that will be involved in successful IOU.

The Business Philosophy

Business also has a philosophy

Having found out as much as possible about the community in which the business is located, the next step in the scientific fact-gathering operation is to find out as much as possible about the particular business enterprise for which we will be working. If it's a manufacturing concern, what is the product? What is the reputation of the company, and what are its personnel policies? Is the management considered liberal or conservative? Does the company promote from within or hire managers from the outside? If it's a government office, what is its relationship to other offices? What is its general mission, and at what level is it in the government hierarchy? How much employee turnover is there? What is the average pay level and educational level of the employees? If it is a service organization, what is the volume of business? What is its general reputation in the community? What is the average age of the worker? How many people work for the industry, and how successful is it? These are just a few of the things we need to find out in order to determine how liberal, conservative, progressive or backward the particular operation may be. After all, the organization is made up of the people. If it has a certain image, then we can perhaps expect that this image is a reflection of the behavior of key people and that most of the people in the organization will reflect this image. What we are really trying to find out is—knowing ourselves and our own philosophy—do we think we can adjust in the company? Or, how much work on our part is successful IOU going to take?

Group Philosophy

You can not know a group until you join

As far as the group goes, we will have little prior knowledge when approaching a job. All we know is that the work group with which we will become associated is going to display the characteristics discussed in Chapter 3. That is, it is going to have norms, role relationships, power and influence and a degree of cohesion. Knowing this, we may want to adapt to the existing patterns of group behavior and attempt to find a secure position from which to operate. This will involve observing what other members of the group do, how they act, how they behave and what demands they make upon us. While this is going on, we'll have to observe the actions of the group and determine which members have the power and the influence and which members may be important to us. Although we can see how people behave, initially we really won't know why they behave in the manner in which they do. We will not know the subtle power relationships and status symbols between the members of the group. Only with time can we identify the true meaning of action and determine how we may have to adjust our behavior if we want to be completely accepted by the group.

We may have to compromise in order to be accepted

We might wonder why we have to adjust our behavior if we want to get along with the group. It's because the group was there before we arrived. We are trying to gain the acceptance. In many cases the group didn't ask us to join. In fact, the more cohesive the group is the more difficult it may be for us to be accepted. Some groups might even impose a trial period very much like a fraternity initiation in which a newcomer has to prove himself. He must show that he is willing to live up to the norms of the group, that he has an acceptable personality, and that he accepts his status within the group. This exclusiveness may come as an unpleasant shock to the unprepared employee.[5]

Because groups are made up of individuals, it is sometimes hard to distinguish between relationships with individuals and a relationship within the group. We have to remember that in many circumstances in order to have interaction with an individual, we first have to become accepted as a member of the group, at least in a work situation. So that would be the reason for entering or approaching the group with what might be called a "low profile" or self-depreciating modesty; that is, purposely playing oneself down until one finds out more about the individuals, their goals, and the goals of the group.

Sex Roles

Sexual differences

Up until this point we haven't mentioned sexual differences, because everything said so far applies to both sexes. At this point, however, we feel it is important to consider that there are differences between men and women in working situations and that these differences can have a profound effect upon the individual approaching the group. These interactions break down into three basic categories: (1) man/man, (2) man/woman, and (3) woman/woman. Everyone has his own viewpoints about men and women in the working situation. We can find support for any viewpoint we want to take based upon something that someone has written somewhere at some period of time. Based upon the scientific method, studies have been completed and results have shown that there are differences between attitudes and values of women and men in the working situation. For example, it has been shown that many women view getting along with their peers as an achievement goal, while the majority of men do not. Whether we believe the results of the studies or not really doesn't matter as long as we are aware of them in our attempt at successful IOU.

Sex roles in the labor force

Before reviewing the results of the studies, however, we should look at some facts concerning women in general that are often overlooked by the average male. In the first place, most women in the labor force work because they or their families need the money—some work to raise family living standards above the level of poverty or deprivation; others to help meet rising costs of food, education for their children, medical care, and the like. Relatively few women have the option of working solely for personal fulfillment.[6] Women make up 55 percent of the voting population; they control 75 percent of consumer spending; they are genetically speaking the stronger sex based upon the fact that the male mortality rate is higher at birth, men die younger, and have a higher suicide rate. Unfortunately, the majority of men think of women as the weaker sex and in terms of sex only. They often fail to realize that women have brains. In fact, according to the Department of Labor Statistics, woman's average IQ is slightly higher than man's.

Joining the all-male group

Now, let's get back to the three situations mentioned above. First of all, a man entering an all-male work group generally has no particular problems regarding sexual differences. On the other side of the coin, however, the woman joining an all-man work group in the majority of cases won't be coming in as an equal even though she might be as good as or better than the men in the group. She will normally be brought in at a lower salary; despite the equal employment opportunity laws, excuses are often found to hire a woman at a lower salary than a man. Again, talking in generalities, she will probably not be accepted as an equal and for herself. The men will feel that they can't "level with her" because she may cry. Efforts on her part to get along as an equal with the men in the group may often be looked at with suspicion because the men not involved might think that a little "hanky-panky" might be going on. In any case a woman approaching an all-man work group is going to have problems that she would not face if she were joining a mixed group.

Joining mixed sex groups

The second category, a mixed group of men and women, is probably the most common. In this situation we are told that women are less self-assertive and less competitive than men, that they use eye contact as a form of communication more frequently than men, and they conform to majority opinions more than males. Furthermore, if a coalition exists between women, it will be less disruptive to the social relationships in the group.[7]

In general, a man approaching a mixed work group will be accepted sooner by the women than the men. In this situation age differences often become important. An older woman may accept a younger man on the basis of a mother-son relationship, often overlooking his bad traits. A young woman conversely may accept an older man into the group on the basis of a father image. These are but examples of the many complex relationships that can develop.

A woman joining a mixed group also will be accepted differently on the basis of age differentials and the number of men and women in the particular group. She will be better accepted by the men than the women in the initial contact. Women often see another woman as a threat to their position in the hierarchy in relationship to the males.

Joining the all-female group

The all-women group would, in general, be the easiest for a man to approach and the hardest for a woman to approach. If we were speaking of a completely liberated group, this would not be the case; but, because there are still women who consider a man as being superior, the man, in general, should have few problems in being accepted by the group. Women, by themselves, on the other hand, tend to have a rigid hierarchy, definite norms, and values, which often result in a difficult problem for a new woman approaching the group.

Sexual roles of the supervisor

In all three of the situation or role relationships mentioned above—that is, man/man, man/woman, woman/woman—the sex of the group supervisor has a lot to do with the relationships established within the group. We could go back and consider first a woman supervisor, then a man supervisor in each of the three situations. But the interpersonal relationships would be so great and varied that we could almost write a book on each one. Because the relationships can become so complicated, what we must be aware of is that sex does play an important part in job relationships and that even though we would like to consider everyone as being equal and treated accordingly, this, in practice, just isn't the case. Women will be discriminated against many times; men will often feel that they have a superior position, and the woman supervisor will often have to work far harder to maintain her position than will the man supervisor.

The Individual

We really can't find out much about individuals until we're on the job. As we pointed out earlier, we can, in approaching the job, find out about the community environment and the organization itself. And we can approach the group knowing what to expect. So now let's approach the situation from the on-the-job standpoint and start from the bottom up with the individual.

Find out about individuals

Once on the job, it is essential for successful IOU to find out as much as possible about the individuals with whom we work as well as our group leader. Remember, each person has a philosophy based upon beliefs and attitudes as modified by values. Also each person has a behavior pattern based upon philosophy as modified by needs, frames of reference, past experiences, the present situation and future expectations. By asking certain questions of our co-workers, we should be able to determine something about their personal philosophy. Also, by questioning we might be able to determine their need structure. General conversations should lead to information on church affiliation, political party, where a person grew up, what he thinks about work, play, entertainment, cars, the government, and life in general. Unfortunately, so many of us are so interested in talking ourselves that we don't listen to what other people say and we don't ask the right questions. The important thing for successful IOU is to find out as much about the other person as possible, aimed toward the discovery of how compatible our unique philosophy is going to be with his.

Personal philosophy

Because we're speaking about interaction in a work situation, we next have to make some assumptions about a person's managerial philosophy. The assumptions should not be based solely upon what a person says, since people pay lip service many times to what they think they should, but on

The individual managerial philosophy

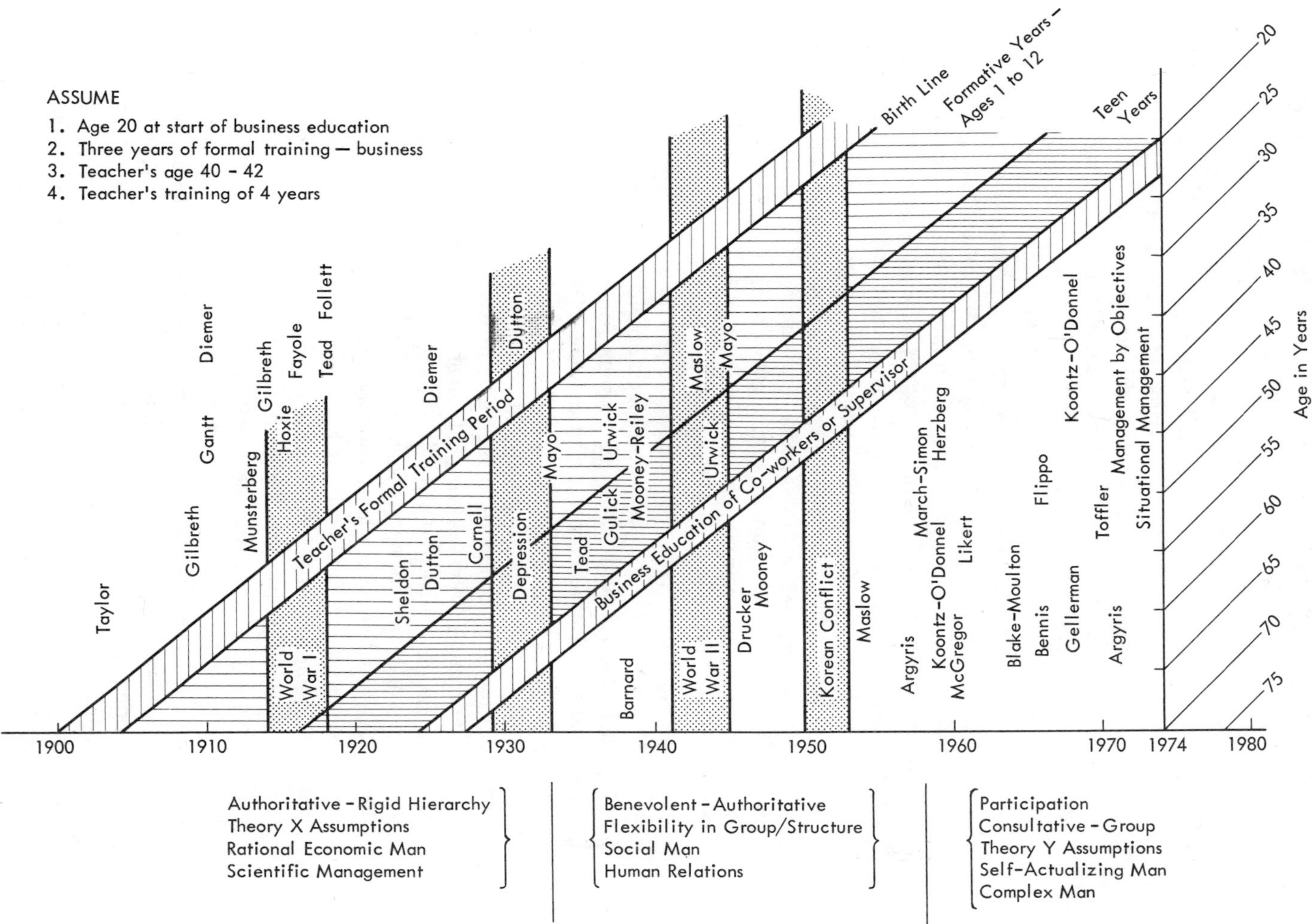

FIGURE 1
Frames of Reference

what he really might think based upon his life—where and when he went to school, what his educational and social frames of reference have been.

In our introduction to managerial philosophy in Chapter 4, we showed a chart by which we might determine what a person's managerial philosophy is. Now that we have reviewed changing managerial philosophies through time periods, Figure 1 from Chapter 4 is reproduced here as Figure 1 with indications of managerial styles and with particular contributors to management thought placed in applicable time periods. The major breakdowns are assumptions concerning people. You'll note from Figure 1 that the period from 1900 to 1930 was based predominantly on McGregor's Theory X assumptions about people. There would have been authoritative leadership, rigid hierarchy in the organization, the rational economic man assumption—thinking of man perhaps as an interchangeable part. Scientific management was in vogue and the Protestant Ethic held sway. In the 1930 to 1957 period we find the Social Man Ethic, the emergence of the human relations school, and a benevolent-authoritative type leadership. The organization is rigid but less rigid than it was in the previous period. From 1957 through 1970 we see the Theory Y assumptions of people, the Self-Actualizing Ethic, the pyramid beginning to crumble, and the emergence of consultative management, participative management, and management by objectives. Finally, from 1970 on, we find more acceptance of general systems theory, the electric approach, and situational management.

Frames of reference

If our co-worker or supervisor does not have formal training, he still would have received on-the-job training from someone who went to school and would have been exposed to some of the managerial philosophies or thinking indicated in Figure 1 and covered in prior chapters.

Assuming that our own managerial philosophy is current, that we are aware of everything contained in Figure 1, then we have to compare this with that of our fellow workers and supervisor based upon their managerial frame of reference to see if it is going to be compatible with ours.

Using Figure 1

To use Figure 1, first locate the intersection of the *Age in Years* line with the vertical year line, which has been drawn in for 1974. Next strike a line from this intersection point horizontal and parallel to the year axis to determine date frames of managerial reference. As an example, assume that one's boss is 45 years old. Figure 1 shows that his business training would probably have taken place between 1949 and 1952, when the human relations approach was popular. His training probably would have been under a professor who went to school just before the Depression and was schooled in the authoritarian Theory X scientific management principles. If this particular boss had not kept up with the times, you wouldn't expect him to be receptive to participative management, the hierarchy of needs or Herzberg's satisfiers and dissatisfiers. He would still probably be more interested in the retirement program, fringe benefits, and conformity by co-workers rather than in new ideas and participation in planning. Now perhaps this might not be the situation, but it would be well to find out before charging in with new ideas. One way, of course, would be to bring up one of the new ideas in a conversation and note reactions.

The next question to be answered in depth concerns what we do with all the information we've obtained about individuals, the group, the company, the community, and possible managerial philosophies of our co-workers and boss? The first answer would be nothing. In fact, we didn't have to go to all the work in the first place. We can take the traditional approach and practice complete conformity. We'll go along with the group; we'll let them change us; we'll compromise all our own beliefs, attitudes, values, and future expectations so that we can be an accepted member of the group. We won't make waves, and we'll go along with the system completely and unquestioningly. There are many people who will do this. However, we believe that in this day and age their number is dwindling.

What do we do with all the information?

Forget it?

The second answer is to use all the information gathered in a Machiavellian tactic wherein the plan of action is "anything to succeed." We do not want to change any of our beliefs, attitudes, values, or philosophies. We are unwilling to back off and see the other person's viewpoint. Our desires are so strong that by hook or crook somehow we're going to get ahead. We alone matter; no one else does. No sacrifice of friendship or other people is too great if it leads to our success, self-esteem, and self-actualization. Again, we would hope that this is an extreme, but some people, unfortunately, do operate this way.

Scheme?

The third answer is in our opinion the most practical. Realize that everybody and every group is unique, has different desires, different goals, and a different need-hierarchy. Be willing to give and take in order to get along, because in the final analysis all of us want to succeed. We would like to be satisfied on the job and gain a measure of meaning from our work experience. We're willing to give and take, to see the other person's point of view. If this is the case, then we want to develop a logical plan of action for rewarding and successful interaction. We use the information we have found to plan a course of action, to get along with the other person, to see his point of view, to appreciate his frame of reference and his background, to realize that it might or might not agree with ours, and to act accordingly. We also realize that to reach group or individual goals we often do not use the direct approach. We gather the facts, go slowly, adopt a plan of action, and compromise if necessary to have meaningful relationships on the job.

Compromise?

No—Plan for successful interaction

Each one of us has to decide how far he is willing to go in order to be accepted. Remember the little boy in Chapter 2 who had to weigh value systems when he was urged by the other members of his group to throw stones at a passing car. Although he didn't realize it, he wanted to be accepted by the group in order to satisfy his needs for belongingness. However, to be accepted, he would have had to modify his own value system to conform with that of the group—thus the conflict arose. What he decided depended, of course, on which value and need system was the strongest at the time.

Each must decide his own course of action

Basically, this is what we all face when we join the group; and join we must, because whenever we work for someone else by definition we

Most of us must join

belong to a group. It's a hard decision to make—that is, how much to modify our own philosophy in order to be accepted by the group. Many times we have to ask ourselves, is it worth it? Unfortunately, many of us, in fact most of us, are not comfortable acting as loners. We will, therefore, try in some way to get along and interact favorably giving up as little as possible and perhaps trying to change the other person and at times the opinions of the whole group. Many times this will require thorough analysis of the other members and judgments about their particular behavior and actions in certain situations. Thus it is necessary to understand as much as possible about the other members based upon their beliefs, attitudes, and values as they have been developed during different time frames.

Attaining Successful IOU

Even in a compromise situation in which we conscientiously want to understand as much about the other person as possible and to really get along, *successful IOU is very difficult*. Argyris found this out in his study of organizational development.[8] Most people are unwilling to express feelings and to experiment with ideas. They take the "I" position and are usually not open to other people's points of view. Most people won't tell each other how they really feel about a situation, much less tell their supervisor. This leads to most difficulties in interaction outward. It most certainly leads to difficulties in interaction upward, because, in general, most of us never want to "level" with the boss.

The second factor that makes interaction very difficult is that *most of us don't adopt a scientific adult attitude*. The word *adult* does not refer to the normal definition of adult as, "a grown-up, mature person." [9] It refers to the definition of adult in the recent best-seller *I'm OK; You're OK*.[10] In the book, subtitled "A Practical Guide to Transactional Analysis," Dr. Harris develops the theory that when people interact, they are often not on the same level of mental information-processing and even internal personalities. He points out that observation supports the theory that there are three states of existence in all people—the parent, the adult, and the child. If we think of the brain as a sophisticated computer, then, "the Parent is a huge collection of recordings in the brain of unquestioned or imposed external events perceived by a person in his early years, a period which we have designated roughly as the first five years of life." [11] The *Parent* records all the rules, laws, beliefs, attitudes, and value systems that the little person hears from his parents and sees in their living. He records this through such things as tone of voice, facial expression, cuddling, or noncuddling. It includes the thousands of "no's" directed at the toddler, the repeated "don'ts" that bombard him, the looks of pain and horror in mother's face when his clumsiness brings shame in the family.

A different view of "adult"

Harris goes on to point out that while the external events are being recorded in the *Parent,* there is another recording being simultaneously cut. "This is the recording of internal events, the responses of the little person to what he sees and hears. . . . It is this seeing and hearing and feeling and understanding body of data which we define as the *Child*. Since the little person has no vocabulary during the most critical of his early experiences, most of his reactions are feelings."[12]

Finally, we come to the *Adult,* "a data processing computer which grinds out decisions after computing the information from three sources: the *Parent,* the *Child* and the data which the *Adult* has gathered and is gathering."[13] The *Adult* has to examine the data in the *Parent* to see whether or not it is true and applicable today, then accept it or reject it. It must examine information of the *Child* to see whether its feelings are appropriate to the present or are archaic in archaic *Parent* data. In most interactions, or as he calls them transactions, we often think, act, and speak not with *Adult* processing but often with *Parent* and *Child* processing. An interesting example is as follows:

Lady 1: (Looks at her watch, winds it, mumbles, catches the eye of the lady next to her, sighs wearily.)
Lady 2: (Sighs back, shifts uncomfortably, looks at her watch.)
Lady 1: "Looks like we're going to be late again."
Lady 2: "Never fails."
Lady 1: "You ever see a bus on time—ever?"
Lady 2: "Never have."
Lady 1: "Just like I was saying to Herbert this morning—you just don't get service any more like you used to."
Lady 2: "You're absolutely right. It's a sign of the times."
Lady 1: "It costs you, though. You can count on that!"[14]

Harris points out that the above discussion proceeds without the benefit of reality, and the ladies are giving the same judgments that they probably overheard their mothers give about riding streetcars.

In general, he gives us some clues to help identify stimulus and responses as *Parent, Adult,* or *Child*. *Parent* physical clues include the furrowed brow, pursed lips, pointed index finger, foot-tapping, hands on chest, and others. *Parent* verbal clues include words such as "asinine," "lazy," "nonsense," "absurd," "cute," "not again," "always," and "never." *Child* physical clues include tears, a quivering lip, shrugging shoulders, downcast eyes, laughter, and others. *Child* verbal clues include: "I wish," "I want," "I don't care," "I guess," "bigger," "biggest," "best," and many superlatives. *Adult* physical clues consist of attentiveness and straightforward listening, while verbal clues consist of "what," "why," "when," "where," "how," and expressions such as "I think I see" and "in my opinion."[15] It is important to be aware of these transactional clues in our interactions with other people. We need to realize that many people are not processing data with their *Adult* but are verbalizing *Parent* and *Child* information. They are not telling us their true feelings and opinions and are often masking what they really think. We should, therefore, realize the true significance of what is said and particularly answer on an *Adult* basis and not on the relationship of *Child* to *Child* or *Parent* to *Parent*. Only *Adult* to *Adult* relationships will result in successful IOU.

Many people are not acting as *Adults*

IOU GUIDELINES

In summation, successful IOU is difficult to achieve, but it is not impossible as long as we realize that it will require work on our part and we must act in an *Adult* manner. In general, we must

1. Find out as much as we possibly can about the community, the business, and the people with whom we are to interact regarding
   a. personal philosophy
   b. beliefs
   c. attitudes
   d. values
   e. managerial frame of reference
   f. group relationships
   g. cultural background
   h. political affiliation
   i. religion.
2. Decide in what areas we might have similar views and in what areas there may be controversy.
3. Avoid introducing sensitive areas and subjects if not pertinent.
   Sensitive subjects make many people uncomfortable and, in the long run, their discussion may interfere with the development of satisfying interpersonal relationships.
4. Back up opinions with facts.
   In most situations the person who speaks on the basis of facts rather than opinion has a better chance of developing effective interaction.
5. From information gathered in (1) above plus knowledge that (a) openness and frankness are rare in most people, and (b) many people do not interact on an *Adult* level, you must decide in what areas you are willing to compromise in order to achieve successful IOU.
6. Determine when a direct approach will not work in upward interaction and guide our actions accordingly.
   Many times it's easier to go around a brick wall rather than through it.
7. Be willing to give and take; win a few and lose a few.
   Successful IOU is not possible with all people in all situations. Sometimes it will not be possible to be liked by everyone and be accepted by the group.
8. Proceed slowly.
   Successful IOU requires time. People have to get to know each other and the group before complete acceptance can occur.

This guideline should work well in the attempt to develop successful interaction—outward with peers—and upward with supervisors.

MODUS OPERANDI

At this point let's go back to Chapter 1 and review the story of Jim and Al and see how Al might have operated to achieve successful interaction rather than abject frustration.

Let's review the situation. First of all, Al had been with the company for one month. On the basis of one of his college courses in quantitative analysis, he saw a way to reroute deliveries that would save his company about $120 a month. It involved changing routes, deliveries to customers, drivers, and a long-established pattern of delivery. Acceptance required interaction with a manager who had been with the company for many years.

The biggest thing involved in Al's idea is a change. And he certainly should have known that people are resistant to change. Second, his boss, Mr. Able, at age 50, had received his managerial training during World War II (see Figure 1) and probably might not be aware of the latest ideas in linear programming. Al had been told that people might not like the change. Let's see how he might have interacted if he had planned for successful IOU.

Al Allen was in the middle of a phone call to Daisy Distributors. "Yes sir, Mr. Daisy, you say it would not make any difference if we made two deliveries every day rather than one a day—you're sure, now, that would be satisfactory? No, sir, we aren't changing for sure. I was just checking it out. Thank you very much—I'll advise well in advance if we decide to change." With the final remark Al replaced the phone on the hook and made a check mark behind the name of Daisy Distributors. "By golly, every single one of the distributors is willing to go along if we install a new system. It looks pretty good to me. I've worked it out on paper, and we can save a $100 per month at a minimum. I haven't said anything else about it to anyone though, because I don't want to get them upset," he thought to himself, "until at least I find out whether the distributors are willing to go along with it. It wouldn't do any good to suggest a change here if the distributors wouldn't agree." Al thought a few minutes more, then picked up the telephone and dialed the personnel office. After one ring, Sally answered with a cheery, "Hello."

"Sally, can I talk to Mr. Sullivan? This is Al Allen calling."

"Why of course, Mr. Allen—one moment please."

Shortly Mr. Sullivan's voice came over the phone, "Hello, Al."

"Mr. Sullivan, as I remember when I was going over the personnel policies last month when I was hired, we have a suggestion award system, don't we?"

"That's right, Al. Any suggestion that amounts in a savings to the company is shared on a fifty-fifty basis with the employee for the first year if the saving amounts to less than $2,000."

"That's what I thought, Mr. Sullivan. Now, something else—can the employee who earns the suggestions award share it with anybody?"

"Of course, Al," shot back Sullivan. "He can do anything he wants with it."

"OK, Mr. Sullivan, that's all I wanted to know."

"Hey, wait a minute, Al; do you have a good one cooking?"

"Could be, Mr. Sullivan. I just wanted to check."

"OK, Al, I hope we'll be hearing from you." With that remark Sullivan hung up.

As he put down his receiver, Al thought to himself, "Now for Phase II. I know there's going to be resistance in this company to any change.

That's obvious. All I have to do is look around at the ages of the fellows and, particularly, Mr. Able. Mrs. Allen didn't raise a completely stupid boy, though. I've spotted Butch Brady as the informal leader of the truck drivers. They all hang on his every word, and whatever he says goes. If I can get him on my side, things might look up."

Later, Al walked into the lunch parlor and saw Butch Brady sitting on the stool at the counter. Al slid into the seat next to Butch and said, "Hi, Butch."

"Hi, Mr. Allen. You going to have a Sloppy Joe today?"

"Yes, I think so, Butch. What's new?"

"Ah, nothing much. Number three rig's shut down, but we got the boys switched around so everything looks OK. The boss driver liked my idea, so I'm getting along as good as can be expected. I ain't got no complaints."

"That's good, Butch." Allen ordered his lunch, and they shot the breeze about things in general and nothing in particular. As he was finishing his sandwich, Al mentioned to Butch, "Butch, how do you think the drivers would like to split $400 between them?"

"You gotta be kiddin, Mr. Allen. They'd like it fine. Whata ya gonna do, rob a bank or something?"

"No, Butch, I have a suggestion idea that might save the company some money, but it would require the cooperation of the drivers. It would be my suggestion, and I'd be glad to share the suggestion awards fee if you think the drivers would go along."

"Good gosh, yes, Mr. Allen. But you know you don't have to share money with my boys. They have the good of the company at heart too. Of course it would be nice of you if you just want to share. What's involved?"

"Well, I can't exactly tell you, Butch—how about stopping by my office after lunch, OK?"

"OK, Mr. Allen, I'll be over as soon as I finish."

Later, "By golly, Mr. Allen, that's a pretty good idea," exclaimed Butch Brady after being shown the warehousing linear program solution to the truck distribution problem. "Yes, sir, that's pretty logical. I wouldn't have thought about it that way. I know it's a change in our system, and the fellows might have to adjust a little bit, but it's not going to hurt them any. And, besides, it's going to save the company some dough. You just leave it to me."

"OK, Butch, but look; I don't want to do it—yet. And when I do do it, I only want to try it for a couple of weeks or so, because this is a change in procedures; and I don't know how the old man's going to take it. I've cleared it out with the distributors, and they're agreeable. Now if you say you can sell it to the truck drivers, I'll only have to worry about the shipping and receiving boys—and they're mine—and the suppliers. So just sit on it until I get everything squared away."

"OK, Mr. Allen. Say, incidentally, I've got a buddy down in your department if you need any help."

"I appreciate that, Butch. But let me see if I can handle it on my own, first."

"Sure, Mr. Allen." With that, Butch turned and left the office.

As soon as Brady left, Al went into the shipping and receiving office and sat down with his three assistants. "Fellows, I've been thinking of an idea that might be able to save us some money, and I wanted to talk it over with you all to see what you think of it."

"OK, Al, fine, fine," came from one of the men.

Al explained his plan in detail telling them how the distributors agreed and that Butch thought that he could line up the truck drivers. They all thought it was a pretty good idea but pointed out several changes that should be made because of road and terrain conditions. Al accepted these plus another minor route change, and they all agreed that it was a workable plan and certainly would save the company some money. Sam said he'd be sure to check the suppliers to be sure there wouldn't be any hitch there, and they agreed that nothing would be done until the suppliers agreed.

Later in the week the final word came in from the suppliers that they could accommodate the shift in supply schedule. Al gave the assistant shipping and receiving boys the go-ahead; Butch Brady got the truck drivers lined up; and Al, himself, called the distributors. Promptly at 7:30 the following Monday, the new schedule was put into effect.

Luckily it was only three weeks until the end of the month, and Al was able to get the cost reports from Jim Dee. As he was looking them over, he got a phone call. "Hey, Al, this is Jim Dee."

"Oh, hi, Jim."

"Say, I noticed we had a saving in mileage costs last month of almost $90. What in the world happened? Business falling off?"

"Not so, Jim—on the contrary, business is picking up. I just changed the distribution schedule."

"You did what!"

"Changed the distribution schedule."

"You mean you changed the schedule like you were talking to me about a month after you came?"

"Yeah, I sure did, and it's working out just fine."

"Well, how in the world did you get the old man's approval?"

"Fact is, I haven't yet."

"What? He's going to you know what when he finds out."

"No, I don't think so. I have everybody working with it on a trial basis, and I'm going up this afternoon and tell him about it."

"Well, good luck, old boy; you're sure going to need it."

After hanging up, Al picked up his phone and dialed the plant manager's office. After a buzz, Sally, answered, "Mr. Able's office."

"Sally, this is Al Allen in shipping and receiving."

"Oh, hello, Mr. Allen, what can I do for you?"

"Well, I was wondering if you could check Mr. Able's calendar and see if I could get an appointment with him some time today."

"Just a minute." In about half a minute Sally's voice came back over the phone. "Yes, Mr. Allen, I can make an appointment for you at three o'clock this afternoon if that would be convenient."

"Oh sure, Sally, that's fine with me, any time."

"All right, then, I'll make the appointment for three o'clock."

At five minutes to three Al approached the plant manager's office with his notebook and some cost sheets under his arm. He grinned as he approached Sally's desk. Before he could speak Sally looked up and said, "He's expecting you; go right in."

As Al walked through the door of the general manager's office, Mr. Able looked up from his desk, nodded, and greeted him with "Have a chair, Al. What can I do for you this afternoon?"

"Well, Mr. Able, I've been doing a little analysis work on our shipping operation, and I've discovered a way that can save us over $100 a month," Al began rather gingerly.

"Sounds interesting."

"Yes, sir," continued Al, a little more sure of himself after Mr. Able's remark. "Yes, sir, I've figured a way that with our two warehouses and three distributors, we can save money by rerouting our trucks. Our situation is very similar to a problem that I had in one of my courses. In fact it's similar to a sample problem. I worked out a solution based upon the model, and we can save ourselves a $100 a month in mileage costs."

"Oh, how do you figure that?"

"Well, the way it works, sir, is that we change our shipping routes so that all of our deliveries are not made to the nearest outlet. There's a combination of units per truck per delivery—"

"Wait a minute," interrupted Mr. Able. "Our drivers then have to get used to different schedules and different routes?"

"Yes, sir, they do, but I've already talked to them, and they're perfectly agreeable."

"Oh, I'm surprised at that. Well, what about the deliveries to the distributors? What are they going to say about that?"

"I've already checked it out, sir, and its agreeable with all of them."

"Well, I certainly didn't think they'd go along with something like that. But how about the people in your department—what do they think about this? You know we've been doing things for a long time and—"

"Yes, sir, I know, and I've checked this out with them; and they're agreeable too."

"It seems you've checked everything out, but you know this is a rather quick change; and I just don't know whether people are going to like it or not."

"To tell the truth, Mr. Able, knowing how concerned you are with profit, we've actually been trying the system for the last three weeks, and the cost sheets show that we've saved over $80 in the shipping department last month."

"Well, well—that's interesting. Well done, Al, let's keep up the good work. I'm proud to see that you're coming along so nicely."

"Thank you, Mr. Able. Do I have your permission then to continue?"

"You most certainly have, young man."

"Thank you."

With that, Al turned and almost ran out of the room. As soon as he got back in the office, he picked up the phone and dialed Jim Dee.

"Hey, Jim, the old man bought it hook, line, and sinker. I told you he would."

"Well, more power to you, Al, old boy. I guess you figured out how to get along with him. I'm glad someone finally has."

Notice that Al handled the situation in this second story much differently than in the first one. In order to achieve successful upward interaction with his boss, he realized that he would have to overcome resistance to change. He found out about the boss's managerial frame of reference; he backed up opinions with facts, and he determined that the direct approach would not work. Next he identified the informal leader of the group and convinced him to work on the men. After getting the drivers to approve his plan, he got his own people to participate, even make suggestions so that they were committed to the plan. He lined up all the distributors and suppliers, had all his facts in a row, went ahead and implemented the plan, then told the plant manager about the results. He anticipated what his problems might be based upon the scientific attitude. He achieved his objective by proving that his system worked. The beauty of his approach was that if the system had not worked out as planned, he could have gone back to the old system without disturbing too many people or the operations of the overall system. In any case, he achieved successful upward interaction.

Now let's take another example of a different occupational setting in which the scientific method is used in an attempt to assure successful interaction outward and perhaps upward.

Suzy was excited, and why shouldn't she be? Here she was at 22 about to graduate with her associate degree in Business Administration with an Accounting major. And on top of that she was being interviewed for the position of cost analyst with Central Distributor Corporation.

She was excited as she picked out one of her nicest daytime dresses, the one that matched her shoes and pocketbook. She laughed when she remembered how her roommate had kidded her about wearing slacks. But after all, she wasn't that dumb. Slacks were OK for school, and jeans were all right on campus. But if you wanted to impress an employer, you certainly wouldn't go job-hunting in slacks. After all, if she wanted to work for the Establishment, she figured she could at least go along with some of their rules on dress even though in her own mind she did think that they were rather square.

Her mind snapped back to reality as she looked at her watch and saw that she had only a half-hour to go. Hurriedly finishing her dressing, she put on what she considered would be just the right amount of make-up, straightened her hair, and dashed out the door.

Riding down town in the cab, Suzy went over some notes in her mind. Dunn and Bradstreet had indicated that CDC was a wealthy, conservative distributor of plumbing fixtures. The majority of the firm's officers were in their fifties and all were from the local area. "Knowing that," thought Suzy, "gives me a little bit of an idea about what to expect. I rather imagine that if the firm's officers think along conservative lines, then probably many of the employees do, especially if they also grew up here in Central City. I know that the government is quite conservative, and many of the leading manufacturers and bankers share the same views. I'm glad I went to school here for the last two years and was able to take part in some of the community activities. I sure know that some of my views aren't exactly in agreement with those of some of the local people, so I'd better not bring politics up, or at least play them down if they come up in my interview today. Maybe if I can look around a little bit, I can also get a feel for their general managerial philosophy. I would rather suspect that they might not be practicing some of the techniques I'm learning about this term."

Suzy's thoughts were so deep that she didn't realize that the cab had stopped until she heard the voice from the front seat say, "Here we are, ma'am."

"It certainly isn't the most modern building," thought Suzy as her heels clunked on the wooden floors of the third-floor corridor. She finally reached the door marked CDC Personnel Office. She gave herself a quick once-over, took a deep breath, opened the door, and walked in. As she entered she immediately saw the middle-aged woman sitting behind the secretarial desk marked "Personnel Receptionist, Miss Johnson." Suzy caught herself about to stereotype Miss Johnson as an old-maid schoolteacher type, but didn't as she remembered her course in behavioral science. "Watch it, Suzy," she told herself. "You're falling into your old pattern."

Miss Johnson looked up with the remark, "May I help you?"

"Yes, ma'am," answered Suzy. "My name is Suzy Smith; I have an appointment with Mr. Curtis about a cost analyst position."

"Ah yes, Miss Smith, I have it marked here on the calendar," Miss Johnson continued in a very pleasant voice as Suzy thought, "She doesn't sound so bad at all. She might look like a hatchet-face, but she has a lovely voice."

Miss Johnson continued, "Did you have to come far for the appointment?"

"No, ma'am, I live just about ten blocks from here. I'm going to Tidewater U."

"Oh how nice," smiled Miss Johnson. "I know several of the teachers there. My late husband used to teach there."

"Oh, I'm sorry," stammered Suzy.

"That's quite all right my dear. It's been quite some time now. And in business I use my maiden name. Now, while you're waiting to see Mr.

Curtis, why don't you sit down over there and relax a little. You look a little tense. I'll get you a cup of coffee and a magazine to read."

"Gee, thanks, Miss Johnson, that's awfully nice of you."

"That's perfectly all right, my dear; I know how nervous you can get about a first job interview. And I assume it is your first one."

"Yes, ma'am, it is."

"Well, relax. Mr. Curtis will be available shortly."

Ten minutes later the intercom on Miss Johnson's desk buzzed. She flipped the button and answered, "Yes, Mr. Curtis?"

"Miss Johnson, has Miss Smith arrived yet?"

"Yes, Mr. Curtis, she's been here for about ten minutes."

"All right, would you send her in?"

Having heard the conversation, Suzy was already on her feet.

"Right this way, Miss Smith."

Suzy followed Miss Johnson through the door in the back of the room, down a short hallway and through the door marked MR. CURTIS, PERSONNEL DIRECTOR.

Miss Johnson turned to Suzy and said, "Miss Smith, this is Mr. Curtis. Mr. Curtis, Miss Smith."

"Good afternoon, sir," said Suzy.

"Good afternoon, Miss Smith," answered Mr. Curtis. "I hope I haven't kept you waiting too long."

"No, sir, not at all. In fact, Miss Johnson gave me a cup of coffee and we had a nice little chat."

"Well, I'm glad to hear that. Miss Johnson always tries to put prospective employees at ease. We all understand that you get a little nervous in these situations."

"Yes, sir, I certainly do," remarked Suzy.

"Sit down, Miss Smith, and let's go over your qualifications and the job that's open here with Central Distributor Corporation.

During the interview Suzy learned that she would be working with a group of about six other cost analysts, all older men and women. There were three women and two men in the group. Two of the women and one of the men were married. One man was a bachelor and the woman was a divorcee. Mr. Curtis had seemed a little surprised that Suzy had asked so many detailed questions about the group she was going to work with. But she explained that she felt that she would know how to get along better if she knew some of the background of the people with whom she would be working. Mr. Curtis thought this was a pretty good idea. At this remark Suzy made a mental note that he hadn't realized this before, that he looked like he was about fifty, and that perhaps she'd been right in assuming that the company hadn't kept pace with the latest behavioral science thinking as far as managerial relationships go. But, then maybe it didn't matter. She wouldn't know until she reported to work.

Finally, Mr. Curtis said, "Well, Miss Smith, I'm satisfied with your credentials, and the opening is available; if you would be interested, I'll show you around our offices, and you can start the week following your graduation."

"That would be wonderful, Mr. Curtis. I am certainly looking forward to it."

Back in his office after the tour, Mr. Curtis continued, "Fine, Miss Smith—now if you'll just come outside again, I'll have Miss Johnson get you all the necessary papers so that we can get you processed and on the payroll by the time you report aboard."

As Suzy walked out toward Miss Johnson's desk, she couldn't conceal her pleasure any more. She wore a big grin on her face as she said, "I got the job."

"I'm so pleased Suzy; I believe your first name is Suzy, and if you don't mind, I'll call you that. You seem like such a nice young lady. I'm sure you'll be very happy with us."

"I surely hope so, Miss Johnson."

"Now Suzy if you'll just fill out these papers, we'll have everything ready for you when you report to work next month."

At home that night, Suzy thought about her new job. "Boy," she thought, "I'm sure glad I found out all I could about CDC before I went down for that interview. They're as conservative as I thought they might be, at least from looking at the secretaries in some of the offices; and if Mr. Curtis is any indication, from some of his comments I'm sure that he hasn't kept up with the latest managerial thinking. And if he's the personnel director, he's probably in charge of training; probably no one else has either. They are conservative, so I knew not to bring up any sensitive issues in my conversation, like the fact that I'm for Women's Lib. I know to other people some of my ideas might be far out from their frame of reference, but I do need the job, so I'm sure not going to rock the boat, at least not until I feel my way around. Now that was something interesting about the cost analysis group. If one of those men is a bachelor and one of the women is a divorcee, she might just have designs on him. She might see me as a threat. I mean I might as well admit I'm not the worst-looking thing in the world. In fact, I've been told I'm fairly good-looking. And older men sometimes go for younger girls, so I might have a little trouble with her. But if I can put her at ease right off the bat—let's see, maybe I can talk about a mythical fiancee. Oh, that wouldn't be right, but I'll have to do something so that right off the bat she gets the message loud and clear that I'm certainly not out for any man in the group. Now I'll probably have to watch the married man, too. He's probably either going to be a flirt or think of me as his daughter. Perhaps I'm being overly anxious. Maybe he'll just treat me as another human being. But, unfortunately, many men think they're God's gift to women and feel that they have to strut in front of an attractive young lady. Now as to the other two women, I don't know what they're going to be like until I really meet them. They can treat me as an equal; they can see me as a threat to them and their position; or they can even think of me as in a mother/daughter situation. Anyway, I'd better take it pretty easy and see how the land lies. Mr. Curtis didn't mention who our supervisor's going to be, but I remember looking at the organizational chart and seeing the name Selina Starr in that slot. In fact, come to think of it, it's rather odd that Mr. Curtis didn't introduce me to her, because I'll be working for her. That seems real odd. Well, she could have been on vacation, or perhaps she wasn't there. In any case I should probably look into that, find out a little bit about what she's like. I certainly don't want anybody thinking I'm out to get her job as a young upstart. I'll just have to play it cool until I find out what the group's norms are, who gets along with whom, what role they expect of me, and anything else pertinent. If they're as conservative as I think they are, they can probably stand some improvements in that cost analysis section, particularly in light of some of the courses I've just completed. But I know I can't charge in and expect people to accept my ideas, because they'll probably look at me like I'm not dry behind the ears yet. And of course I'm a girl and nobody, well I shouldn't say nobody, maybe I'm prejudiced too—very few people, at least men, think a girl has any brains—but in any case, I do want to get along. I want to be accepted by the group, and I want to have an atmosphere such that I'll enjoy working there. I realize that to be accepted, I'm probably going to have to back off on some of my ideas. In the long run it really doesn't matter that much. If it comes right down to it, I'll stand up for some of my more basic principles. But I don't think people are going to argue with them anyway. So I'll concentrate on completing my exam next week and starting work right after graduation."

It's obvious from the above that Suzy Smith has adopted a scientific attitude and is truly interested in developing satisfactory interaction outward and upward in her new job. She found out as much as she could about the company and the position and the people for whom and with whom she will be working. She avoided sensitive subjects in her interview. She got facts on which to base her opinions. She laid out her plans, and figured out an approach to take based upon knowledge of relationships, and assumptions based upon how the relationships might work out. Finally, she is willing to give a little and take a little in order to be accepted.

This, in general, is the proper attitude and plan to adopt for successful IOU. Although the above story shows the procedures or techniques that might be developed in approaching the job situation, the techniques on the job are identical. Consider the following situation.

Jim Sullivan was a most unhappy man. He'd been with the City Planning Commission for the last three months as a junior planner, exactly the job that he had wanted. So he should have been happy—but he wasn't. He was never asked out to lunch by any of the other members of the group. Everyone seemed to clam up when he tried to join in, and he got the icy treatment from the group's secretary. Sure, the actual work he was doing was fine, and he seemed to get along all right with Bob

Barton, but as for the rest of the members, it was pretty miserable. In fact, he disliked it so much that he was seriously thinking about quitting.

"I just have to find out what's wrong," he thought to himself. "I don't think I've got leprosy. There has to be some reason that the fellows give me the cold shoulder."

With these thoughts in mind, he walked to Bob Barton's desk. "Bob, do you have any plans for lunch today?"

"No, Jim, as a matter of fact, I haven't."

"Hey, that's terrific. How about we go up to the Greasy Spoon and have a couple hamburgers. I'd like to talk a little bit—away from the office, that is."

"OK, Jim, I think I can arrange that. How about we go around 12:15?"

"Fine, Bob."

Later, "That wasn't a bad hamburger," exclaimed Jim as he wiped his mouth with a paper napkin. "How was yours, Bob?"

"I'll agree with you, Jim; it wasn't bad at all. "And," looking at his watch, "it's only twenty minutes to one, so we've got a little while to talk."

"Yes, we do, Bob. As you probably have gathered, I'm not too happy at the job. I mean, I'm not unhappy with what I'm doing. It's just that I don't seem to get along very well with the rest of the group, and I can't quite figure why. Now, I wish you'd level with me, and tell me if *you* know why. Because I really would like to get along, and I do like the job. But the atmosphere is just getting me down. So please level with me. So it hurts my feelings—I really want to know."

"OK, Jim," answered Bob, "you really want it straight?"

"Yeah, I really want it straight."

"So, I'll tell you. You try too hard, and it turns the rest of the men off. Now, I'll be specific. The first couple of days you were on the job you offered to take everybody out to lunch, and you were going to pay the bill. You acted like the big man on campus with plenty of money. Now, the rest of the guys just don't go for that. Next, you tried to be the joker. In fact, you still do. You're always coming in with jokes to tell Harry and Joe, and they don't particularly like jokes. In fact, if you'd taken time to get to know the group a little bit, you'd find out that Margie's the joker in the group. And another thing, besides the fact that Margie's the joker and usually is the one that the guys look to for jokes, you told a couple of off-color Jewish jokes."

"Well, what's wrong with them?" interrupted Jim.

"That should be obvious," replied Bob. "Margie's Jewish. I know you're Catholic and you probably never thought about it, and this is a predominantly Catholic community. But Margie's Jewish, and you know, that kind of a joke just doesn't go over too well. To make matters worse, you made a couple cracks about Margie being a pretty sexy secretary and that you could, or that you'd really like to make out with her. Well, that was the wrong thing to say. Harry and Joe feel very fatherly toward Margie and to think of someone wanting to—well, make out with her, as you said, really rubbed them the wrong way."

At this point Jim gave a low whistle and said, "Wow, I sure did get off to the wrong start, and it looks like I'm still on the same far-out track."

"You sure are, Jim," countered Bob. "I hate to say it, but you *can* be a little obnoxious at times. Me, I don't mind it. I know you're young; you'll get over it; and personally I like you—but Harry and Joe—no way in that case. And the way they feel about Margie and what Margie tells them—nope, you've really got a lot of work to do if you want to get along with that group."

"Well, Bob, I certainly appreciate the information. I guess there's nothing much I can do about it, or is there?"

"To be truthful Jim, maybe there is something that you can do about it. You can do now what you should've done in the beginning. First of all, find out as much as you can about everyone in the group. As an example, Harry likes cars. He's fairly conservative in clothes and political thinking; he's southern and a little slow-moving; and he likes to take life at an easy pace. Joe, on the other hand, likes yard work; he's from the North, fairly liberal, and knowing that, doesn't talk politics with Harry. Margie's young and Jewish and has had a little problem getting along in the community, but she gets along well with the rest of the group. Stan gets along pretty well with everybody. He plays the straight man to Margie's jokes and, in turn, Tommy is the butt of a few of their jokes. He's an easy-going kid but has had a very strict upbringing and feels guilty if he takes one minute over on his lunch hour or leaves one minute before five o'clock. The guys kid him about it, but he doesn't seem to mind it as long as he thinks they like him. My suggestion to you would be to back off, take it easy, no more jokes, try to go slow with each one, and develop some mutual topic of conversation so that they can find out that you're really not as bad as they think you are now."

"Gee, Bob, I sure appreciate that. You know, I never thought about it that way. I guess that I did just sort of charge in without finding out about any of the group. And I know I shoot off my mouth a lot. I'm very opinionated, and most of the time I can't back it up."

"Well, it looks like you know yourself pretty well," remarked Bob. "You do have a tendency to shoot off your mouth without backing it up with any facts. Actually, it doesn't really matter in the long run. You know, in most of the arguments and discussions we have, it doesn't matter whether you make a point or not. Hey, it's about that time. We better start heading back."

"Yeah, I guess so, Bob. Well, thanks a million. I think maybe now I can work on a course of action that might get me into the good graces of all the fellows and the group as a whole."

"OK, Jim, I sure hope so."

With that they left the diner and walked back to the office.

The next morning Jim Sullivan reported to work as usual at nine o'clock. About five minutes after nine, with a magazine tucked under his arm, he walked over to Harry's desk. "Morning, Harry," said Jim.

"Mmm," mumbled Harry.

"Harry, I was looking at this magazine last night, and I noticed an article on the new Wankel engine. It's better than any of the other articles I've seen, and I thought you might like to read it."

At this, Harry perked up, "Well, thanks, Jim, I appreciate it."

"That's OK, Harry. You know, I'm interested in cars, and I overheard you and Bob Barton talking about them the other day. I hadn't realized you were interested too."

"Yeah, I am, Jim—funny, I didn't know you were interested."

"Yeah, well, see you," said Jim and turned back to his desk.

At lunch Jim picked out a magazine on yard work and read it during the lunch hour. After lunch he walked by Joe Day's desk with the remark, "Well, it looks like with warm weather coming we might see the crocus a little earlier this year. What do you think, Joe?"

"Yeah, maybe," mumbled Joe.

"I was just reading it here in *House and Garden.* I'm interested in yards, and I have a new variety of crocus that I hope will bloom this year."

At this remark Joe showed a little interest. "Oh, I didn't know you were interested in gardening."

"Yeah, I play around at it a little bit. I haven't mentioned it to too many people though. I didn't think anybody here in the office was interested."

"Well, I am," said Joe. "What kind of a place do you have?"

"Oh, just a small piece of yard outside the duplex, but I try to take care of it a little bit. And it's a lot of fun. Incidentally, would you like to see the latest garden book here?"

"Thanks, Jim, I might get a chance to look at it during the break this afternoon."

"OK, Joe, keep it as long as you want." And Jim went back to his desk. His plan of action was obvious. He would find out as much as he could about cars, so that he could converse on a common subject with Harry. He would find out as much as he could about gardening, so that he could talk and have something in common with Joe.

Following this routine, he found out as much as he could about Stan and Tommy and soon was on good terms with them. In the meantime he'd apologized to Margie, accusing himself of being pretty much a clod for telling jokes like that and, to really get back in her good graces, sent her a dozen red roses and a box of candy—to the office, of course.

Three weeks later Jim was sitting at his desk at about ten minutes to twelve. As he looked up, he noticed Harry and Joe, Stan, Tommy, and Margie heading his way. "Hey, Jim," yelled Harry, "we're going down to the Greasy Spoon; how about coming along with us?"

"Gee, thanks, fellas. Can we pick up Bob and make it an office party?"

"Hey, sounds great. Let's go!" yelled Stan.

"Yeah, Joe," remarked Harry, "if this one works out all right, maybe we can try that other diner next week."

"Say, that's a good idea," chipped in Margie. "Maybe we can have an office party every week at a different restaurant. It sure is nice when we all get along so well together."

"It sure is," breathed Jim. "It truly is."

Jim really had to plan in order to achieve his successful outward interaction. First of all he had to find out that he had been violating group norms and had not recognized the established group roles. He had not realized the strong cohesiveness of the group or taken time to explore religious and ethnic backgrounds. Luckily, Bob was willing to level with him and give him the word—sometimes a rarity today. Armed with the facts about the group, which he should have found out himself, he was able to change—alter his behavior—so that he would be accepted.

Finally, let's take an example of a situation in which detailed planning and research for successful IOU was necessary before the fact.

David Levy read the letter from Charleston Fertilizer, Inc. one more time.

Dear Mr. Levy:

We are pleased to offer you the position of Junior Industrial Engineer at an annual salary of $10,000.

As we discussed during your visit to the plant, you may have a little trouble being accepted in the community because of your background. However, I think you'll find the members of your work group will provide a congenial atmosphere.

As I promised, the information you requested concerning your supervisor and the other industrial engineers in your new section is as follows:

Sumner Smith—supervisor—born and raised near Charleston—Baptist—age 51—24 years with the company;

Harry Clauzowitz—born and raised in western Pennsylvania—Methodist—age 45—9 years with the company;

John McClarty—born and raised in the state of Washington—Catholic—age 36—5 years with the company;

John Radcliff—born and raised in South Carolina—no religious preference—age 28—2 years with the company.

Sincerely,

Robert Montgomery

Robert Montgomery
Personnel Director

RM:jml

David put the paper down and thought to himself, "Well, here it is. I've been on pins and needles waiting for the offer. Now that I have it, I don't know what I should do. I know I'm likely to have problems. Here I am a young, New York City Yankee invading the Southern Bible Belt. But I really think I can get along. I want the job; it provides the challenge I'm looking for. I like the area, and I like the company's frankness. Mr. Smith told me I was technically qualified and that he would like to have me. But he pointed out that I might have a little trouble being accepted by his group based upon their background and mine. Well, he didn't say exactly that it would be impossible, but he implied that I might have a little trouble getting accepted. And certainly, Mr. Montgomery told me the same thing. In fact, he pointed out that an outsider has quite a problem getting into Charleston society—that is, if I even wanted to.

"I really want the job, though, and I think I can get along if I take some time to find out about the background of the people I'll be working with, and particularly Mr. Smith, and also the community in general. That's why I asked for the information on my co-workers and Mr. Smith. It was nice of Mr. Montgomery to give it to me.

"Yep, that's what I'm going to do. I'm going to anticipate problems and therefore find out as much background information as I can, make one more visit to the plant to test out my information, then decide whether I'll be able to get along."

Having made the decision, David gathered up the pertinent notes from his human relations class and headed toward the public library. Once there, he wrote each of the names contained in Mr. Montgomery's letter on a separate piece of paper, then began his analysis of information. When he finished, his papers appeared as follows:

SUMNER SMITH—Baptist—51—24 years with Co.
Born and raised near Charleston.
Charlestonians want it known that there is no place in the world like it. The only way to enter the upper crust is marry in.
Ku Klux Klan still active.
Democratic Party—to 1960—only active one.
Some changes now.
Middle of Bible Belt—Methodists
Presbyterians
Lutherans
Episcopalians } majority
Conservative Democrat?
51 - 24 = 27 when started with Co.
1974 − 27 = 1947—born 1923—Depression.
Was probably in the war and finished college afterward.
Probably has not been exposed to behavioral scientist movement (didn't start until about 1960).
Social man philosophy.

Benevolent-authoritative.

Probably paternalistic, not interested in participative management.

Might make work for work's sake.

Protestant Ethic.

Square?

Probably not society since only supervisor at 51.

Probably resistant to any change.

HARRY CLAUZOWITZ—Methodist—age 45—9 years with Co.

Born and raised in western Penna.

Iron, steel, and coal.

European extraction—probably changed religion— name sounds Catholic.

Probably a conservative Democrat.

Take life easy—9 years and only in a group.

Protestant Ethic.

Might have been in Korean Service.

1974 − 45 = born 1929, grew up during Depression—bad times in Pa.—would have known value of hard work.

Management training around 1950.

Benevolent-authoritative—the group the "in" thing.

Social man (and how in Pa.!).

Would not have been exposed to behavioralists—probably hasn't kept up in management philosophy because hasn't been promoted.

Resistance to change.

Go easy with him. But might be kindred soul.

JOHN McCLARTY—Catholic—age 36—5 years with the Co.

Born and raised in state of Washington.

1974 − 36 = 1938.

Probably went to college in 1958 to 1962.

Should have been exposed to human relations movement plus all that went before.

Grew up in a permissive society.

Washington made up of mostly Swedes and Norwegians who migrated from Mid-west.

Catholics in minority—would have had to get along well or have been isolated —based upon where he grew up he would be a liberal Republican—with Catholic background is probably conservative Democrat from state history.

Participative management & Theory Y.

If worth his salt is probably getting ready to move on.

JOHN RADCLIFF

A native South Carolinian—probably a Bible Belt conservative instilled with the Protestant Ethic—that is if he hasn't changed—probably will depend on his parents.

1974 − 28 = born 1946.

Should have been exposed to much of the same training that I have had.

Participative management.

Consultative-group.
Self-actualizing man.
Management by objectives.
Theory Y assumptions.
Complex man.
Wonder how he gets along with Smith?
No religion—maybe he has changed.

Back in his Bronx apartment, David studied the four sheets of notes.

"Well," thought Dave, "I certainly shouldn't have too much trouble getting along with Harry. I would suspect that his parents came over from the old country, but so did mine. And I certainly understand the Protestant Ethic. The fact that we're probably both Democrats would help too. I would suspect that he had just as much trouble as I might have in getting accepted in the community. But he should be a kindred spirit.

"As far as McClarty goes, I'm not sure on that one. If he's a conservative Catholic, we might not see eye to eye, but all I have to do is be careful of subjects that might be controversial with him—at least suspecting now what his background and philosophy might be like.

"Now let's take a look at Radcliff. If he's a local boy, he's probably quite conservative. Although I know I have liberal views and have also been taught the latest theory, I might have a little trouble getting along with Radcliff. My own upbringing in New York was probably a little rougher and a much faster pace of life than his. But, knowing his background and his managerial philosophy, or at least what I think his managerial philosophy might be, I think I can try very hard to get along.

"Based upon my analysis, I probably shouldn't have too much trouble getting along with John McClarty or Clauzowitz, but Radcliff might be a different matter. I'll just have to be prepared for the eventualities now that I have a little bit of background to go on. As far as Mr. Smith goes, I'd be willing to bet he'd believe strongly in the Protestant Ethic and is not going to be amenable to change based upon modern managerial practices. If I want to suggest any improvements in management at the plant for the betterment of the overall business, I'm going to have to move pretty slowly and carefully.

"I would suspect that if any coalitions develop, Radcliff might line up with the boss. I can probably get along best with Clauzowitz because we're both sort of outsiders.

"I know my Jewish background is going to be a strike against me in general—so I'll just have to be like Avis—try harder.

"Based upon my assumptions, I'll go down to the plant next week, and test them out. I'll take the job if I think I will be able to develop successful interpersonal relationships. If I'm way off base, and it looks like there is going to be a personality clash between individuals, then I certainly don't think the job will be worth it."

Armed with the assumptions that he had made concerning his supervisor and co-workers from research information available on states and localities plus facts from his human relations course, David Levy visited the Charleston Fertilizer Plant early the next week.

Arriving in Charleston, he drove to the plant and went immediately to the personnel office. After being ushered into Mr. Montgomery's office, he began, "I'll bet you didn't expect me today, Mr. Montgomery, but I wanted to visit the plant one more time before I acted upon your offer. Would it be all right to visit the group?"

"Of course, Mr. Levy, I'd be most happy to have you visit the group again. And perhaps if Mr. Smith is free, we might all go to lunch."

"That sounds fine, Mr. Montgomery," answered David. "I'll go down to the Industrial Engineering Office and then meet you back here about noon."

"OK, David."

David went down to the plant and renewed acquaintances with McClarty, Clauzowitz, and Radcliff. By asking certain leading questions he was able to find out that his assumptions about the three men were, in essence, correct. Not only could he get along, but he found out that he could be accepted as a member of the group.

At lunch he found out that his assumptions about Mr. Smith were a little right and a little wrong. Smith's original thinking had not been along the behavioral science approach, but he had attended a few management courses in order to keep up with the times and had been exposed to some of the newer techniques. Although he didn't exactly buy them hook, line, and sinker, he was willing to listen—to an extent.

After lunch, David Levy told the personnel director that he would be happy to accept the job now that he realized that he could interact successfully with the group and his supervisor. As far as being accepted in the town, he'd work on that.

In this example, David really had to accomplish a detailed amount of research and homework just to make some assumptions on the chances of successful IOU in his new job situation. He then had to test his assumptions and act accordingly.

In the final analysis, successful interaction within an organization is not easy to achieve. It is necessary to go through many of the steps outlined in this chapter and discussed in our stories, then decide how much give-and-take is necessary and perhaps how much planning is involved to develop satisfactory IOU and in the long run to accomplish objectives; for all of us have objectives that we wish to achieve in any organization. We want to be accepted, be recognized, be appreciated for what we can do for the organization, and obtain self-satisfaction from the job.

Each one of us in our own particular way, being a unique individual, comes in contact with other individuals in our progress through life. Some contacts are temporary; some are permanent, but in each one interaction takes place. Each interaction causes us to bend, give a little, and hopefully, become a better person. We learn from each other to give and take. And in the final analysis that's what successful IOU is all about.

I have a circle
So do you
But it's not always
Round
Sometimes it's
Oval
On occasion it's
Square
And sometimes
(If you're lucky)
It's concentric
With another.
But it doesn't happen
Very often.
Most of the time
The circles
Only intersect
Randomly
And wait for
Another
To pass by
Or change
Shape.[16]

EXERCISE QUESTIONS

1. What three propositions make up the attitude of everyday life? How would you recognize whether or not a person had this attitude?
2. Give an example of routinization.
3. Cite an example of how personal perspective has caused a problem for you in an interaction situation.
4. Give an example of how typification can adversely affect interaction.
5. What three propositions make up the scientific attitude? How would you recognize whether a person had this attitude?
6. Why do women work?
7. List and explain the eight guidelines for successful IOU.

DISCUSSION QUESTIONS

1. What are the difficulties in adopting a general perspective?
2. Is it possible to always pursue a posture of doubt? If not, why not?
3. Is it difficult to make realistic typifications? Cite situations pro and con.
4. Can you see attitudes changing toward women in the work force?
5. What affect could religious background have on successful interaction?
6. Give some examples of controversial subjects that might have a bearing on successful IOU.
7. Give some examples of a nondirect approach in an upward interaction.
8. Why is it necessary to proceed slowly in IOU?

PROJECTS

1. Make a report on your local community. See if you can determine what its philosophy might be based on the factors discussed under the *Community Philosophy* heading.

2. Determine the business philosophy of several industrial, government, and service organizations within your community.

3. Select another classmate and role-play an interaction situation between a person with a 1970 managerial frame of reference and one with a 1940 managerial frame of reference.

4. Obtain information on two or three states that shows how people who grew up in the particular states may have different personal philosophies.

NOTES

1. Clovis R. Shepherd, *Small Groups* (Scranton, Pennsylvania: Chandler Publishing Co., 1964), pp. 9–10.
2. Carroll Quigley, "Needed: Revolution in Thinking," *NEA Journal* (May 1968), p. 8.
3. Timothy W. Costello and Sheldon S. Zalkind, *Psychology in Administration* (Englewood Cliffs, N.J.: Prentice-Hall, Inc., 1963), pp. 6–7.
4. Shepherd, *Small Groups,* p. 14.
5. Leonard R. Sayles and George Strauss, *Human Behavior in Organizations* (Englewood Cliffs, N.J.: Prentice-Hall, Inc., 1960), p. 101.
6. "Why Women Work," U.S. Department of Labor, Wage and Labor Standards Administration, Women's Bureau, December 1970.
7. Marvin E. Shaw, *Group Dynamics* (New York: McGraw-Hill Book Co., 1971), pp. 112 and 182.
8. See p. 181 in Chapter 11.
9. *The Random House Dictionary of the English Language,* unabridged ed. (New York: Random House, 1966).
10. Thomas A. Harris, *I'm OK—You're OK* (New York: Harper & Row Publishers, 1967, 1968, 1969).
11. Thomas A. Harris, *I'm OK—You're OK,* p. 18. Copyright 1967, 1968, 1969 by Thomas A. Harris, M. D. Reprinted by permission of Harper & Row, Publishers, Inc.
12. Ibid., p. 25.
13. Ibid., p. 30.
14. Ibid., p. 69.
15. Ibid., pp. 65–67.
16. Ira H. Schöen, "Circles," an unpublished poem, with permission.

Bibliography

Ackoff, Russell L., "The Development of Operations Research as a Science," *Operations Research,* 4 (June 1956), p. 265.

Allen, Louis A., *Management and Organization* (New York: McGraw-Hill Book Company, 1958).

Anderson, A. C., *Industrial Engineering and Factory Management* (New York: The Ronald Press Company, 1928).

Anderson, E. H., *The Process of Internal Organization* (Chapel Hill: The University of North Carolina Press, 1937).

Anthony, E. James, and Koupernik, Cyrille, ed., *The Child in His Family* (New York: Wylie Interscience, 1970).

Argyris, Chris, *Executive Leadership* (New York: Harper & Bros., 1953).

_________. *Integrating the Individual and the Organization* (New York: John Wiley & Sons, 1964).

_________. *Interpersonal Competence and Organizational Effectiveness* (Homewood, Ill.: Irwin-Dorsey, 1962).

_________. *Personality and Organizational* (New York: Harper & Row, 1957).

Aron, Raymond, and Burchard, John E., et al., eds., *Daedalus,* Journal of the American Academy of Arts and Sciences (Richmond: American cademy of Arts and Sciences, 1967).

Asch, Solomon E., *Social Psychology* (Englewood Cliffs, N.J.: Prentice-Hall, Inc., 1952).

Atkins, P. M., *Factory Management* (Englewood Cliffs, N.J.: Prentice-Hall, Inc., 1926).

Babbage, Charles, *On the Economy of Machinery and Manufactures.* (London: Charles Knight, 1832).

Barnard, Chester I., *Organization and Management* (Cambridge: Harvard University Press, 1948).

Bass, Bernard, *Leadership Psychology and Organizational Behavior* (New York: Harper & Row, 1960).

________. *Organizational Psychology* (Boston: Allyn and Bacon, Inc., 1965).

Beach, Dale S., *Personnel: The Management of People at Work,* 2nd ed. (New York: The MacMillan Company, 1970).

Beer, Stafford, *Cybernetics and Management* (New York: John Wiley & Sons, Inc., 1959).

________. *Cybernetics and Management* (London: English University Press, Ltd., 1968).

Bennis, Warren G., *Changing Organizations* (New York: McGraw-Hill, 1966).

Bennis, Warren G., Benne, Kenneth D., and Chin, Robert, eds., *Planning of Change: Readings in the Applied Behavioral Sciences.* (New York: Holt, Rinehart & Winston, 1961).

Blake, Robert R., and Mouton, Jane S., *Corporate Excellence through Grid Organization Development* (Houston, Texas: Gulf Publishing Co., 1968).

________. *The Managerial Grid* (Houston, Texas. Gulf Publishing Co., 1964).

Blanchard, Kenneth H., and Hersey, Paul, *Management of Organizational Behavior* (Englewood Cliffs, N.J.: Prentice-Hall, Inc., 1972).

Brisco, Norris A., *Economics of Efficiency* (New York: The Macmillan Company, 1914).

Campbell, John P., Dunnette, Marvin D., Lawler, Edward E., III, and Weick, Karl E., Jr., *Managerial Behavior, Performance, and Effectiveness* (New York: McGraw-Hill, Inc., 1970).

Caruth, Donald L., and Rachel, Frank M., *Business Systems* (San Francisco: Canfield Press, 1972).

Chess, Stella, and Thomas, Alexander, eds., *Annual Progress in Child Psychiatry and Child Development* (New York: Brunner/Mazel Publishers, 1971).

Church, Alexander H., *The Making of an Executive* (New York: D. Appleton and Company, 1923).

________. *The Science and Practice of Management* (New York: The Engineering Magazine Co., 1914).

Churchman, C. West, Ackoff, Russell L., Arnoff, E. Leonard, *Introduction to Operations Research* (New York: John Wiley & Sons, Inc., 1957).

Clausewitz, Karl von, *Principles of War* (Harrisburg: Military Service Publishing Company, 1832).

Cornell, William B., *Organization and Management in Industry and Business* (New York: The Ronald Press Company, 1928).

Costello, Timothy W., and Zalkind, Sheldon S., *Psychology in Administration* (Englewood Cliffs, N.J.: Prentice Hall, 1963).

Dale, Ernest, *Readings in Management: Landmarks and New Frontiers* (New York: McGraw-Hill Book Company, 1965).

D'Aprix, Roger M., *Struggle for Identity* (Homewood, Ill.: Dow Jones-Irwin, Inc., 1972).

Davis, Ralph C., *Industrial Organization and Management* (New York: Harper & Bros., 1951).

Davis, Ralph C., *The Principles of Factory Organization and Management* (New York: Harper & Bros., 1928).

Dennison, H. S., *Organization Engineering* (New York: McGraw-Hill Book Company, 1931).

Diebold, John, *Business Decisions and Technological Change* (New York: Praeger Publishers, 1970).

Diemer, Hugo, *Factory Organization and Administration* (New York: McGraw-Hill Book Company, 1910).

_________. *Factory Organization and Administration* (New York: McGraw-Hill Book Company, 1914).

_________. *Industrial Organization and Management* (Chicago: LaSalle Extension University, 1919).

Dowling, William F., Jr., and Sayles, Leonard R., *How Managers Motivate: The Imperatives of Supervision* (New York: McGraw-Hill Book Co., 1971).

Drucker, Peter F., *The Age of Discontinuity* (New York: Harper & Row Publishers, 1968).

_________. *The Effective Executive* (New York: Harper & Row, 1967).

_________. *Managing for Results: Economic Tasks and Risk-Taking Decisions* (New York: Harper & Row, 1964).

_________. *The Practice of Management* (New York: Harper & Bros., 1954).

Drury, Horace B., *Scientific Management: A History and Criticism* (New York: Columbia University Press, 1915).

Dubin, Robert, *Human Relations in Administration.* (Englewood Cliffs, N.J.: Prentice-Hall, Inc., 1961).

Duncan, John C., *The Principles of Industrial Management* (New York: D. Appleton and Company, 1911).

Dutton, H. P., *Business Organization and Management* (Chicago: A. W. Shaw Co., 1925).

_________. *Principles of Organization as Applied to Business* (New York: McGraw-Hill Book Company, 1931).

Emerson, Harrington, *Efficiency as a Basis for Operation and Wages* (New York: The Engineering Magazine Co., 1900).

_________. *Efficiency as a Basis for Operation and Wages* (New York: The Engineering Magazine Co., 1911).

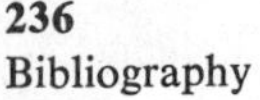

————. *The Twelve Principles of Efficiency* (New York: The Engineering Magazine Co., 1913).

————. *Efficiency as a Basis for Operation and Wages* (New York: The Engineering Magazine Co., 1919).

Fast, Julius, *Body Language* (New York: Simon and Schuster, Inc., 1970).

Fayol, Henri, *Administrative industrielle et générale* (Paris: Dunod, 1925). First English trans. 1929; 2nd trans. by Constance Storrs (London: Sir Isaac Pitman & Sons Ltd., 1949).

Festinger, Leon A. *A Theory of Cognitive Dissonance* (New York: Harper & Row 1957).

Filippeti, George, *Industrial Management in Transition* (Homewood, Ill.: Richard D. Irwin, Inc., 1946).

Flippo, Edwin B., *Management: A Behavioral Approach* (Boston: Allyn & Bacon, Inc., 1966).

Follett, Mary Parker, *Freedom and Coordination* (London: Management Publications Trust, 1949).

Ford, Robert N., *Motivation Through the Work Itself.* (New York: American Management Associaton, 1969).

Galloway, Lee, *Organization and Management* (New York: McGraw-Hill Book Company, 1910).

Gantt, Henry L., *Industrial Leadership* (New Haven, Conn.: Yale University Press, 1916).

————. *Organizing for Work* (New York: Harcourt, Brace and Howe, 1919).

————. *Work, Wages and Profits* (New York: The Engineering Magazine Co., 1910).

Gardiner, G. L., *Management in the Factory* (New York: McGraw-Hill Book Company, 1925).

Gardiner, B. B., *Human Relations in Industry* (Homewood, Ill.: Richard D. Irwin, Inc., 1945).

Gardner, John W., *Self-Renewal: The Individual and the Innovative Society* (New York: Harper & Row, 1964).

Gardner, Riley W., and Moriarty, Alice, *Personality Development at Preadolescence* (Seattle: University of Washington Press, 1968).

Gellerman, Saul W., *Management by Motivation* (New York: American Management Association, 1968).

————. *Motivation and Productivity* (New York: American Management Association, 1968).

George, Claude S., Jr., *The History of Management Thought* (Englewood Cliffs, N.J.: Prentice-Hall, Inc., 1972).

Gilbreth, Frank B., *Bricklaying System* (New York: The Myron C. Clark Publishing Co., 1909).

Gilbreth, L. M., *The Psychology of Management* (New York: Sturgis and Walton Co., 1914).

Glover, J. G., *Fundamentals of Professional Management* (New York: Republc Book Company, 1954).

Godwin, E. B., *Developing Executive Ability* (New York: The Ronald Press Company, 1915).

Goffman, Erving, *The Presentaton of Self in Everyday Life* (New York: Doubleday & Co., 1959).

Gowin, E. B., *The Selection and Training of the Business Executive* (New York: The Macmillan Company, 1918).

Greenwood, Willam T., *Management and Organizational Behavior Theories* (Cincinnati, Ohio: South-Western Publishing Company, 1965).

Gross, Bertram M., *The Managing of Organizations* (New York: Cromwell-Collier Publishing Co., 1964).

Gulick, L., and Urwick, L., eds., *Papers on the Science of Administration* (New York: Institute of Public Administration, Columbia University, 1937).

Haire, Mason, *Modern Organization Theory* (New York: John Wiley & Sons, Inc., 1959).

———. *Organization Theory in Industrial Practice* (New York: John Wiley & Sons, Inc., 1962).

———. *Psychology in Management* (New York: McGraw-Hill, 1956).

Hamachek, Don E., *Human Dynamics in Psychology and Education—Selected Readings,* 2nd ed. (Boston: Allyn and Bacon, Inc., 1972).

Harris, Thomas A., *I'm OK—You're OK* (New York: Harper & Row Publishers, 1967).

Haynes, W. Warren, and Massie, Joseph L. *Management Analysis, Concepts, and Cases* (Englewood Clffs, N.J.: Prentice-Hall, Inc., 1961).

Herzberg, Frederick, *Work and the Nature of Man.* (Cleveland, Ohio: World Publishing Co., 1966).

Herzberg, Frederick, Mausner, Bernard, and Snyderman, Barbara, *The Motivation to Work,* 2nd ed. (New York: John Wiley & Sons, 1959).

Holden, P. E., Fish, L. S., and Smith, H. L. *Top Management Organization and Control* (Stanford, Calif.: Stanford University Press, 1941).

Hoxie, R. F., *Scientific Management and Labor* (New York: D. Appleton and Company, 1915).

Hunt, Edward E., *Scientific Management Since Taylor* (New York: McGraw-Hill Book Company, 1924).

Jay, Antony, *Management and Machiavelli* (New York: Holt, Rinehart & Winston, Inc., 1967).

Jevons, W. S., *Theory of Political Economy* (London: Macmillan & Co. Ltd., 1888).

Johnson, Ellis A., *The Application of Operations Research to Industry.* (Chevy Chase: Operations Research Office, 1955).

Jones, E. D., *The Administration of Industrial Enterprises* (New York: Longmans, Green & Co. Ltd., 1916).

Jones, Edward D., *Industrial Leadership and Executive Ability* (New York: The Engineering Magazine Co., 1913).

Jones, Manley H., *Executive Decision Making* (Homewood, Ill.: Richard D. Irwin, Inc., 1957).

Jung, C. G., *Analytical Psychology: Its Theory and Practice (The Tavistock Lectures)* (New York: Pantheon Books, Inc., 1935, 1968).

Juran, J. M., *Managerial Breakthrough* (New York: McGraw-Hll Book Company, 1964).

Kaufman, Herbert, *The Limits of Organizational Change* (Alabama: The University of Alabama Press, 1971).

Kildahl, John P., and Wolber, Lewis R., *The Dynamics of Personality* (New York: Grune and Stratton, Inc., 1970).

Kimball, Dexter S., *Plant Management* (New York: Alexander Hamilton Institute, 1918).

————. *Principles of Industrial Organizaton* (New York: McGraw-Hill Book Company, 1913).

Koontz, H., and O'Donnell, C., *Principles of Management* (New York: McGraw-Hill Book Company, 1964).

Koontz, H., and O'Donnell, C. *Principles of Management* (New York: McGraw-Hill Book Company, 1955).

Learned, Edmund P. D. C. S., and Sproat, Audrey T., *Organization Theory and Policy* (Homewood, Ill.: Richard D. Irwin, Inc., 1966).

Leavitt, Harold J., *Managerial Psychology* 2nd ed. (Chicago: University of Chicago Press, 1964).

Leavitt, Harold J., and Pondy, Louis R., eds., *Readings in Managerial Psychology* (Chicago: University of Chicago Press, 1965).

Levinson, Harry, *Emotional Health in the World of Work* (New York: Harper & Row, 1964).

————. *The Exceptional Executive* (Cambridge, Massachusetts: Harvard University Press, 1968).

Lewin, Kurt, *A Dynamic Theory of Personality* (New York: McGraw-Hill, 1954).

————. *Field Theory in Social Science: Selected Theoretical Papers* (New York: Harper & Row, 1951).

Lichtenberg, Philip, and Norton, Dolores G., *Cognitive and Mental Development in the First Five Years of Life* (Chevy Chase, National Institute of Mental Health, 1970).

Likert, Rensis, *New Patterns of Management* (New York: McGraw-Hill, 1961).

________. *The Human Organization* (New York: McGraw-Hill, 1967).

Lincoln, James F., *Incentive Management* (Cleveland: The Lincoln Electric Co., 1951).

Lippitt, Gordon L., This, Leslie E., and Bidwell, Robert G., Jr., *Optimizing Human Resources* (Philippines: Addison-Wesley Publishing Company, Inc., 1971).

Maier, Henry W., *Three Theories of Child Development* (New York: Harper & Row Publishers, 1965).

March, J. G., and Simon, H. A., *Organization* (New York: John Wiley & Sons, Inc., 1958).

Marrow, Alfred J., *Behind the Executive Mask* (New York: American Management Association, 1964).

Marrow, Alfred J., Bowers, David, and Seashore, Stanley E., *Management by Participation* (New York: Harper & Row, 1967).

Marshall, Alfred, *Elements of Economics of Industry* (London: Macmillan & Co., Ltd., 1892).

Marshall, L. C., *Business Administration* (Chicago: University of Chicago Press, 1921).

Maslow, Abraham H., *Eupsychian Management: A Journal* (Homewood, Ill.: Irwin-Dorsey, 1965).

________. *Motivation and Personality* (New York: Harper & Row, 1954).

________. *Toward a Psychology of Being,* 2nd ed., (Princeton: Van Nostrand Company, 1968).

Massie, Joseph L., *Essentials of Management* (Englewood Cliffs, N.J.: Prentice-Hall, Inc., 1964).

Mayo, George Elton, *The Human Problems of an Industrial Civilization* (Boston: Division of Research Harvard Business School, 1933).

________. *The Social Problems of an Industrial Civilization* (Boston: Division of Research, Harvard Business School, 1945).

Mee, J. F., *Management Thought in a Dynamic Society* (New York: New York University Press, 1963).

Merrill, Harwood F., ed., *Classics in Management* (New York: American Management Association, 1960).

Metcalfe, Henry, *The Cost of Manufactures and the Administration of Workshops Public and Private* (New York: John Wiley & Sons, Inc., 1885).

Metcalf, Henry C., *Scientific Foundations of Business Administration* (Baltimore: The Williams & Wilkins Co., 1926).

Metcalf, Henry C., and Urwick, Lyndall, *Dynamic Administration—The Collected Papers of Mary Follett* (New York: Harper & Bros., 1942).

Mill, James, *Elements of Political Economy,* 3rd ed. (London: Baldwin, Cradock, and Joy, 1826).

Mill, John Stuart, *Principles of Political Economy,* Sir W. J. Ashley, ed. (London: Longmans, Green & Co. Ltd., 1926).

Mills, Theodore M., *The Sociology of Small Groups* (Englewood Cliffs, N.J.: Prentice-Hall, Inc., 1967).

Mitchell, W. N., *Organization and Management of Production* (New York: McGraw-Hill Book Company, 1939).

Mooney, James D., *Principles of Organization,* rev. ed. (New York: Harper & Bros., 1947).

Mooney, J. D., and Reiley, A. C., *Onward Industry!* (New York: Harper & Bros., 1931).

________. *The Principles of Organization.* New York: Harper & Bros., 1939.

Munsterberg, Hugo, *Psychology and Industrial Efficiency* (Boston: Houghton Mifflin Company, 1913).

McClelland, David C., et al., *The Achievement Motive* (New York: Appleton-Century-Crofts, 1953).

McCormick, Charles P., *Multiple Management* (New York: Harper & Bros., 1938).

________. *The Power of People, Multiple Management Up to Date* (New York: Harper & Bros., 1949).

McFarland, Dalton E., *Management Principles and Practices* (New York: The Macmillan Company, 1958).

McGregor, Douglas, *The Human Side of Enterprise* (New York: McGraw-Hill, 1960).

________. *Leadership and Motivation.* W. G. Bennis, and E. H. Shien, eds., with McGregor, Caroline (Cambridge, Massachusetts: M.I.T. Press, 1966).

________. *The Professional Manager.* Caroline McGregor and W. G. Bennis, eds. (New York: McGraw-Hill, 1967).

McKinsey, J. W., *Business Administration* (Cincinnati: South-Western Publishing Co., 1924).

Newman, William H., *Administrative Action. The Techniques of Organization and Management* (Englewood Cliffs, N.J.: Prentice-Hall, Inc., 1951).

Newman, William H., and Summer,Charles E., Jr., *The Process of Management: Concepts, Behavior, and Practice* (Englewood Cliffs, N.J.: Prentice-Hall, Inc., 1961).

Nobile, Phillip, ed., *The CON III Controversy* (New York: Pocket Books, 1971).

Odiorne, George S., *Management by Objectives* (New York: Pitman Publishing Corp., 1965).

__________. *Management Decision by Objectives* (Englewood Cliffs, N.J.: Prentice-Hall, Inc., 1969).

Parsons, C. S., *Office Organization and Management* (Chicago: LaSalle Extension University, 1918).

__________. *Perceiving, Behaving, Becoming* (Association for Supervision and Curriculum Development, NEA, 1962).

Person, H. S., ed., *Scientific Management in American Industry* (New York: Harper & Bros., 1929).

Pigors, Paul, and Myers, Charles A. *Personnel Administration* (New York: McGraw-Hill Book Company, 1956).

Potter, Charles Francis, *The Faiths Men Live By* (New York: Ace Books, Inc., 1954).

Reich, Charles A., *The Greening of America* (New York: Random House, 1970).

Ricardo, David, *The Principles of Political Economy and Taxation* (New York: E. P. Dutton & Co., Inc., 1960). Original published in 1817.

Robinson, Webster, *Fundamentals of Business Organization* (New York: McGraw-Hill Book Company, 1925).

Rochlin, Gregory, *Man's Aggression* (Boston: Gambit, 1973).

Roethlisberger, F. J., *Management and Morale* (Cambridge: Harvard University Press, 1941).

Roethlisberger, F. J., and Dickson, William J., *Counseling in an Organization: A Sequel to the Hawthorne Research* (Boston: Harvard University, Graduate School of Business, 1966).

__________. *Management and the Worker* (Cambridge: Harvard University Press, 1956).

Rowntree, B. S., *The Human Factor in Business* (London: Longmans, Green & Co., Ltd., 1921).

Sayles, Leonard R., *Managerial Behavior* (New York: McGraw-Hill, 1964).

Sayles, Leonard R., and Strauss, George, *Human Behavior in Organizations* (Englewood Cliffs, N.J.: Prentice-Hall, Inc., 1966).

Schein, Edgar H., *Organizational Psychology* (Englewood Cliffs, N.J.: Prentice-Hall, Inc., 1965).

Schulz, Edward, Spriegel, William B., and Spriegel, Willam R., *Elements of Supervision* (New York: John Wiley and Sons, Inc. 1957).

Selye, Hans, *The Stress of Life* (New York: McGraw-Hill, 1956).

Shaw, Marvin E., *Group Dynamics* (New York: McGraw-Hill Book Co., 1971).

Sheldon, Oliver, "The Art of Management," *Taylor Society Bulletin,* (December 1923), p. 209.

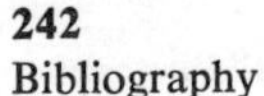

———. *The Philosophy of Management* (London: Sir Isaac Pitman & Sons Ltd., 1923).

———. *The Philosophy of Management* (New York: Pitman Publishing Corp., 1966).

Shepherd, Clovis R., *Small Groups* (Scranton, Pa.: Chandler Publishing Co., 1964).

Simon, Herbert A., *Administraitve Behavior: A Study of Decision-Making Processes in Administrative Organization,* 2nd ed. (New York: The Macmillan Company, 1957.

Smith, Adam, *An Inquiry into the Nature and Causes of the Wealth of Nations* (New York: Modern Library, Inc., 1937).

Smith, Frederic, *Workshop Management: A Manual for Masters and Men,* 3rd ed., (London: Wyman and Son, 1832).

Special Task Force to the Secretary of Health, Education, and Welfare, *Work in America* (Cambridge: MIT Press).

Stacey, Chalmers, and DeMartino, Manfred, compilers and eds., *Understanding Human Motivation—A Book of Selected Readings* (Cleveland, Ohio: Howard Allen, Inc., 1963).

Strauss, George, an Sayles, Leonard R., *Personnel: The Problems of Management* (Englewood Cliffs, N.J.: Prentice-Hall, Inc., 1967).

Strauss, George, and Sayles, Leonard R., *The Human Problems of Management,* (Englewood Cliffs, N.J.: Prentice-Hall, Inc., 1960).

Sutermeister, Robert A., *People and Productivity,* 2nd ed., (New York: McGraw-Hill Book Company, 1960).

Tannenbaum, Robert, et. al., *Leadership and Organization: A Behavioral Approach* (New York: McGraw Hill, 1961).

Taylor, Frederick W., *The Principles of Scientific Management* (New York: Harper & Bros., 1911).

———. *Shop Management* (New York: Harper & Bros., 1903).

Tead, Ordway, *The Art of Leadership* (New York: McGraw-Hill Book Company, 1935).

———. *Instincts in Industry* (Boston: Houghton Mifflin Company, 1918).

———. *The Art of Administration* (New York: McGraw-Hill Book Company, 1951).

Terry, George R., *Principles of Management* (Homewood, Ill.: Richard D. Irwin, Inc., 1953).

Thompson, C. Bertrand, *Scientific Management* (London: Oxford University Press, 1914).

Toffler, Alvin, *Future Shock* (New York: Random House, 1970).

Tolman, William H., *Social Engineering* (New York: McGraw-Hill Book Company, 1909).

Ure, Andrew, *The Philosophy of Manufactures* (London: Charles Knight, 1835).

Urwick, L., *The Elements of Administration* (New York: Harper & Bros., 1944).

_________. *The Golden Book of Management* (London: Newman Neame, Ltd., 1956).

Vroom, Victor H., *Work and Motivation* (New York: John Wiley & Sons, 1964).

Webb, Sidney, *The Works Manager Today* (London: Longmans, Green & Co. Ltd., 1917).

Weber, Max, *The Protestant Ethic and the Spirit of Capitalism* (New York: Charles Scribner's Sons, 1958). Translated by Talcott Parsons.

Whyte, William H., Jr., *The Organization Man* (Garden City, N.Y.: Doubleday and Co., Inc., 1956).

Wolberg, Louis R., and Kildahl, John P., *The Dynamics of Personality* (New York: Grune and Stratton, Inc., 1970).

Woods, C. E., *Organizing a Factory* (New York: The System Company, 1905).

Wren, Daniel A., *The Evolution of Management Thought* (New York: The Ronald Press Co., 1972).

Zaleznik, Abraham, and Moment, David, *The Dynamics of Interpersonal Behavior* (New York: John Wiley & Sons, 1964).

Index

N

O

P

Q

R

S

T

U

V

W